Keepsake Crafts

A Craft Book Showing How to Display Keepsakes, Collectibles and Antiques.

140 Ideas with History and Illustrations of each Item.

By
V. A. William

Copyright 1977
by
V. A. William

ISBN: 0-87069-195-3

PUBLISHED BY
WALLACE-HOMESTEAD BOOK CO.
BOX BI
DES MOINES, IOWA 50311

Author's Note

PURPOSE

We have written and designed this Craft Book to be of interest and value in serving people with a wide range of talents.

CRAFT AND HOBBYIST

It is for the Craft and Hobbyists, to be a guide for developing a talent to use yesteryear items as the focal point for a craft project. (A delight for ladies to use their decorating skill.)

COLLECTOR

It is for the Collector of keepsakes, primitives and antiques that may want to show off some favorite old piece in an interesting and different display, as well as increase their general knowledge about these items.

PEOPLE THAT REMINISCE

It is for the People that take pleasure in reading and reminiscing about objects of interest in the past; some of which are still workable and enjoyed for their original use.

PROFESSIONAL

It is for the Professional; Interior Decorator, Florist, Art Teacher and etc. to experiment with and develop new ideas for using old items of the past in an interesting way to mix with the new of today.

The purpose of the book is also to encourage anyone to enjoy keepsakes by displaying them in a new and unique way. Show off your "American Heritage" and you will be surprised what an interesting conversation piece it can make.

William

Dedicated to Ginny with love.

Grandmother's Bread Board

Nearly everyone is familiar with a Bread Board and it dates back to the time when Mother had only a table top to prepare three square meals a day. A clean wooden surface proved best for making the daily bread and other goodies associated with baking.

This kitchen necessity was also referred to as a Dough Board, Pastry Board, Meat Board and Slides. This latter term being used for those boards that were included in the kitchen cabinet under the table top for handy storage purposes.

Bread boards were advertised in the 1800's and in a variety of sizes from 16" x 22" to 20" x 30". Smaller boards were also available for use on the table to hold a full loaf of bread for slicing. Some of these boards were circular in design and called bread plates.

GUIDELINES FOR STARTING WALL PLAQUE

Selection of Wood

One ideal board for displaying collectible items of course is the bread board, however if such is not available, then new wood can be used with a most satisfying effect by distressing and staining. The addition of a wood knob at the length end of the board readily gives the "bread board look" when desired. (See illustration on opposite page)

Barnwood is most appropriate for mounting some keepsakes, particularly those associated with farm life dating back to the early 1800's. Also one may already have a wall decor that will enhance a primitive that is used with a weathered piece of wood. Occasionally a piece of barnwood itself may have "keepsake" memories and becomes an ideal conversation piece when used to display a favorite old and cherished item.

Preparing the Plaque for Hanging (backside)

After the board has been cut to size, the first step is to attach the "hardware" to the back of the board for easy mounting on the wall. Attach one or two "sawedge" hangers, depending on the size of the board and the weight of the keepsakes used on the plaque. A small 1/8" thick wood strip attached to the bottom backside of the board as indicated will make the plaque hang in a true vertical position. A strip of masonite is also ideal to use for this purpose.

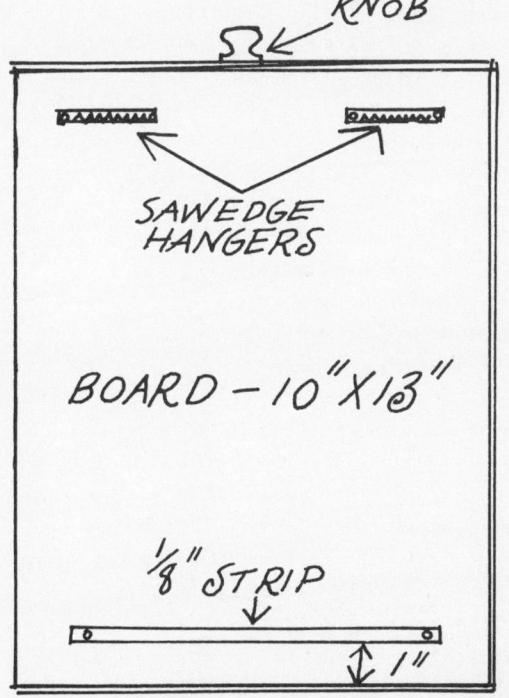

BASIC DIRECTIONS FOR ALL PLAQUES

1. Position board as it will be used for display selected. (See examples below)
2. Nail hangers to top backside 1" from edge and top of board.
3. Nail or glue strip to bottom of board.
4. Sand and distress front of board as desired.
5. Finish board with light stain or as preferred to fit wall decor.
6. Stain or paint knob white and glue to top of board. (Use white porcelain knob if preferred.)

Position of Board

The size and shape of the "keepsake" will determine the use of the board in a Vertical or Horizontal position.

Note: Every plaque in this book has simple and easy directions for making same. Also on pages 162 and 163 there are directions for attaching shelves and towel bars along with other useful ideas.

Contents

Grandmothers Bread Board 4
Preparing the Plaque for Hanging 5
Old Brace with Auger Bit 8
Egg Beater in Drawer 10
Stereoscope 12
Washboard — Medicine Chest 14
Washboard — Using Back 16
Washboard — Bulletin Board and Towel Rack 18
Washboard — Wooden Bowl and Mirror 20
Small Tin Scoop and Old Drawer 22
Old Wood Shovel Handle 23
Kraut Board with Biscuit Cutter 24
Hay Bale Hook 26
Match Box with Old Knife and Fork 28
Coffee Mill — Wall Type (Side Mounting) 30
Coffee Mill — Modified Side Type 32
Coffee Mill — Table Type 34
Coffee Grinder — Wall Type 35
Coffee Mill with Picture Cards 36
Toy Popgun and World War I Soldiers 38
Toy Gun with Wooden Soldier 40
"Thumb" Sugar Scoop and Bowl 42
Spoons, or Knife and Fork 43
Hat Blocking Frame 44
Duck Decoy Heads in Drawer 46
"Tourist" Folding Curling Iron 48
Canning Lifter and Jar 50
Foot Warmer 52
Ice Skates 54
Shoe Cobbler's Tools 56
Egg Grading Scale 58
Curry Comb 60
Wooden Horse Stirrup 62
Enamelware Cup on Shelf 64
Grain Scoop in Picture Frame 65
Steel Stirrup and Horse Bit 66
Square Match Safe and Stove Ash Shaker 68
"Cereal" Stove Lid and Toy Bank 70
Hay Pulleys 72
Wheel Making Tools 74
Ice Tongs and Toy Ice Wagon 76
Stove Cover Lifter and Match Box 78
"Patent" Medicine Bottle 80
The "Show Off" Shelf 82
Vanity Hand Mirror and Curling Iron 84
Hand Mirror and Graniteware soap Dish 86
Old Hand Mirror with Wire Type Soap Holder 88
Pipe and Tobacco Can 90
Butter Paddle and Tea Strainer 92
Broken Butter Paddle 94
Old 1750 Pistol with Book 96
Enamelware Funnels 99
Sewing Machine Drawer and Sewing Items 100
Flour Sifter and Wood Spoon 102

Soap Saver	104
Spring Balance Hand Scales	106
Biscuit Cutter	108
Irish Cop Bank and Jail Key	109
Carpenter Tools in Frame	110
Lincoln Picture Drawer Using Old Bookend	112
Enamelware Ladles and Dippers	114
Comb and Brush Case with Vanity Mirror	116
School Slate and Wooden Bowl	118
School Slate with Shelf	120
Spigot with Old Tin Bucket	122
Wooden Spoon with Towel Rack	124
Wooden Spoon with Bowl of Eggs	126
Kraut Box as Horse Stall	128
Kraut Box as Chicken Nest	130
Vegetable Grater	132
Ice Cream Dipper and Sundae Dish	134
Recipe Booklets	136
Mincing Knives (Chopping Knives)	139
Potato Mashers	140
Patent Medicine	143
Wooden Shipping Boxes	144
Silver Evening Purse and Vanity Mirror	146
More Ideas Using Old Kitchen Utensils	149
Old Milk Bottles	150
Cream Skimmers	152
Horse Curry Comb with Wooden Handle	154
Horse Saddles	156
1898 Shoe and Harness Repair Box	158
Hay Barn Pulleys of Yesteryear	160
Shelving Construction	162
Old Bible, Eyeglasses and Ink Bottle	164
Simulated Handcuffs	167
Old Vanity Hand Mirror and Candle Holder	168
More Ideas Using Old Kitchen Untensils	171
Grandfather's Shaving Items	172
Bathroom Fixtures of Early 1900's	174
Old Canning Jar Lifters	176
Bee Smoker	178
Grocery Bill Holder of the 1920's	180
Rolling Pin and Friends	182
Old Mirror Frame	184
Trivets	186
Old 'Lava' Soap Box	187
Kitchen Funnels	188
Butter Paddles	190
Old Eggbeaters	192
Other Ideas for Using Plastic Eggs	194
Old Moonshine Still	195
Household Graters	196
Firetorch (1800-1850)	198
Old Railroad Keepsakes	200
Abraham Lincoln Book	202

Old Brace with Auger Bit

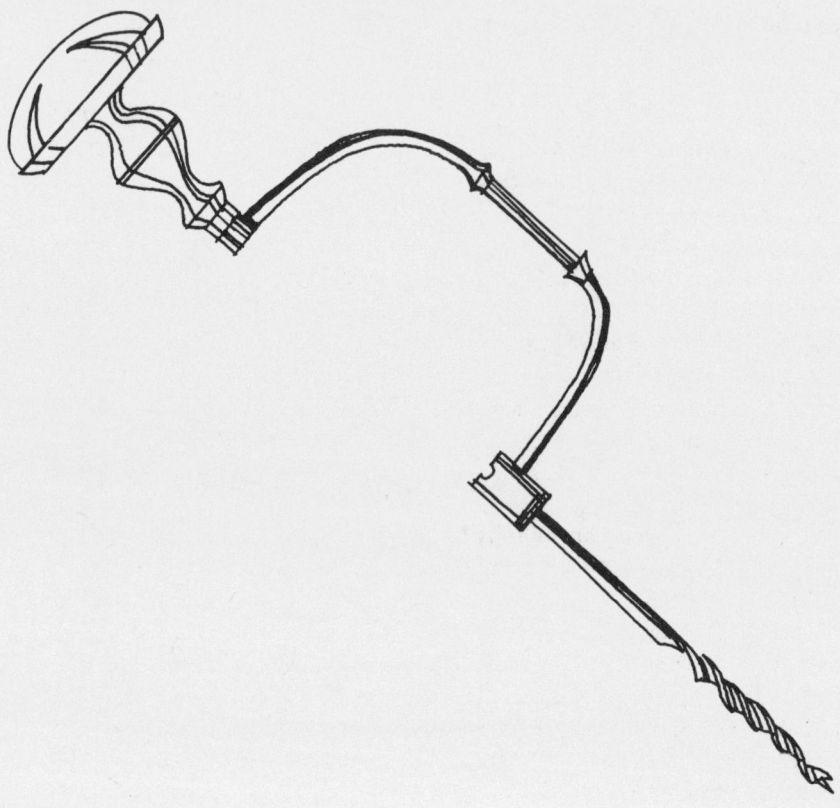

    Many of the bit braces prior to 1900 had fancy wood handles and make a handsome wall hanging. Some of the older ones do not have a revolving wood handle in the sweep and were good blister and callus makers.

    The open distance between the head handle and the bit holder is called the sweep. The measurement was usually 8" to 16". The bit holder, instead of being of a ratchet design as today was simply a split metal head with a thumb screw to tighten the bits for drilling.

    The auger bit for this project needs to be about as long as the brace (12"). The candle when placed in the holder should be about 3" shorter than the top of the bit to allow the cutting end to show.

How To

The board used for mounting should be at least two inches longer than the brace. Our board measures 12" x 17". To attach the brace drill an eighth inch hole in head handle a half inch deep and cut an inch length dowel rod to glue into it. Position on board, drill hole to receive dowel rod and glue in place. Also at the bottom of the brace, drill a small hole through the board at each side of the piece and wire securely. The bit is secured by drilling a small hole on each side at both the top and bottom and attaching with black wire.

The cast-iron black candle cup is not old but fits in well with the arrangement. It is secured with a screw and placed just below the auger bit. Insert white candle and the piece is ready to hang.

Egg Beater in Drawer

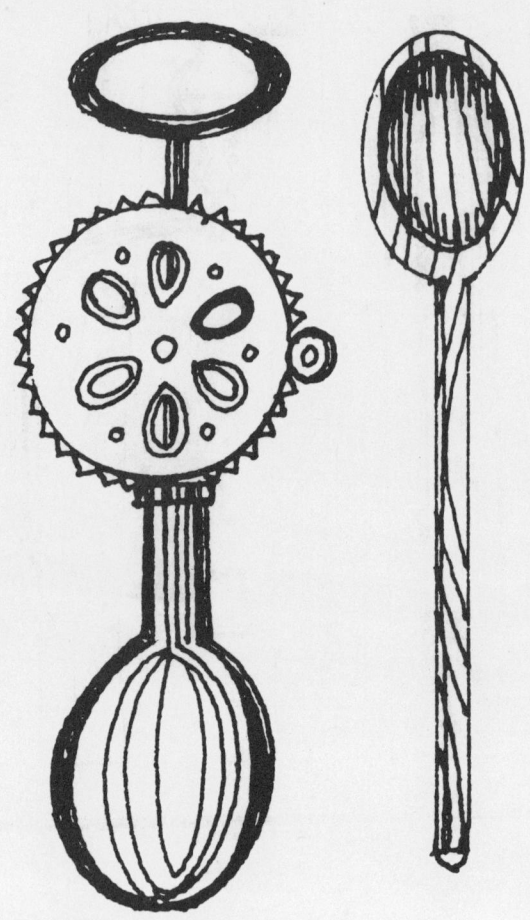

For this plaque we used the Dover egg beater dating back to 1899. These came in at least three different lengths. Nine, ten and 12 inches were the more popular sizes. The larger size was more usable for bakeries or hotels. If available, the smallest size is best for this plaque. This makes a most delightful piece for the kitchen or dining area.

How To

The "drawer" is made from quarter to three-eighths inch wood to a depth of 3" to 3½". The one we made measured 12" x 14". Eighth inch plywood was used for the backing. It could well be that an old existing drawer similiar in size would be most suitable for this purpose. After attaching the two saw-edge hangers to the back, attach an old wooden knob to give the "drawer" appearance. Then

make and nail together the partitions, allowing sufficient space for the egg beater and wooden spoon you have selected. Before nailing the partitions in the drawer, cover the "bottom" of the drawer with contact paper of your choice. We used a red and white check.

Make and attach the half wooden bowl (see page 162 for detail). Also secure the egg beater. Near the top of the beater handle drill a small hole through the wood on each side of the shank and secure with wire. In this decorative piece, the beater is in more of a "storage" position, so we did not include the eggs for the bowl but placed them above.

The next step is to make the nest for the eggs and fasten the excelsior and eggs securely in the compartment. Spray glue is good for this purpose.

The spoon is in a leaning position. Other bottles or items can be added to compartments as desired.

Stereoscope

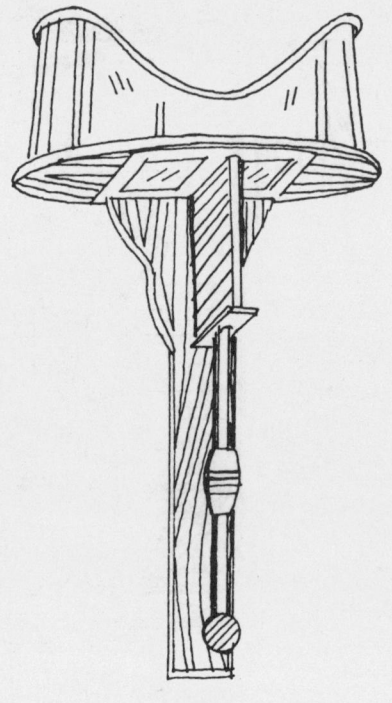

    The stereoscope is an optical instrument to show pictures with a three dimensional effect. It was found in the best parlors around 1900. The "views" were usually provided in a packet with 12 to 24 pictures of a given subject, or each could be purchased separately. Typical sets of views were "A Visit to Washington," "Wonders of the Old World," "Wedding Bells," "The Life of Christ," "A Tour of the Big Cities of the U.S." There were even comic series.

    Patent dates we have seen are 1895 and 1904. Even many of the folding handles were patented. The frames were made from cherry, walnut, and other hard woods. The "hood" piece was quite often made from rosewood, tulip, cherry, or was of nickelplated metal.

    We do not suggest that you use a workable stereoscope for this piece—but quite often you can find a broken one. They may be found with broken eye glass, handle missing or damaged in some other way and can be purchased for a few dollars.

How To

The cutting board used should be about 8" x 18" in size. Finish the board as desired and attach hanger to backside. Locate the stereoscope on the board (handle will have to be removed if there is one) and attach with small finishing nails or use dowel rod attachment. The ivy decoration will cover nail heads.

Drill hole at angle near edge of eye piece (hood) to receive ivy. If bottom part of the stereoscope is not ornate, use small round wooden balls and dowel rod to improve looks. If the handle is available, it can fill this spot. Attach greenery and fill with artificial flowers.

Washboard—Medicine Chest

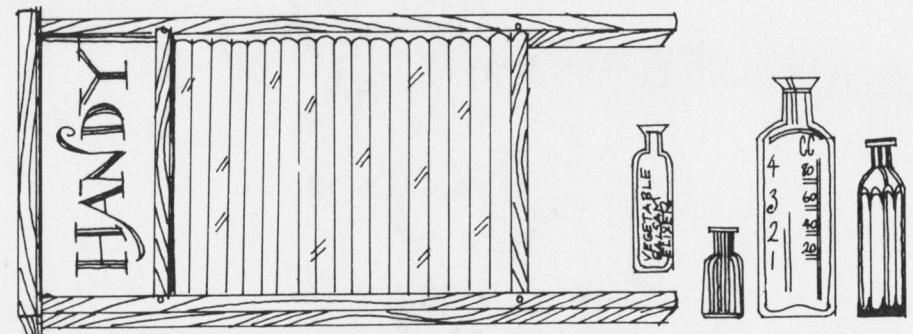

These washboards measure about 9" x 18" and were of the type used in a pail or sink for washing small articles. The larger boards were for the family wash and used in a regular wash tub. Some of these boards are still around and date back to about 1900. The old ones can be identified by their "washed out" appearance. The rubbing surface was made from spring brass, tin, zinc, or even wood. The ridge crimping to make the rubbing surface was made in various styles. The aim of course was to design a crimping to take out the dirt without excess rubbing on the part of the user.

These boards had a hardwood frame which was very durable and strongly constructed. Some manufacturers even guaranteed the boards up to five years' usage. The wood backing and cross support pieces gave added stiffness to the rubbing surface and helped to prevent a sag in the board. The top of the boards have a rectangular space about 4" x 8". This provided a place to hold the soap when not in use, and to show the name and advertising of the manufacturer.

For the "medicine chest" select old bottles of suitable size.

How To

To convert one of these into a "medicine chest," first stain all of the wood on the front side. Next attach a saw-edge hanger to the back of the top horizontal board. Then drill a hole and insert the procelain knob.

To make the frame for the medicine chest, use wood lath or wood lattice stripping a quarter inch thick and 1½" to 2" wide. Measure the rubbing surface so that the frame will fit into this area. After cutting the four frame pieces nail these together, and then across the bottom of the frame attach a piece of wood (same as used for the sides) to hold the bottles in safely. Put a similiar piece at the top for looks. Stain the chest and attach to rubbing sur-

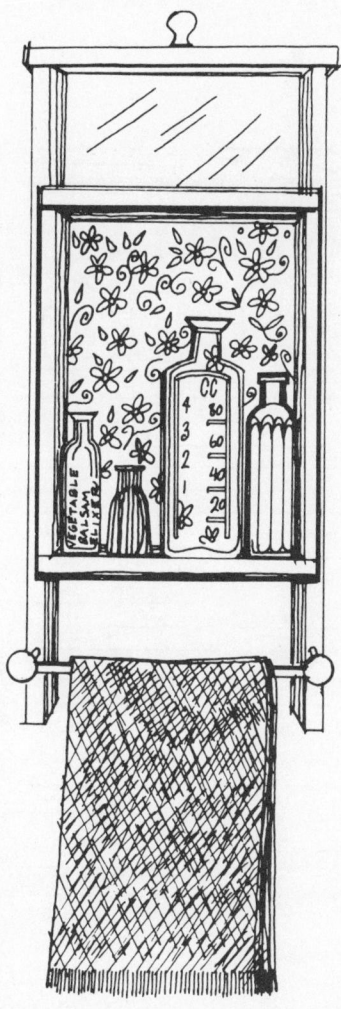

face with dowel rods. Then cover the area inside the frame with contact burlap or a pattern paper to finish the medicine chest.

To make the towel holder use two wooden knobs of approximately 1″ diameter. Drill an eighth inch wide hole into center of knob and another hole at a 90 degree angle. See illustration.

Cut two dowel rods in 2″ lengths. Insert in knob and glue. Next drill an eighth inch wide and half inch deep hole into each "leg" of the washboard 2″ from the end. Measure distance between these holes to determine length of towel bar to be made from eighth inch dowel rod. Insert towel bar into knobs and attach to washboard. Measure the top panel of the board and have a mirror cut to fit.

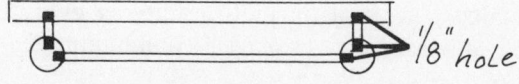

Washboard—Using Back

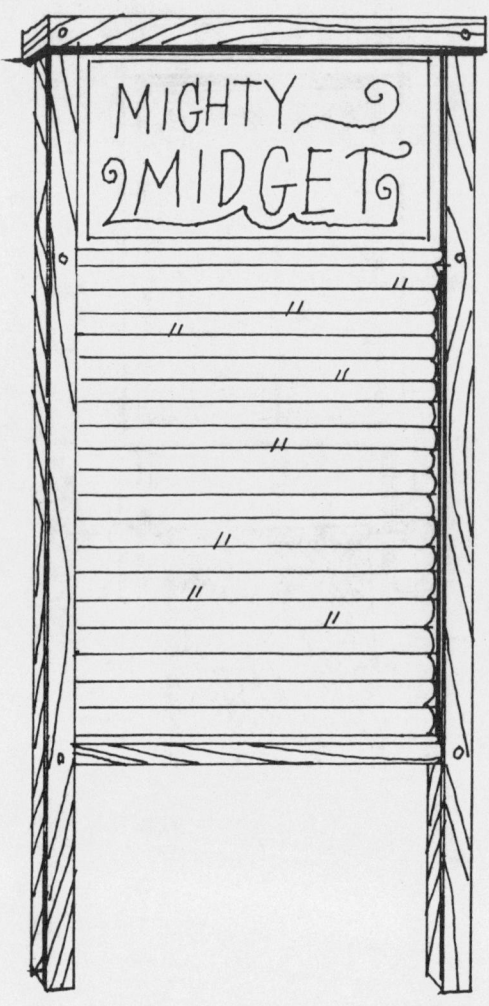

    Some of the older small washboards have a thin wood covering on the backside to give support to the rubbing surface. This is the type we used for this piece.

    The petite girl in the frame is from a picture card provided in cans of coffee years ago as an advertising gimmick. The back of the card reads: "Use Banner coffee guaranteed to be the best packaged coffee in the market. A combination for purity and flavor unequaled. A beautiful picture card in every package. Banner coffee once used always used." Manufactured by the Indiana Coffee Co.

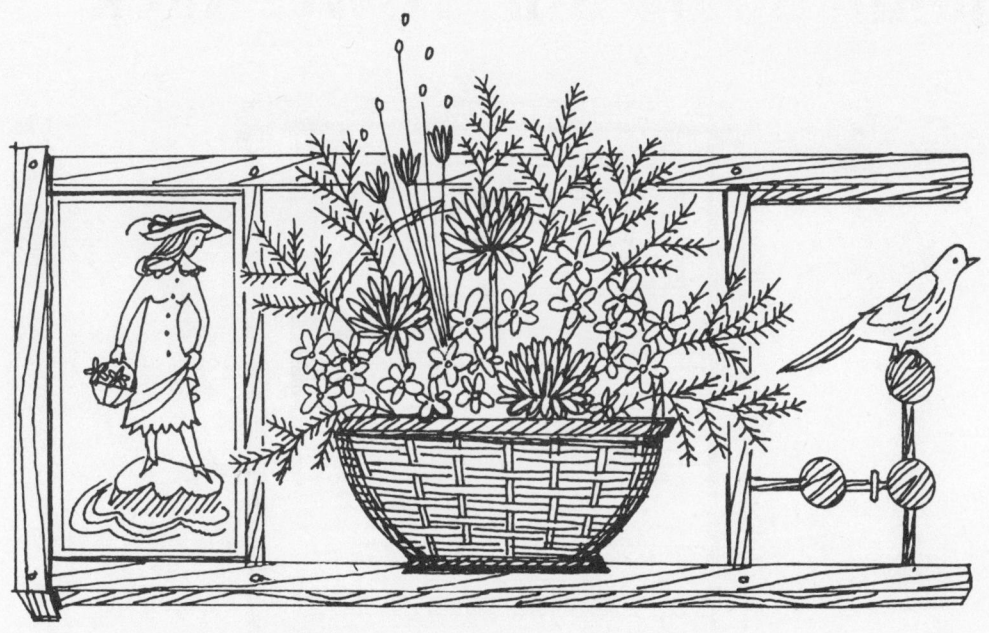

How To

First attach two saw-edge holders 12" apart on the backside of the top horizontal board. Next stain the wood and then drill eighth inch holes for the bird perch. It is made from 1" round wood balls and eighth inch dowel rods. The picture card is then decoupaged to the board.

To complete the piece, take a small woven basket about 5" wide and cut in half. Use the half with the handle and drill small holes in the board to wire through the basket and out the other side of the washboard. After it is secured, fill with flowers to complement the picture.

Washboard
Bulletin Board and Towel Rack

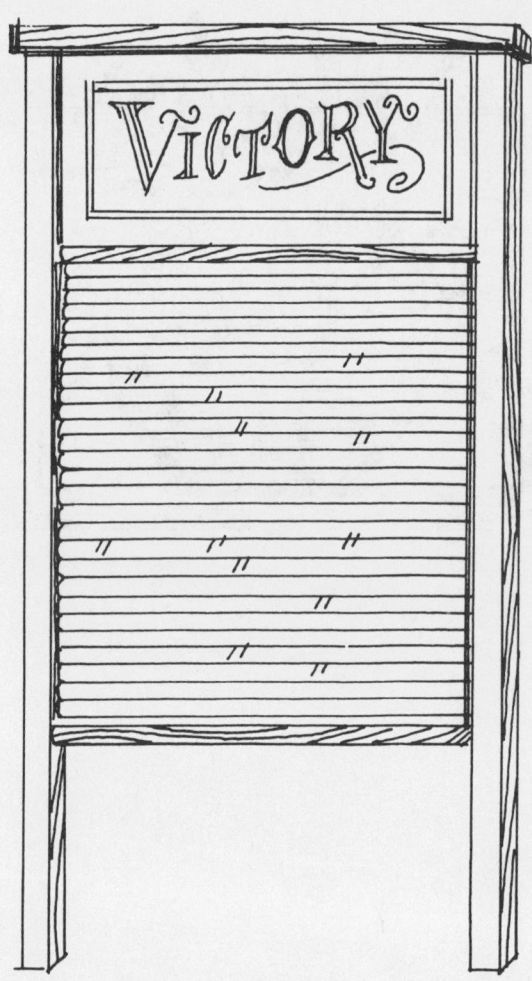

These small washboards were apparently a popular item for many manufacturers as there seems to be an almost endless variety of brand names. Some of these are Victory, Scanti, Handi, Federal Brand, Midget, and Baby Grand. In size these are about 18" long and 9" wide. For this particular piece, the rubbing surface needs to be tin or zinc to permit use because of magnets to hold the notes of the day.

How To

First stain the wood on the washboard and then nail two saw-edge holders to the top backside. This will keep the board from tipping when you take off or add the magnets. After the stain has dried, cover the wood around the rubbing surface with masking tape and then spray the surface with gold or brass paint. Let the

paint dry for four or more hours and then go over lightly with fine steel wool to remove the shine and give an aged look. The directions for the towel rack are on page 163.

Have a mirror cut to fit the panel above the rubbing surface and glue it in place. After this has dried well, cut an eighth inch diameter piece of dowel rod three-fourths inch long. Drill two small holes near one end of the rod to stick in the wires for the feet of the small bird. Drill a hole into the wood alongside the mirror to insert rod that holds bird. The bird should be looking into the mirror so you can see the reflection of its face.

Washboard— Wooden Bowl and Mirror

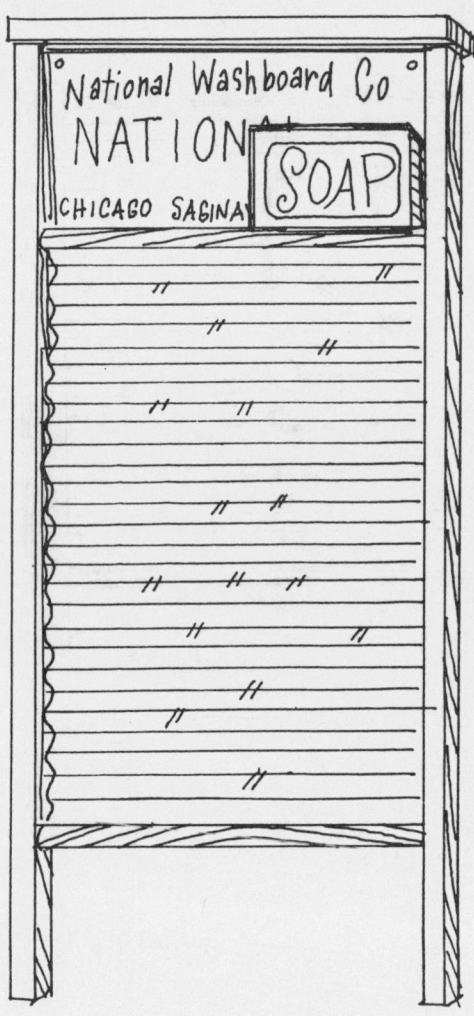

The small washboards seem to hold a certain nostalgia for most people. To grandmothers, however, they are a reminder of the days when washing and drying clothes was an all day affair. Usually Monday was the designated wash day, depending partly of course on the weather for "hanging out" the clothes to dry in the sun. To the modern mother the washboard is more fun as a decorative item.

How To

A small washboard approximately 9" x 18" is used. First antique with gold or silver the rubbing surface or leave as is if it cleans well with steel wool. Next stain the wood part of the front of the washboard. Then you are ready to add the saw-edge hanger to the back of the top horizontal board and the white knob to the top

of the washboard. Cut a 6" diameter wooden bowl in half (see page 162 for details). Stain or paint the bowl as desired. Place on rubbing surface to mark for drilling holes to receive dowel rods from bowl. Then glue the bowl in place. Fill the bowl with mushrooms, strawberry or vegetable picks. For towel rack detail, see page 163.

For the mirror to fit into the panel above the rubbing surface, it is best to take the washboard to a mirror shop where they can make an exact measurement and cut to fit. Insert and glue in the mirror as the last step.

Small Tin Scoop and Old Drawer

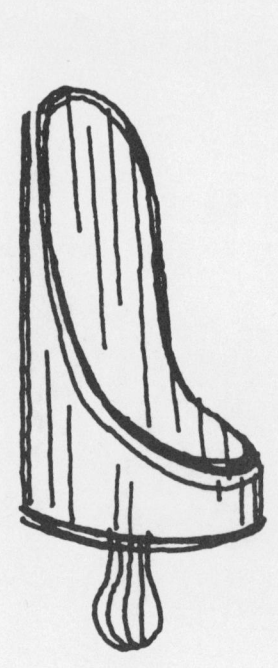

Small tin scoops had many uses both in the home and at the old time grocery store. A primary use was for measuring out sugar, bulk tea, and of course candy.

A small, shallow desk or dresser drawer to hold the scoop works great for this piece. We were fortunate to find one measuring about 6" x 7" x 2½" deep for the original piece. A drawer as the one in this illustration can be made from scratch, using quarter inch wood slats 3" wide. Make the drawer a 6" x 7" rectangle.

How To

After you make or find a drawer, attach a saw-edge hanger to the back. Next put on a white small knob. Then place the backing in the drawer. Here again we used a red and white check contact paper.

The scoop should be 3" wide x 4" long. Nail it through the top edge of the rim to the drawer side and at an angle as shown. Insert nest and bird. Drill a small hole in the bottom of the shelf to receive the ivy and then curve this up and over toward the scoop.

Old Wood Shovel Handle

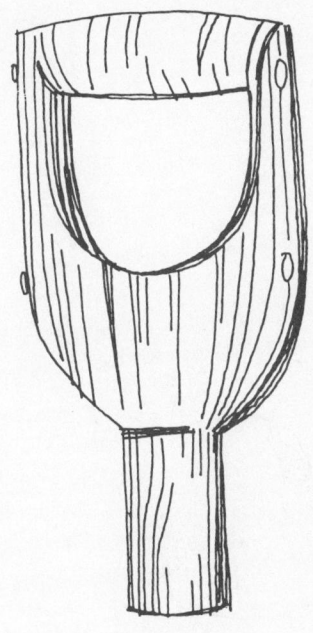

Most shovels today of the spade type have a combination wood and metal handle grip. Years back many of the handles were all wood. Some of these go back to the 1850-1900 era. The handles were referred to as D handles because of their shape.

How To

The shank of the handle is cut to 6" and mounted on a piece of barn wood. The barn wood is 6" to 8" wide and 6" longer than the shovel handle. Attach saw-edge hanger to backside of board. Drill two holes an eighth inch in diameter and a quarter inch deep into handle. Insert dowel rods letting these extend out a half inch. Place on board and mark for drilling receptive holes for rods.

Mount handle on barn wood and make nest from excelsior to glue into handle hole. Use two small birds in the nest and further decorate with ivy and wheat as desired.

"Kraut" Board with Biscuit Cutter

    Although this board, used to cut cabbage, is commonly referred to as a kraut board or cutter, technically it is a slaw cutter. These measure about 6″ x 16″ in size. The board is equipped with cutting knives.

    The kraut board is much larger, being 8″ to 10″ wide, with a length up to 30″ or more. The true kraut cutter is also identified by the "slide box" that fits in a groove running the length of the board. The purpose of the box is to hold a cabbage head and make it easy to push the head across the knives for shredding. The cutting blades are adjustable for making fine or coarse kraut. Some boxes had a wooden lid with handle so that the operator could press down on the cabbage while keeping the fingers away from the sharp blades.

    Sometimes you will find for sale the sliding box minus the kraut board. These have interesting possibilities as described elsewhere in this book.

The biscuit cutter is made of tin. A two inch width is a common size. Quite often these were given away by flour manufacturers. Such were made with raised lettering on the cutter telling the merits of the flour. The biscuit maker used for this plaque has the wording "Davis—Positively Pure Baking Products—None Better." Another we have makes this direct statement, "Use U.S. Flour."

How To

You may wish to stain or varnish the board or let the natural, worn finish of the wood show. Attach saw-edge hanger to back top of board and an old drawer pull on the front side near the top. Next mount the biscuit cutter in upside down position at bottom of board with a small nail. Hang ivy from the drawer pull and attach the bird. Fill the biscuit holder with styrofoam and add mushroom pick and star flowers. The piece is finished and ready to hang.

Hay Bale Hook

    Hay is alfalfa, clover, or some other grass plant grown in the field, mowed and cured as fodder to feed livestock. For years the procedure was to load the hay onto wagons using pitchforks and taking this to the barn for storage in the haymow. A daily chore was to climb the ladder into the loft and throw hay into the chutes which ran from the loft down to the feeding troughs for the cows and horses.

    Hay baling equipment, or presses as they were also called, was available in the late 1800s. Baled hay was expedient for transporting any long distance. The size of the bale varied, some being as small as 18" x 22". Today a typical bale measures 20" by 4' in length.

    Bale hooks were devised to make it easier to handle the bales for loading on the wagon in the field. These hooks were also known as "box hooks," as they were useful to pick up or pull about any large item in the barn. Some of these were simply a piece of steel in the form of a pointed hook with a hardwood handle on the opposite end. However, for this project you will need the hay hook with the D shaped wood and steel handle. It was made to give an easier and firmer grip. Also for our purpose it holds the cozy bird nest.

How To

Select a piece of barn wood with "character" about 7" x 13". If the board is not slanted or weather beaten at the top end, cut at an angle. Attach saw-edge holder to back of board. Drill an eighth inch hole into the backside of the wood handle about a quarter inch deep and insert a piece of dowel rod three-fourths inch long. Position hook on board and drill receptive hole for dowel rod. Glue in place. Where the "hook" curves away from the board, drill a small hole on each side and fasten with black wire. Next make a small nest from excelsior and place in the handle. We used two birds and added a cluster of small berries for color. Decorate as desired, using ivy and wheat.

Match Box with Old Knife and Fork

Old knives and forks were made with handles of iron, wood, bone and ebony. Many patterns for the handles were available. The set we used for this piece is a "double ring" pattern with a ring at both the top and bottom. The better handles had "bolstered" ends, that is a metal covering over the tip end of the handle to give added strength and life to the implement.

The match holder used was originally called the "twin match safe." Two small receptacles are provided for the wood matches, with a striking surface in the center. This was one of the several varieties of match holders offered through the stores into the 1900s. This twin type is somewhat scarce and therefore more expensive than some of the match holders found today.

How To

For this piece you will need a board about 12" x 13". After preparing the board, attach two saw-edge holders on backside 2" from each end and 1" from the top of board. See page 163 for instructions on mounting the half bowl. The knife and fork are secured with elastic banding at the top and bottom of each handle. Position these utensils and drill holes on each side of the handle and make a loop of the elastic. Pull tight and tie on backside. Center the match holder above the bowl, allowing space for the arrangement of greenery in the bowl. Attach the match holder with small wooden drawer pull or white porcelain knob. Fill bowl and the piece is finished.

Coffee Mill—Wall Type (side mounting)

    The wall type coffee mill or grinder dates back to the 18th century and predates the box type used on the table. These were first crudely made of wrought iron and then of cast-iron. Some of the older ones were mounted with two small bolts to a piece of wood about 6" x 12". The bolts extend through the backside of the board. The tin hopper to feed the roasted coffee into the grinding gear had only three sides and was attached to the front of the board with small nails. The board then immediately behind the hopper became the backside of the hopper chute and was notched out three-eighths inch for this purpose. Some of these mills have a tin lid to cover the hopper top, hinged to the top of the board.

    On the backside of the board is a cylinder flange giving an opening to the shank end of the grinder handle. A wing nut screws into the flanged opening to control the coarseness of the coffee. The wing nut extends out about an inch and had to be accessible to operate the mill. Because of this, the grinder mounting could not be flush against the wall and was usually attached to the end of a cabinet or doorway opening. This particular model was referred to as a "side" coffee mill. You will find these with three mounting holes at the right end of the wood piece.

    The ideas and workmanship on this mill are most interesting and well worth the cost of the piece. The several mills of this type that we have seen or used have a brass oval attached to the tin hopper with the wording, "Increase Wilson's—Best Quality—New London" or "Wilson's Improved—Patent—Coffee Mill."

How To

Use a board 8" x 14". Stain this to contrast with the wood on the grinder. The 14" length is on a horizontal plane so it is desirable to use two saw-edge holders on the backside. Then drill a hole in the end of the 8" length for a white knob. See illustration. The board now gives the appearance of a "pull out" bread board from a kitchen cabinet. Position the handle of the grinder as you want it to appear permanently and tighten the wing nut. If desired the wing nut can be removed and you can retain the tension on the handle with a piece of dowel rod in the flange hole. We followed this procedure and then attached the wing nut to the front of the plaque.

The grinder is attached to the board by using the top and bottom holes of the three that originally held the grinder in place on the cabinet. Center the mill on the board and drill holes for the screws and secure tightly. This will make the left end of the grinder board extend out one to two inches from the cutting board which gives the effect of the original appearance of the grinder in use.

We placed ivy along the left end of the grinder and nut and berry clumps in the hopper opening.

Coffee Mill, Modified Side Type

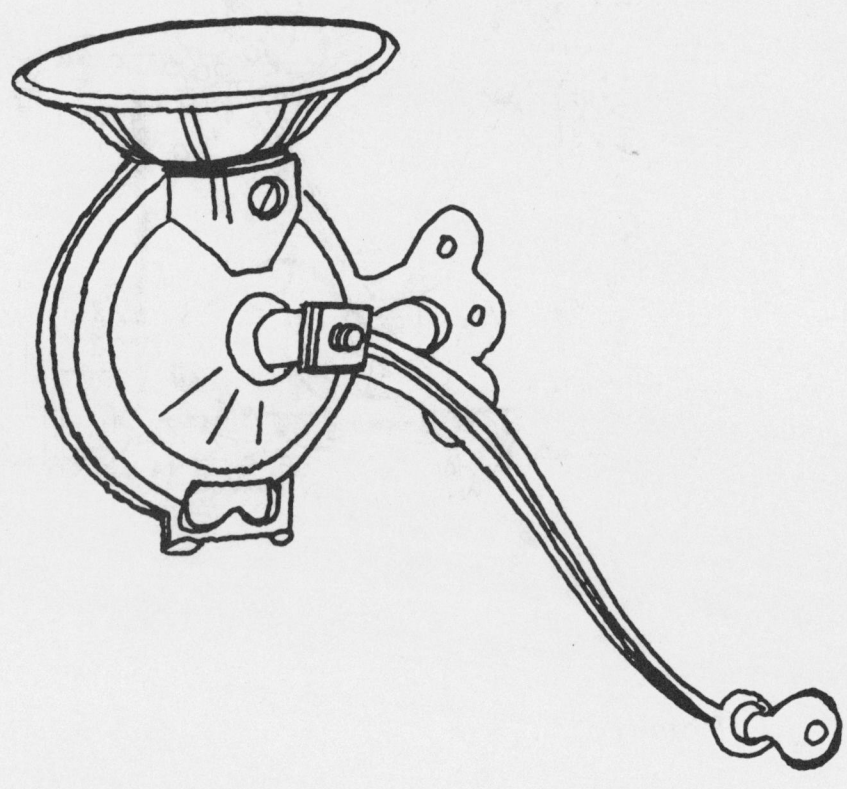

We assume that the inventor of this coffee mill (patent 1901) was making an improvement on the mounting of the much earlier "side mill" grinder. The "modified side type" is our terminology, as the mounting bracket allows the mill to be attached to any flat wall surface, but the handle is angled toward the wall and operates in this position. See illustration. This makes the piece different from all other wall types. The construction of the grinding box is flat on the backside but the 3" wide circular tin hopper extends out 1½" on the backside and necessitates this unusual mounting. The hopper to receive the roasted coffee is held on the grinder top with a small screw. The backside of the grinder is covered with tin instead of iron and is "clamped on" for easy removal to dismount the grinding burr.

The discharge opening for the ground coffee has a small hook-like piece that must have held some kind of tin container to catch the coffee.

How To

We used a board 10″ wide and 12″ high. It was stained light cherry to contrast with the black iron of the grinder. Attach a saw-edge holder to the backside of the board and white knob to the top. Positioning of the grinder is important for the right balanced look. It is attached by simply using two screws in the holes provided in the mounting arm. The left side of the grinder will extend out from the board about two inches. To fill in this "gap" we attached small mushrooms individually with eighth inch dowel rods and then finished the decorating with ivy.

Coffee Mill—Table Type

The table coffee grinder is more plentiful than the wall type. However, the demand has kept the price in the $15 to $25 range for the more common variety. We look for those that have been damaged in some way but yet not beyond repair to make an attractive table piece.

These box type coffee mills were sometimes made entirely of heavy tin but mostly of cast-iron and wood. The top was cast-iron with a hinged cover as the hopper opening. The hopper for pouring in the roasted coffee was either raised above the hardwood box, which had dovetail corners, or was sunk into the box. The cheaper mills had an open hopper which was mounted on top of the box. Some of these mills are quite ornate and even have a carrying handle as part of the top or a handle mounted on the side of the box.

How To

The one used for this particular project is of heavy tin construction. It was rusty and the drawer was missing. Also the "dish" in the hopper mill was cracked. After rubbing with steel wool it was sprayed flat black. We were careful to cover the wood knob on the handle before painting. A new drawer was made from wood, sprayed black and white, and knob added. The tin hinged cover for the "sunken hopper" is left open to hold the nest for the little partridge bird. Make the nest from excelsior and glue in place. The drawer is filled with strawberry picks and small greenery.

A previous coffee mill we repaired was of the hardwood box type. Not only was the drawer missing but the complete bottom. It was made up in a similiar manner. For the bottom we used a small bread board and centered the mill on it.

Coffee Grinder—Wall Type

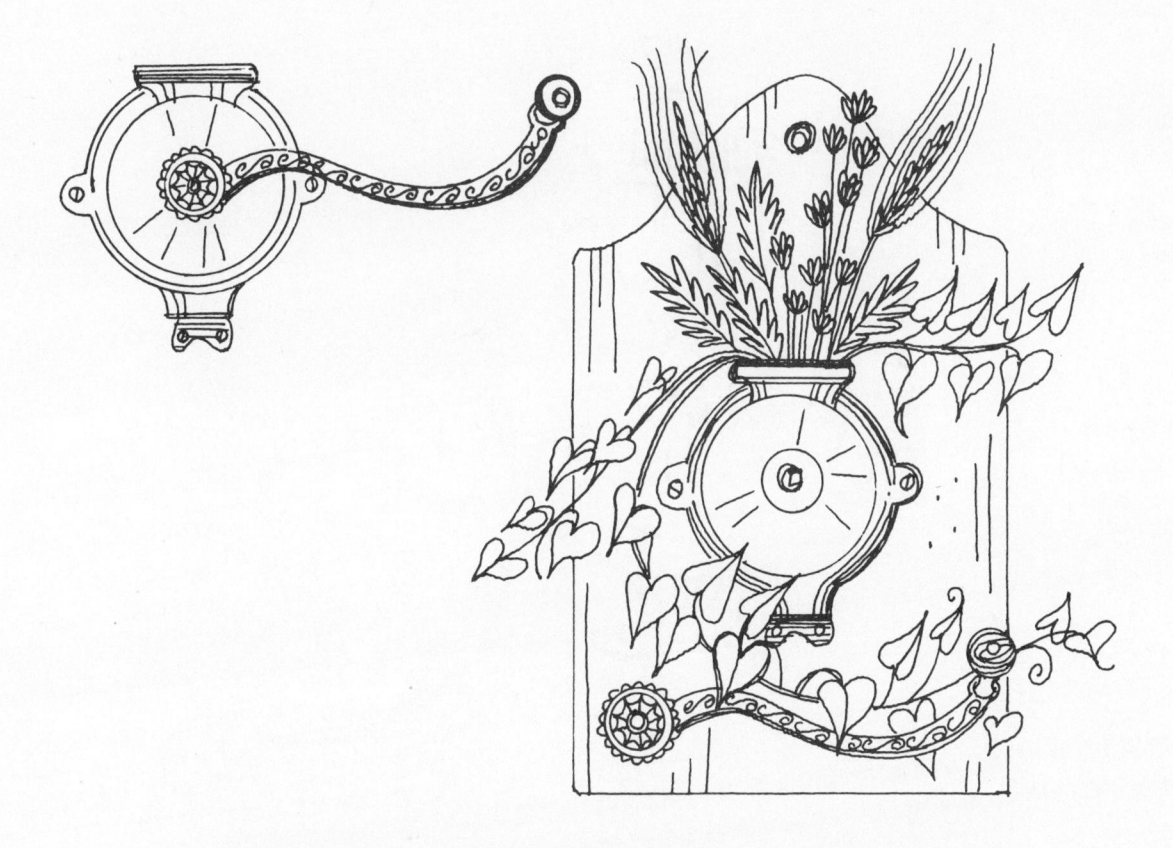

The coffee grinder used for this plaque was made entirely of cast-iron and had mounting "legs" to attach it to any flat vertical surface. Although the backside of the housing for the grinder wheel is flat, the top of the mill has a circular opening for the glass hopper.

Fortunately for our purpose, the glass hopper to hold the coffee is not essential.

How To

The bread board we used had a natural curve at the top and is ornate in itself. If the board is straight-edged, we suggest a white knob be attached to the center top edge. Stain the 8" x 12" board as desired and nail a saw-edge holder to the backside. Use nails of a size sufficient to support the weight of the mill. Attach same with black screws, using the holes in the "mounting legs."

We removed the handle and placed this below the grinder. Many of the iron handles are quite ornate and mounting below the mill makes the handle stand out even more. Drill hole through board and use a bolt and nut to attach.

Fill the opening in the grinder with an arrangement of dry flowers and ivy and it is ready to mount.

Coffee Mill with Picture Cards

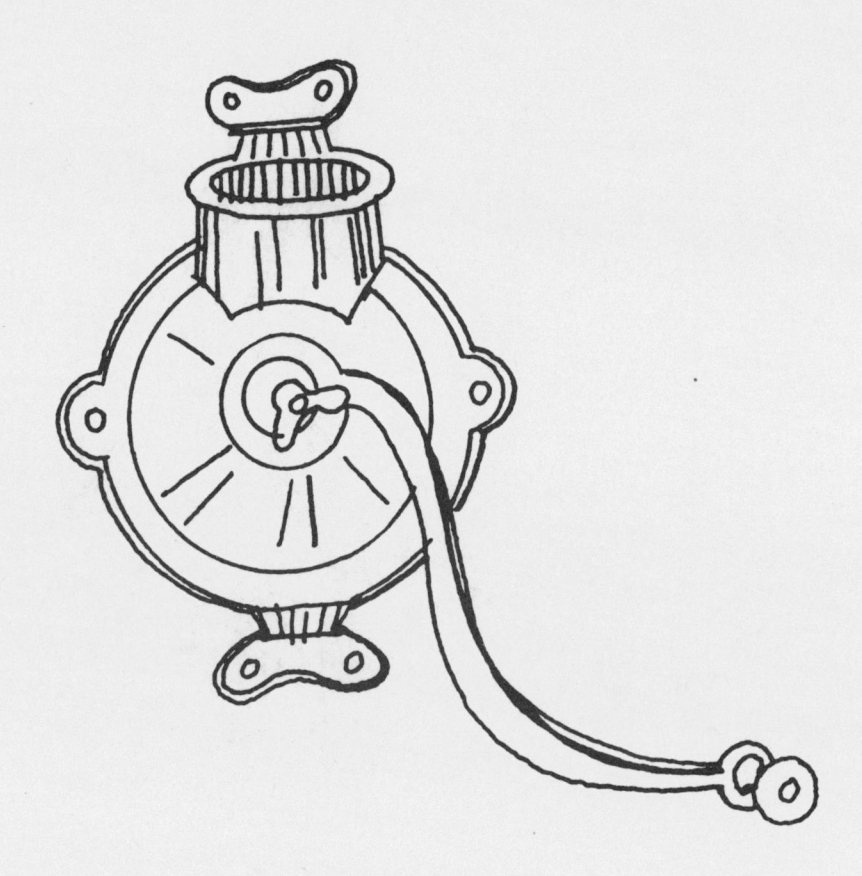

    This plaque not only displays an old coffee grinder but also the gimmicks used for selling the roasted coffee.

    The two picture cards are quite old and were packaged in the coffee cans long ago to entice the consumer to purchase this particular brand. It was customary to advertise the merits of the coffee on one side of the card and display a colored print on the other. In this plaque the card on the left has the side showing the advertising and the other has the colored print. The card with the advertising reads, "To secure a picture like this you have only to buy a package of Lion Coffee! It is composed of a successful combination of Mocha—Java and Rio. It is a roasted with great care, but is not ground. Lion is the king of coffees, manufactured by Woolson Spice Co., Toledo, Ohio." The advertiser made sure that the company name would be seen when looking at the front or back of the card. In the upper corner of the picture in fancy script is the wording, "The Woolson Spice Co's. Midsummer Greetings." Pictured are two pretty young ladies in outfits of the Gay Nineties.

How To

The coffee mill used for this project is similiar in size to the previous one described. The bread board used is 10" x 12". Attach saw-edge hanger to the backside of board. Mount the mill on the board using black screws in the holes provided.

The prints were glued to the board and then a small quarter inch wood frame painted gold was put around each picture. Use a light coat of varnish to protect the cards.

This is a nice conversation piece for your coffee drinking friends.

Toy Popgun and World War I Soldiers

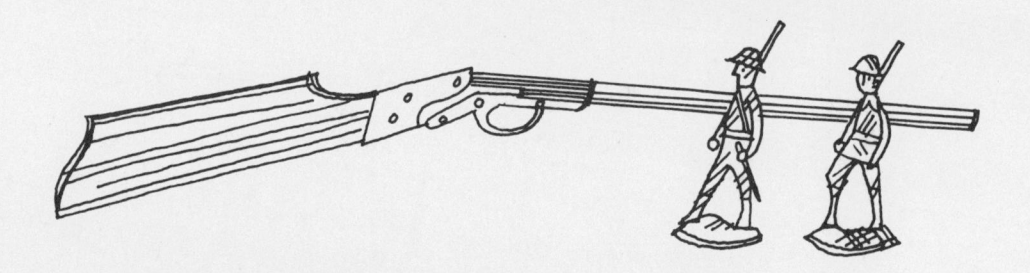

The toy popgun was a favorite for every little boy and dates back to the early 1900s. The stock was made of wood, just like dad's, with the barrel and other mechanism of steel. These will vary in length but most we have seen are about 17" long. It may still "break" to cock the gun and the trigger will work. Or it may fail to operate because of age and rust. Either kind will do fine for this plaque.

The toy soldiers are of lead and were made for several years after World War I. These have now become collectors' items.

How To

The cutting board is 7" x 21" and rounded at the top. Drill hole and insert white knob. Center a saw-edge holder near the top of the backside and then stain the board to contrast with the wooden stock of the gun. If necessary use steel wool on the gun stock and flat black paint on the metal part of the gun. To mount the toy figures we cut a 1½" drawer pull in half. Drill an eighth inch hole in the "cut" surface of the pull to insert a dowel. Let the dowel rod stick out a half inch to be secured to the cutting board later.

Usually the toy soldiers will have a hole running up each leg. Insert dowel rods in the legs and also drill holes in the flat side of the drawer pull to insert the rods to secure the soldiers to the pulls. Then position the gun and drawer pulls (with soldiers attached). Drill holes in the board for the pulls. The gun probably will be light weight enough to attach with elastic banding to board. See Illustration.

Toy Gun with Wooden Soldier

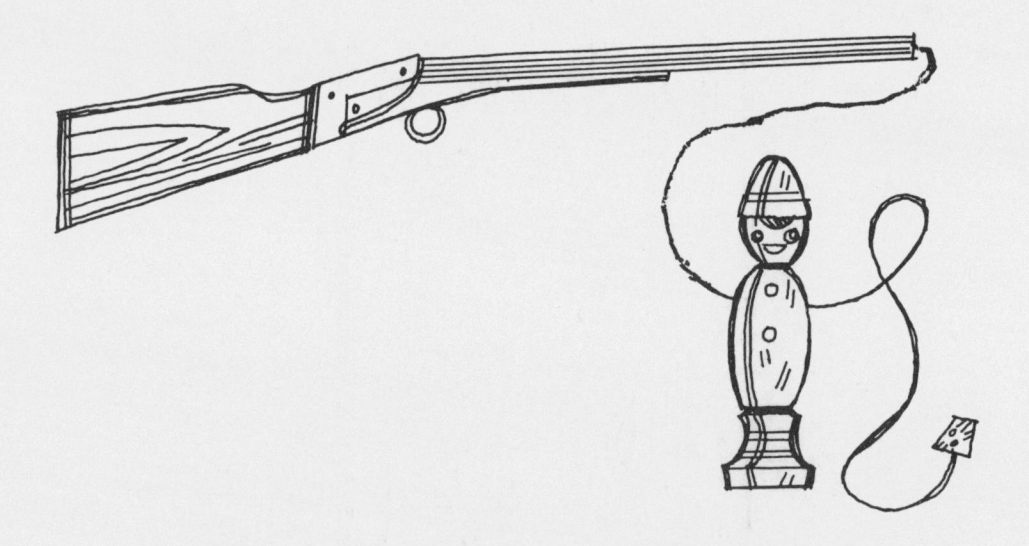

The toy gun used is similiar to the one described on the preceding page. We believe it predates the other one because it has a circle for the trigger. The mechanism doesn't work but we found an old cork still in the barrel. Many of these toy guns were originally sold with a string attached to the cork and gun. For this piece we followed this theme and added an old toy wooden soldier (with arms missing) for the target. A delightful piece for a young boy's room.

How To

The cutting board is 8" x 30" and rounded at the top. Stain as desired and nail saw-edge hanger to backside. Attach the gun with elastic banding. The string is run through the cork and cut off flush with the bottom of the cork. Use a small nail to place the cork on the board. Then run the string back to the gun in a semi-circle and into the muzzle. Glue the string to the board.

The soldier is secured by drilling two eighth inch holes into the backside and inserting three-quarter inch length dowel rods. Place on board and drill receptive holes and attach.

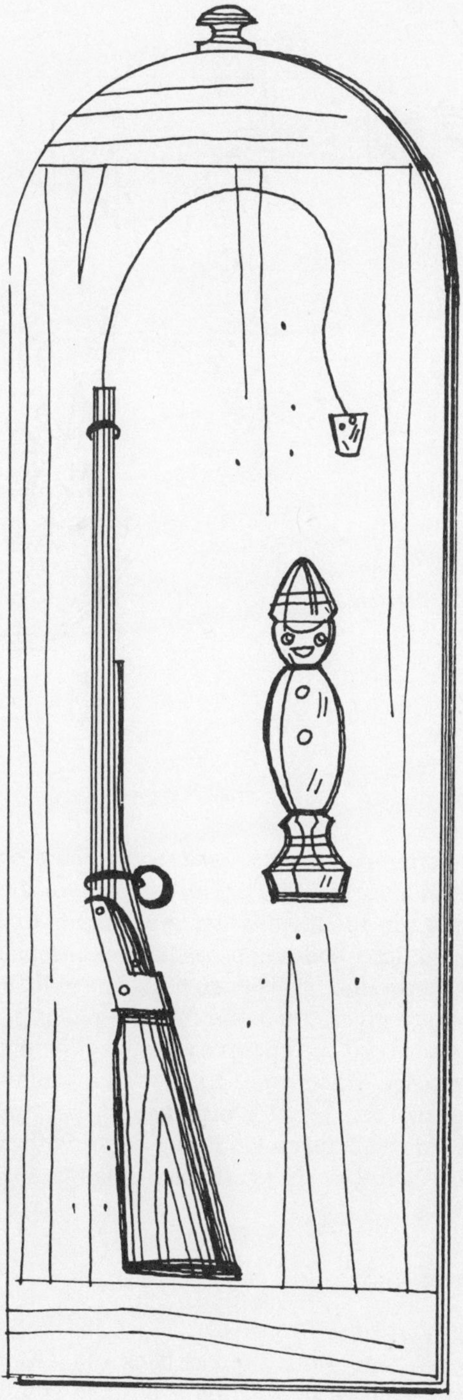

"Thumb" Sugar Scoop and Bowl

Many of the small tin scoops used in the home or at the early grocery store had a curved tin loop at the base for a handle. Some of these, as shown in the illustration, were made to slip the index finger through the loop and had a special resting place on the top of the loop for the thumb. This design made the little scoops easy to hold. They were given the name "thumb scoop."

Again this was a type of item given away by the flour companies for advertising. We found one scoop with a painted button-like piece about the size of a quarter attached to the "thumb spot" on the handle. It was a picture of a flying horse with wings and the wording "E. A. Flour Co.—Everett Aughenbaugh, Waseca, Minn."

How To

The cutting board used measures 11" x 12". Stain the board, then attach the saw-edge holder on the back and a white knob at the top. The scoop is nailed in position using two small nails. Next prepare a half wooden bowl as on page 162 and attach this to the board. In the scoop glue in some excelsior for a small nest and place a bird in it. The bowl is filled with any flower arrangement desired. We used small glossy apple picks and a touch of dried fall foliage.

Spoons, or Knife and Fork

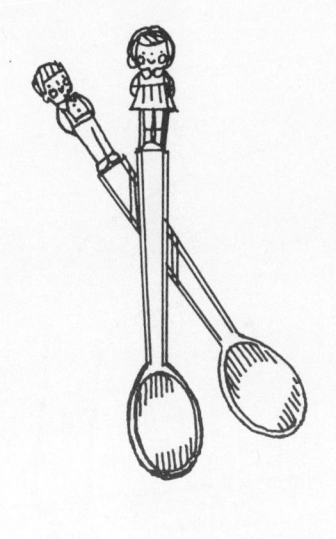

For this plaque we were fortunate to find a pair of the Campbell Kid spoons put out by the Campbell Soup Co. years ago. Quite likely these spoons were originally obtained by sending in labels from the soup cans. The attractive little figures on the tops of the spoons were popular with the children, and they liked the novelty of using such spoons. Also, of course, the spoons were an aid to mother in getting the children to eat the hot soup.

If preferred, other old ornate spoons can be used, or even knives and forks dating back to the late 1800s. These are plentiful.

How To

The board should be at least 12" wide and 10" high. First stain, paint or leave the board natural. Attach the hanger. Then cut a wooden bowl in half (5" to 6" diameter). Paint or stain bowl as desired, and attach to board with dowels. See page 162 for detail. Next place the spoons or knife and fork on the board. Elastic banding should hold each of these lightweight items in place. The design of the utensil will determine the best place to attach the elastic. Drill a small hole on each side of the utensil and just slightly under (to hide hole). Use a three inch length of black elastic putting each end through a hole. Place the utensil under the elastic and draw very tight. Then tie a knot in the elastic banding at back. Now you are ready to fill the bowl with an arrangement.

Hat Blocking Frame

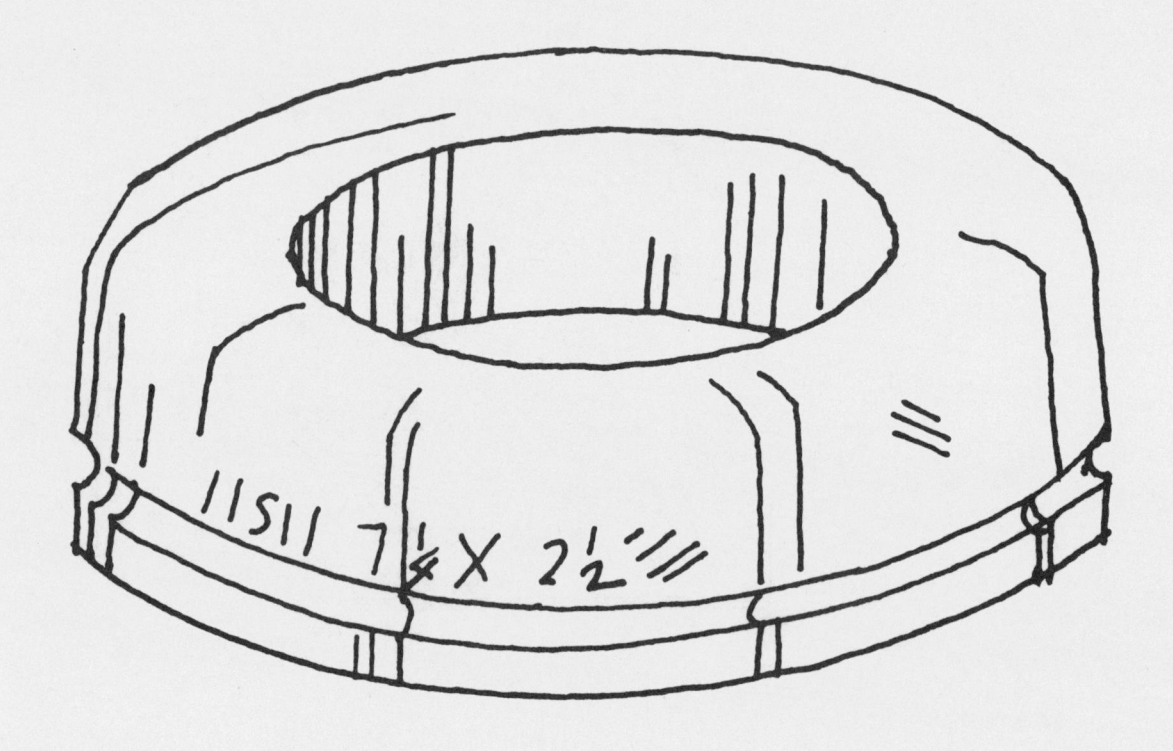

These old hat forms are rare and do make a most interesting frame. Here we found the "brim" of the form separate from the "crown" that in regular use filled the middle opening. Years ago when felt hats were popular with men it was customary every so often to have the hats cleaned and "blocked" to retain their appearance and shape. Such a business was often combined with that of shoe repairing. In fact, there are a few shops that still offer this service. The hat brim form will have a number stamped on the end indicating the hat size. The form we used is a size 7 and the over all width of the piece is 10", the length 12" and the depth 2".

How To

It's best to leave the wood natural and select the item to be "framed" accordingly. To put a "back" in the block, first place the form on a piece of paper and mark the size of the inside oval. Then enlarge this by a half to three-quarter inch. Cut out the pattern and trace on eighth to quarter inch plywood and saw out to size. Cover the plywood with contact burlap of any color and design suitable. Nail the plywood to the back of block and attach saw-edge hanger. We used a cornhusk doll in the frame, as illustrated, and artificial flowers. The cornhusk dolls are made today commercially and as a hobby. These are said to go back to pioneer days when they were made as toys for the children and were copied after those made by Indians.

Duck Decoy Heads in Drawer

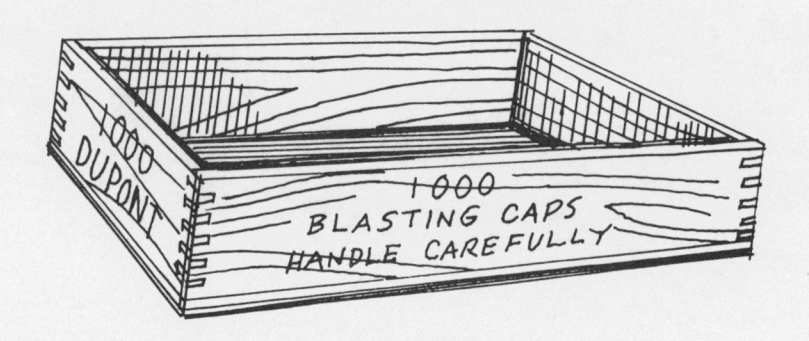

Duck decoys are often found in a sportman's den or family room. The carving and painting of a full size decoy is an art that goes back many years. The ones made of wood, of course, are the most desirable. There were also inflatable canvas ducks in the late 1800s. Later papier-mache types were manufactured at a considerably lower cost than the hand made wood decoys.

Usually the heads of the wood decoys are carved separately and then attached to the bodies with a quarter inch dowel. Sometimes the bodies are destroyed by an eager hunter and for this reason or another spare heads are sometimes available. We were fortunate to find at a flea market two handsome heads (with marks of a few buckshot) in good condition. It seemed appropriate to mount these in a "drawer" that once was a box for dynamite blasting caps.

How To

Find a drawer about 8" x 12" in size or make one. The depth should not be over 3¼". If you find a box suitable but too deep just cut it in two pieces. Stain the box antique maple and add an old drawer pull at one end to give the appearance of a drawer. Then use a piece of red contact burlap in the bottom. Nail a saw-edge hanger to the top backside.

In the backside of each duck head drill an eighth inch hole and cut a three-quarter dowel rod to insert. Position the heads in the drawer and mark for drilling receptive holes for the rods. Put a little glue in the drawer holes, position the duck heads, and the piece is ready to hang.

"Tourist" Folding Curling Iron

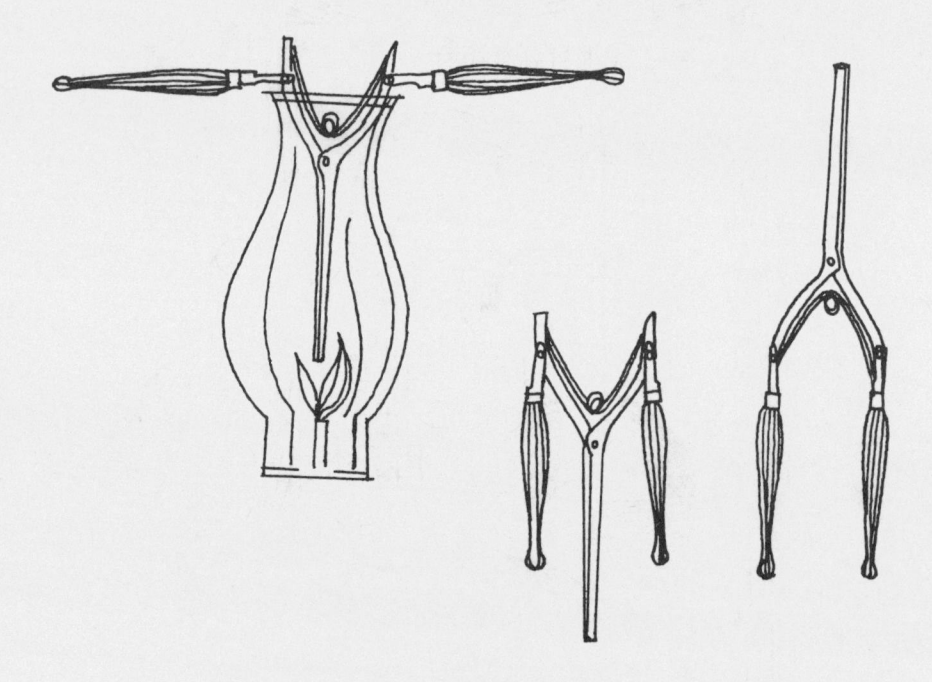

Curling irons were still used in the 1930s and many of these of different sizes and types are still readily available. They are usually made with wood handles of oak or rosewood and polished steel. About one out of 25 curling irons you see may be of the folding handle type, known as the "tourist iron." The handles are cleverly jointed so that for regular use these work the same as the conventional curling iron. However, the two handles easily bend back and were designed in this way for two purposes. For traveling this made the iron more compact and it could be discreetly carried in the lady's purse. Also by bending the handle halfway back, they are placed perpendicular to the steel shaft. In this way the steel part of the iron fits into a kerosene lamp chimney with the bent handles supporting same. The wood part of the handle is away from the heat of the lamp. You will find some curling irons with regular handles that have the wood scorched from the heat of the lamp.

For this project we used a 9" "tourist" folding iron with handsome oak handles, along with an old kerosene lamp. The curling iron is mounted so it can be easily removed to show your friends how it works.

How To

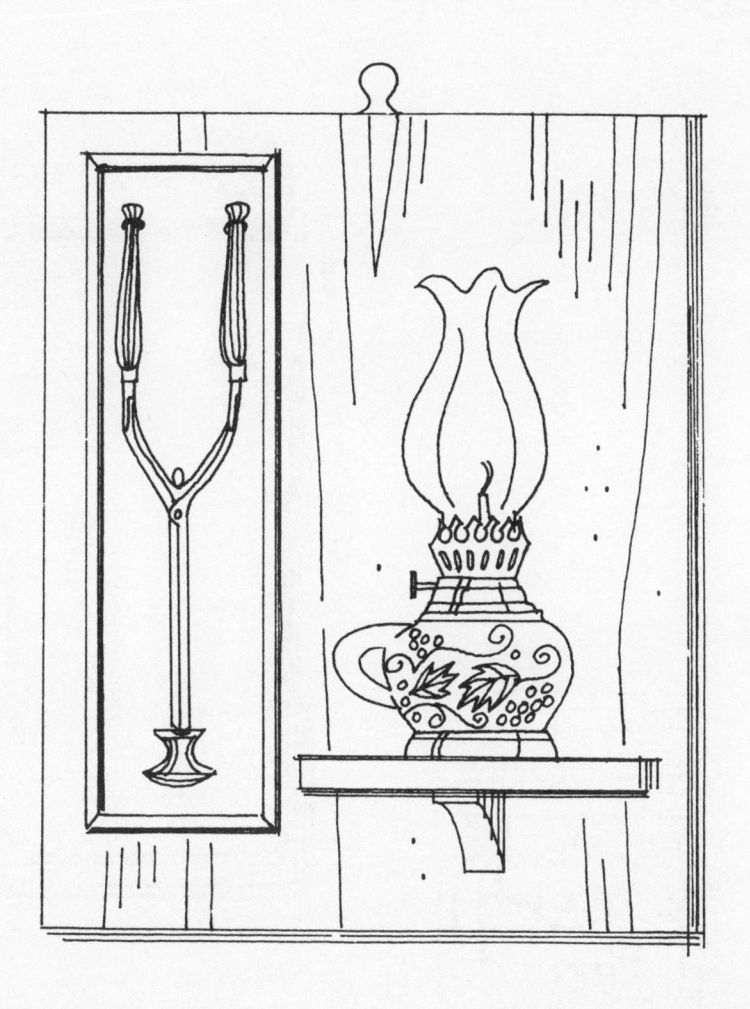

The bread board measures 12″ x 15″. The shelf for the lamp is 3½″ x 5″ and the bracket to support the shelf is 2″ x 2½″. See page 162 for mounting the shelf. Stain the wood as desired and nail two saw-edge holders on the backside top of the board. Also drill a hole and insert the white knob. To give more contrast to show off the curling iron, we used a 4″ x 12″ piece of gold contact burlap as the backing and made a mitered frame of quarter inch wood strips to edge the burlap. The frame was antiqued gold before attaching with nail brads.

The tip end of the iron rests on an old drawer pull. Cut one side off the pull so it will fit flush against the burlap. Drill an eighth inch hole in the backside of the pull so a dowel rod can be used to attach to the board. Secure the wood handles at the top with elastic banding by drilling two small holes in the board on each side of the two handles. The curling iron can then be easily removed to demonstrate how it was actually used.

Canning Lifter and Jar

Here's a fun piece to make, particularly for those ladies who have canned vegetables and fruit in the past. In fact, the canning jar lifter is still quite helpful for those who "put up" a few things today. Its purpose is to lift the hot jars from the boiler and to set them aside for cooling. The lifter is a double wire affair riveted together and has wooden handles. It works something on the principle of hand pliers. The bottom part of the lifter would grip the outside lid thread and hold tightly when the top wooden handles were pressed together. A quarter-pint Ball Mason jar is used along with the lifter.

How To

The board used measures 10" x 16". The shelf to hold the jar and lifter is 3" deep and 5" long. The bracket used with the shelf measures 2" x 2½". See page 162 for attaching the shelf. Secure a saw-edge holder to the top backside of the board and drill a hole for the white knob. We suggest a light stain be used to retain the natural dough board look.

Fill the jar with miniature fruit or vegetables. We used miniature carrots.

To hold the "lifter" on the jar, unscrew the jar slightly and clamp the lifter against the glass threads and tighten the lid. Ivy is intertwined about the handle and down the side. See illustration.

The bird nest is made from excelsior and glued to the top of the jar lid. Include a couple of eggs and place bird in the nest.

Foot Warmer

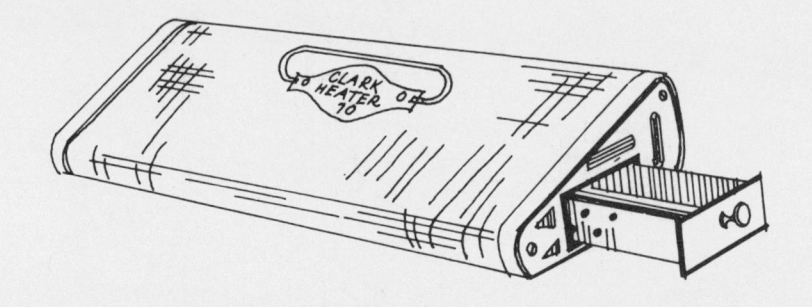

Although the foot stove we have here is not dated, it goes back to the horse and buggy days. It is constructed to be like a small foot stool without legs. See illustration. It is made from steel, with a tin box. The foot warmer measures 13½" long and 8" wide. The fuel box or drawer is 3½" wide and 11" long. The end at the opening for the drawer has air holes, and the opposite end has a ventilation shutter that can be opened or closed to control the fire in the fuel box. A wire handle to carry the stove lies flat on the foot rest side. A metal plate which attaches the handle has the wording, "The Clark Heater #70." The fire box has holes along its side to let air circulate about the coals. Charcoal or candle coal was normally used for fuel. At the front of the firebox there is a partition about 3" long and 3½" wide. This may have been to carry extra fuel.

Except for the two ends, the stove is covered with a carpet-like material which helped to retain the heat but gave off enough to warm the feet. The foot warmer was used in the buggy on the way to church and was even carried inside, for in those days only one small stove in the middle of the room couldn't do the job for the entire congregation.

Other times it was used for trips in the stagecoach and for romantic rides in the sleigh. A fellow with a foot stove may have had a little edge with the girls.

How To

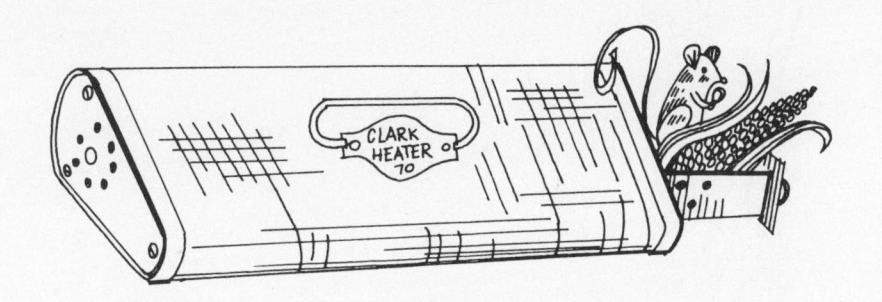

Like the stove we have, you may find the metal ends a little rusty. If so, cover the carpeted part and spray the ends flat black. We placed our foot warmer on the fireplace hearth. In the back chamber (firebox) of the drawer, a box of wooden matches is kept to light the fire. The drawer was pulled out to show the forward compartment. We made a nest of excelsior for a little gray funny mouse. If someone in the family is squeamish about mice, use a bird nest.

Ice Skates

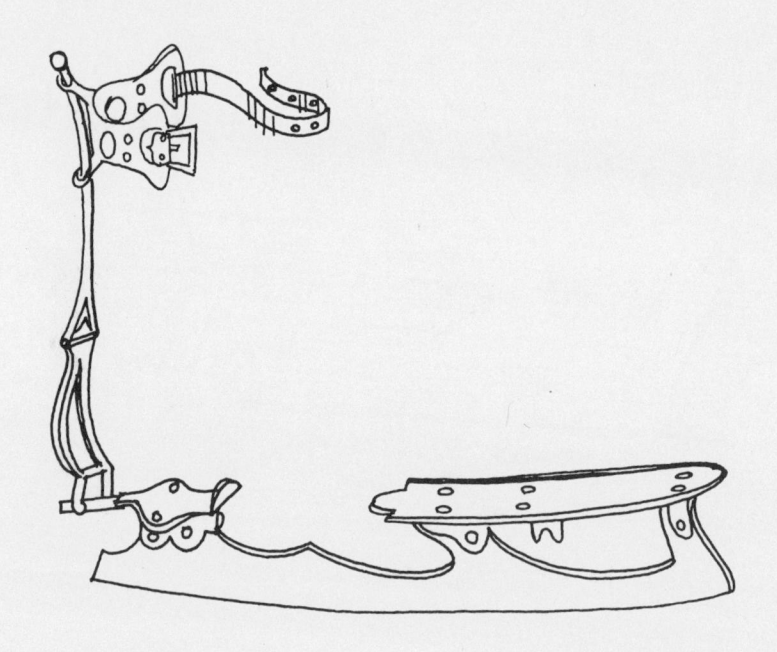

In the 1800s ice skating was one of the popular winter sports. Even then there were several models of skates to choose from, but most common was the type clamped on or strapped to the regular shoe. The skate we mounted is all steel and has patent dates of 1884 and 87. At that time the all-metal skate predominated, although combination wood and steel skates were still available into the early 1900s. The "old-fashioned" skates of that time were of wood upper and steel runner. The wood part which fit against the shoe had a horizontal slit at the heel and also at the toe through which a leather strap was inserted and buckled over the shoe. The all-metal skates were made with and without ankle braces. We used one with the brace as it is more interesting looking.

The skates will often be rusty when you buy them. You can hunt for identifying marks when cleaning. Be sure to use a wire brush and then steel wool on the toe and heel plates (the surface that the shoe rested on) as well as the runner. Usually the manufacturer's name or trademark will appear, possibly a patent date, and also the size of the skate. On cleaning the skate used for this mounting we noted the trademark was a circle around the letters BB. There were also the patent dates, skate size 10½, and on the runner the word "hardened."

How To

The size of the board used was 12″ x 20″. It was well worn and we left it in the natural. Two saw-edge holders were attached to the top backside. A white porcelain knob was placed at one end. After the skate has been sprayed with black flat paint, position on the board, allowing space for the half wood bowl. Mark the board to drill small holes so that the skate can be attached, using black wire at the heel and toe plate, and also where the half-round metal ankle brace touches the board. The directions for the half bowl are on page 162. We used a dark stain for the bowl to contrast with the bread board. The bowl was filled with winter-time delights of nuts, popcorn, and small apples (artificial).

If it is winter time when you are considering this project maybe you will want to try out the skates to see how it really was back then. The author in 1932 learned to skate on such as these. Good luck!

Shoe Cobbler's Tools

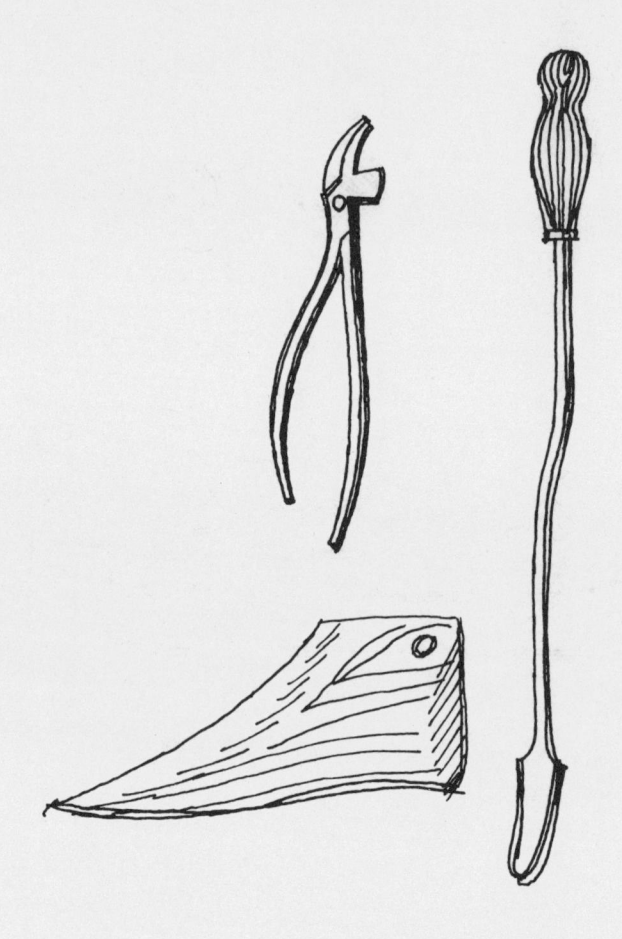

    In the very early days of shoe and boot making the soles were attached to the uppers with pegs of chestnut wood. The pointed end of the pegs protruded inside the shoe and needed filing off for comfort. The tool shown with the long handle has a grooved backing on the tip end which was worked back and forth inside the shoe and had the effect of filing the peg ends smooth. The hammer-like plier tool is a "lasting pincers" used to pound in or pull pegs or nails. The wooden "last" was used to form the shoe and hold it firm while the soles were put on.
    As today people then were style conscious. The toes of the shoes were pointed, round, or square. When shoes were first hand sewn, they were usually made on straight "lasts." One had to wear the shoes to shape them gradually to fit the right and left foot. No doubt this is why there were special tools to stretch out the shoe leather where it fit too tightly.

How To

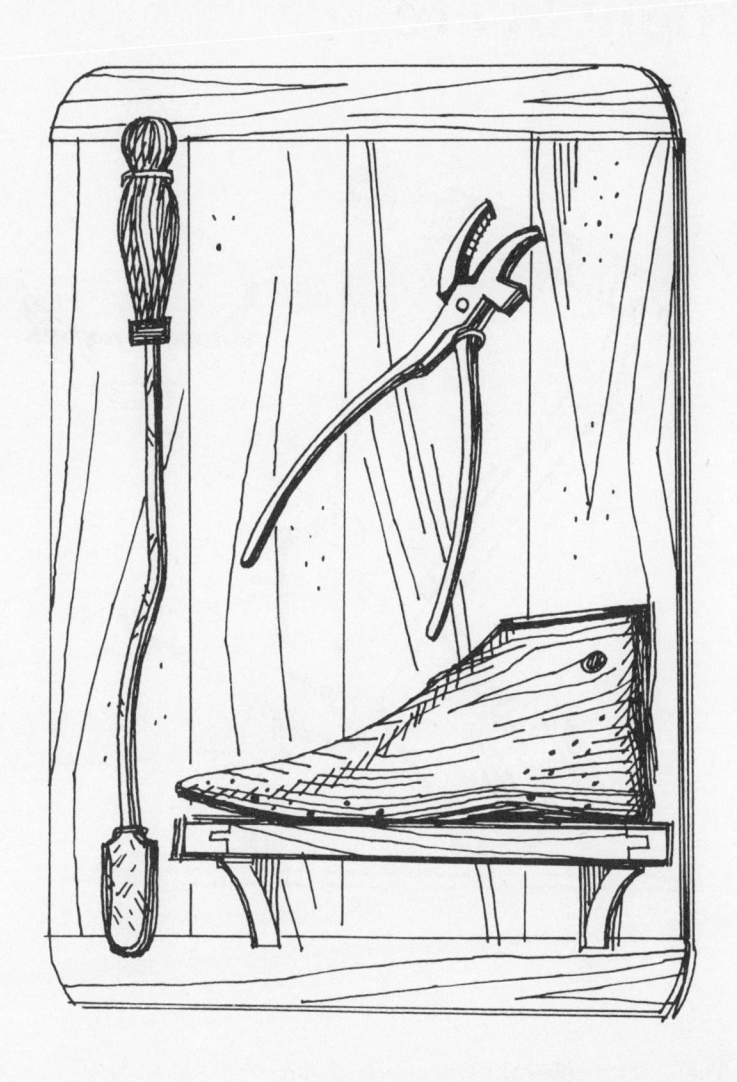

The board used measures 12″ x 17″. Due to the size and shape of the shoe "last," a shelf is used to mount it. The shelf measures 4″ x 9″ and the brackets 2″ x 2″. See page 162 for shelf detail. After the shelf is attached stain the piece and attach two saw-edge holders to the top backside.

Next, the smoothing tool and lasting pincers are mounted with strong elastic banding, 3/16″ size. A small hole is drilled on both sides of the tools to permit inserting and tying the black banding. Use rubber cement to attach temporarily the wooden last to the shelf.

The piece is now ready to display.

Egg Grading Scale

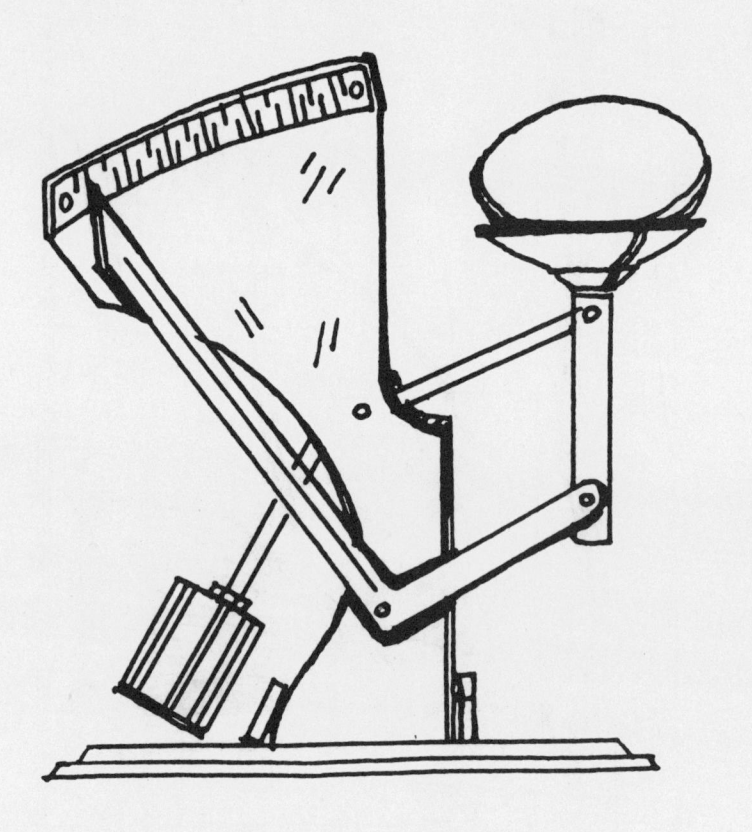

There were several types of egg grading scales to determine if an egg was small, medium, or large. The scale we used had two sets of figures, one showing the weight of the egg in ounces, and above that the equivalent weight for a dozen of the same size egg. Other scales we have seen simply indicated if the egg was in a category of small, medium, large, or extra large. These scales are usually made of heavy tin, with a metal plate showing the weight figures.

How To

You may find the tin on these scales to be rusty. If so, spray with flat white, quick drying paint. The scale part with the grading marks should be cleaned up with steel wool. Be sure to cover this with masking tape before painting the other part of scale.

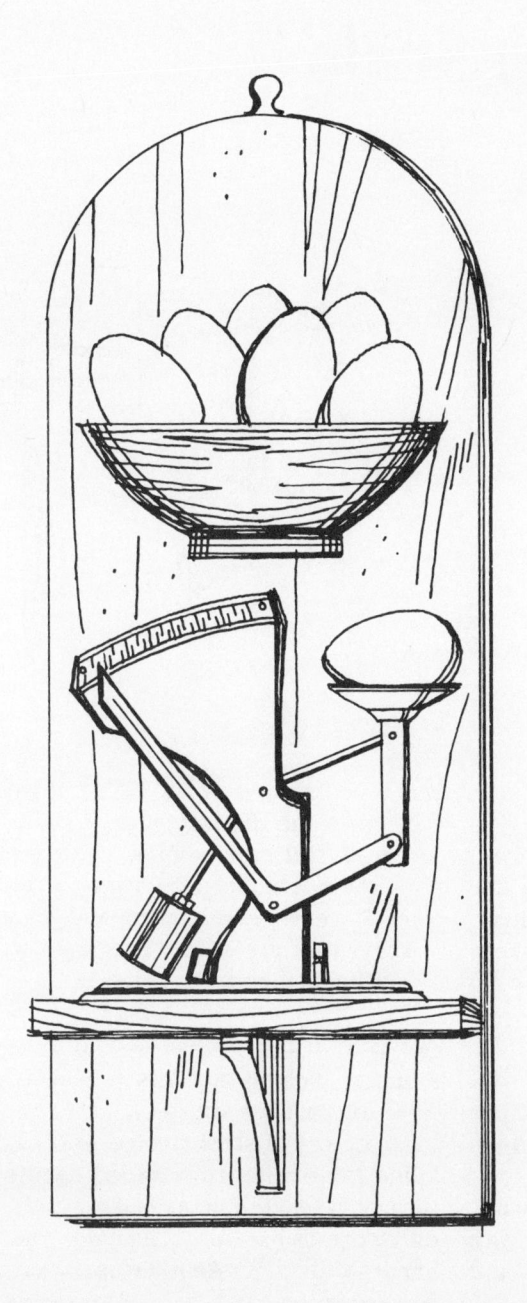

Cut the board to size. We used one 8" x 19". Attach saw-edge hanger and white knob. Then cut the wooden bowl in half and mount. See page 162 for detail. Next make a shelf 4" x 7" and mount. See page 162 for detail. Use one or two mounting brackets as preferred. Fill bowl with excelsior and add plastic eggs. Place scale (do not attach) on shelf and put one plastic egg on scale.

This makes a delightful show-off piece for the kitchen.

Curry Comb

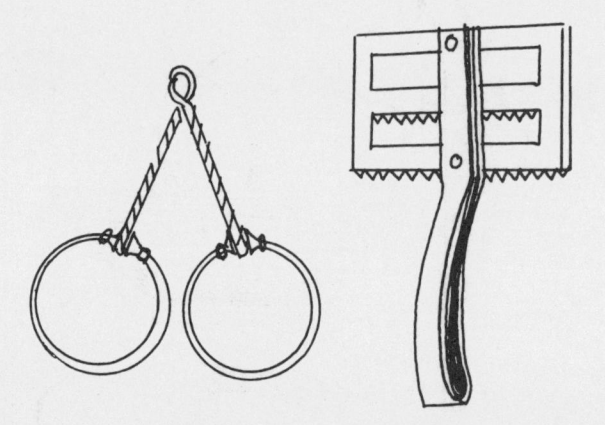

The work horse was used extensively on the farm well into the 1930s, although even at that time the tractor with its tremendous horsepower was becoming a fast replacement. Farmers not only depended on horses for their livelihood but were proud of their looks and pulling power. The curry comb, along with a horse brush, was used to keep the horse well groomed. This not only kept the horse clean but removed impurities from the skin for health reasons.

The curry comb we used in this project is of the "open back" type which is more ornate looking and lets the bird nest show through the bars. The comb part has six steel bars (rows of teeth) and the handle is a looped piece of steel riveted to the comb part. Quite often you will find these with a hardwood handle having a steel shank running through it and the shank end riveted to the body of the comb. Other curry combs have a closed back, and the method of attaching the handle will vary. Another variation that is interesting and could be used is the comb made of circular steel and with a wood handle.

How To

As you will note from the illustration, we included in this plaque a horse bit (mouthpiece). If you prefer a shorter decorative piece and do not have a bit, disregard this part of the project and use the curry comb only.

Barn wood should be used for this piece. This one measures 7" x 30". Attach a saw-edge hanger to the backside. Next drill two holes a quarter inch apart in the wood near the top to secure the twisted wire bit. Also in a similiar manner wire one of the bit "rings" to the board so it will stand out to provide a perch for the small bird.

The curry comb when placed on the board will extend out about two inches. This is where you place the small nest of excelsior. The curry comb is wired to the board. If you should use a comb with a wood handle, drill an eighth inch hole in backside and attach with a dowel rod.

For the bottom of the board we cut a semicircle piece of barn wood 3″ long and attached it with dowel rods. Fill with a small piece of styrofoam, cover with moss and add dried flowers. The mushrooms are plastic and also attach with dowel rods. The piece is now ready to hang and admire.

Wooden Horse Stirrup

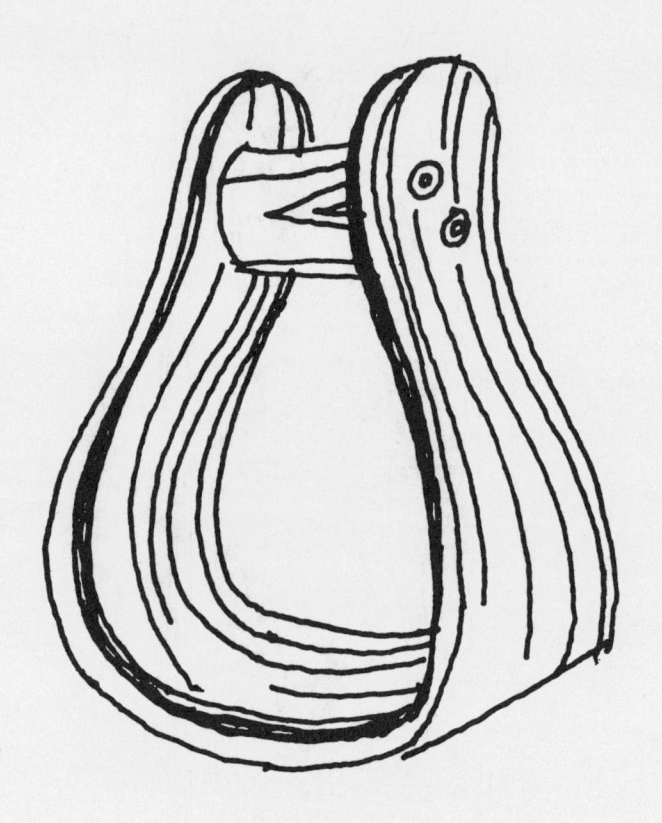

   Old wooden riding stirrups from grandpa's farm or ranch have a "depth" of about 2½" and make an ideal planter. These stirrups were normally used by the men and boys, while the ladies had a light weight brass or metal stirrup. For side saddle riding a "shoe" or "slipper" stirrup was also available for the women and girls.
   The stirrup used for this project was made entirely of wood except for two iron bolts. The bolts reinforced the wooden "bar" through which the leather strap passed to attach the stirrup to the saddle. Fancier stirrups were of wood or steel covered with leather.

How To

Use a piece of barn wood 8" x 14" for mounting the stirrup. After cutting the wood to size, attach saw-edge hanger to back. Then drill two eighth inch holes about a quarter inch deep into the backside of the stirrup to insert dowel rods. Cut two rods three-quarters inch long and glue into stirrup. Place on board and mark for mounting holes. Drill holes and glue stirrup to board. Place styrofoam in bottom of stirrup and cover with moss. Then use mushroom picks, greenery, and pieces of wheat to finish the piece.

Enamelware Cup on Shelf

Grandmother took a liking to a complete line of cooking utensils in enamelware (sometimes referred to as graniteware) because of its light weight and the color it added to the kitchen scene.

The cup we used in this project is a popular collectors' item in a blue and white swirl pattern, sometimes called "tru-blue" enamelware. There are a number of cups of various shapes with interesting handles and a variety of colors that would fit this piece quite well.

Some of the enamelware cups have a hook-like handle. These are similiar to those on some punch bowl cups today. The handle is attached to the cup near the rim and curves down in the normal manner but the end is not attached. With the handle made in this fashion, it could easily hang on a bucket or cooking utensil. We believe these were commonly called the "open end" handle.

How To

A shelf made from a cutting board is the resting place to highlight and set off this particular cup. The "backboard" for the shelf measures 6" x 10" and the shelf itself is 3½" x 6". This size can vary to fit the size of the cup. See page 162 for full details for mounting. Attach saw-edge hanger near the top center on backside of board.

Stain the shelf as desired or leave clear. We used a light stain to retain the early kitchen look.

Fill cup with plastic eggs, flowers, and fernery.

Grain Scoop in Picture Frame

In the early grocery stores large metal scoops were used to measure out bulk dry items. Such scoops were also used on the farm for handling shelled corn and other grains. The one we came across was minus the handle. For our purpose it fitted all the better into the frame. It measures 4½" x 9" and is very handsome in shape.

How To

This scoop is mounted in an old frame 11" x 14". First cut a piece of eighth to quarter inch plywood to fit inside the frame. Next stain the frame and attach two saw-edge holders to back side. Then cover the plywood with contact burlap and nail into frame.

Place the scoop in position and nail securely to board. Secure a small piece of styrofoam in the bottom of the scoop and cover with moss. Then add artificial flowers as desired.

Steel Stirrup and Horse Bit

Some horse lovers like to collect old stirrups, and this plaque was designed for them. We found a heavy metal stirrup supposedly used by cowboys because of its rugged nature and appearance. It is made of heavy iron and with "cutouts" along the side and bottom that make it attractive for all its ruggedness. As the twisted wire horse bit seems to make a nice swing perch for a bird, this was included too. Mamma bird on the nest is just about ready to call for relief from her "setting spell" on the eggs.

How To

The barn wood piece should be about 7" wide and 30" long. After attaching a saw-edge hanger to the top backside, drill two holes about a quarter inch apart to attach the bit to the board. Also, in a similar manner, drill two holes along one of the "rings" to hold it out about an inch from the board and place the bird in this ring. Wire the metal stirrup in the same way to the board in two or three places to secure it well. Next cut a semicircle piece of scrap barn wood about 3" long to be placed in the center of the board for the flower arrangement. This is attached by drilling holes in the backside of the barn wood for dowel rods to go into this piece and the main board. Fill with styrofoam and cover with moss. Then put around this a few mushrooms (attached with dowel rods) and star flowers.

A bird's nest of excelsior is placed in the stirrup along with a couple of eggs and the bird. Above the stirrup, attach a piece of ivy "growing" out of the board. We included a small butterfly.

This can be a very interesting conversation piece.

67

Square Match Safe and Stove Ash Shaker

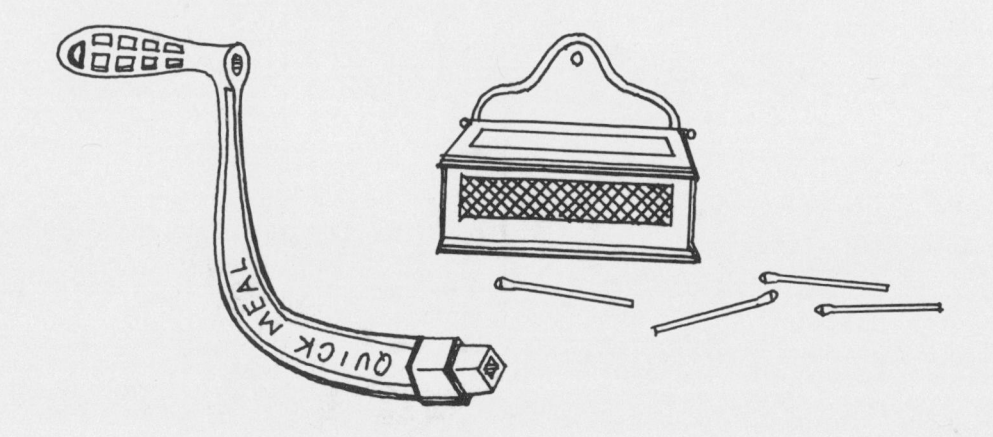

Both the small match box ("match safe" as most were called long ago) and the ash shaker handle from a wood burning kitchen range date back prior to 1900.

At the beginning of the 20th century wood and coal burning stoves were still used extensively for cooking as well as heating the home. Some stoves were made to burn both wood and coal, while others were for wood only. To prepare the meal it was a concern not only to have coal or wood readily available but also to have the fire hot enough to heat the iron lid of the stove. If a fire was kept at a low ebb between meals, ashes accumulated. To revitalize the fire not only was fuel added, but shaking down the ashes was important. The ash shaker handle for this purpose was removable and in some respects resembled the crank for the Model T Ford cars. The importance of shaking the ashes for a red hot fire was emphasized by the wording "quick meal" in raised letters on the shaker handle.

The small tin match box measuring about 2" x 2" x 3" was called a "square match safe." It was designed to hold just a few wooden matches and was kept on a shelf or nailed to the wall, high out of the reach of small children. These are considerably more scarce then the match box holder type that is a receptacle for a full box of wooden matches.

When you find one of these, the tin lid may well be missing. Some of these still have the readable word "matches" on the front face of the box which was also a scratching surface.

How To

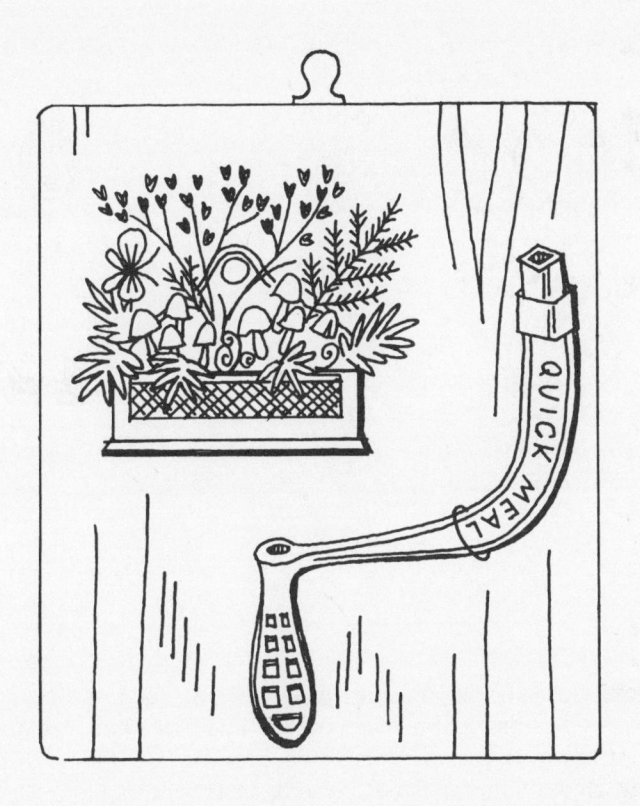

First, a board measuring 10″ x 12″ is stained and saw-edge hanger attached to backside. Then at the top of the board use a wood drawer pull. Position the items on the board to obtain a proper "balance" look, and attach the match safe with a white knob. The shaker is secured to the board in two places by drilling small holes and using black wire looped over the shaker handle. We used small clumps of mushrooms and greenery to fill the match safe.

"Cereal" Stove Lid and Toy Bank

Special lids were sometimes provided for wood and coal burning stoves. The particular one used for this piece has this wording in raised letters circling the outside edge of the lid: "Turn this cover to raise it and prevent cereals from burning."

Many of us today may skip breakfast entirely but in the days when most people were doing hard manual labor, breakfast was one of the "hefty" meals and necessary to keep one going till noon. In the summer months it was customary to burn wood and corn cobs to make a quick fire. In the winter the cooking stove was kept going all the time for heating the room as well as for cooking. When coal was used for the stove, a bucketful was always kept near by. A small coal shovel or one glove was kept on top of the coal to replenish the fire without getting coal dust on the hands.

In the old days, the wood matches to light a fire were used sparingly. In fact, if father wanted to light his pipe, or a fire in the fireplace, he would often use a splinter of pine wood or a rolled piece of paper to "catch" a light from the cooking stove.

The cast-iron "Aunt Jemina" bank is a reproduction of those made of people and objects dating back to the early 1800s.

How To

The board used measures 10½" x 12". Stain as desired and nail two saw-edge hangers to backside. Two hangers are needed because the stove lid measuring 7" diameter is mounted to the right side of the board. Next drill a hole in the center top edge of the board for the white knob. The shelf is 8" long and 2½" wide. The brackets measure 2" x 2". See page 162 for mounting detail. The shelf was made wide to be able to include small objects in addition to the bank figure. We added a miniature brass tea kettle.

To secure the bank, use a dowel rod in the hole running up through the foot and let it extend out a half inch, then drill a hole in the shelf to secure the dowel rod. The lid is attached by drilling small holes through the board at the top and bottom of the lid and running black wire through to the backside.

Hay Pulleys

Even though relatively small, hay pulleys did a big job on the farm handling heavy loads. Many pulleys were made of a combination of wood and iron. The wooden wheel or roller for the pulley was usually made of maple wood for strength and durability. Inside the wooden frame of the pulley was an iron U-shaped shaft with a ring attached to the top. Near the bottom were two holes. These horizontal holes held the iron pin which passed through the wooden roller. The real load of the pulley was borne by the steel shaft.

During the summer, large quantities of hay were stored in the barn loft to feed the stock through the winter. The hay was loaded on a wagon in the field and then horse drawn to the barn. The wagon pulled up just under the hayloft doors which opened out from the second story of the barn. At least three pulleys of the type shown were involved in putting the hay in the mow. Suspended from the peak of the barn ceiling was a steel track which ran the length of the barn. Steel wheels on each side of the track formed a rolling carriage to which pulley No. 1 was attached. A stop block was on either end of the track to prevent the carriage from running off the ends. At the opposite end of the track from the loft doors pulley No. 2 was secured, and pulley No. 3 was attached to the barn about one foot above ground level and directly below pulley No. 2.

A 1" to 1½" rope was secured to a hay fork and then passed through pulleys 1, 2, and 3, in that order. The rope as it passed through pulley No. 3 was attached to a "single tree" which in turn was hitched to a horse. Riding the horse to pull the hay into the mow was the only fun part of this job, eagerly accepted by the youngest boy or girl on the farm.

How To

The metal part of the pulley will probably be a little rusty. Take out the cotter key which holds the pin for the roller, remove same, and the U-shaped shaft with the ring on the end will pull out. Then you can clean this piece with a wire brush and steel wool. Paint this piece flat black if desired. The wood frame of the pulley should clean nicely using a fine grade of steel wool. Leave the wood in the natural or stain with antique maple to make a most handsome piece. After all pieces have been refinished, reassemble the pulley.

The pulley we used had the wording, "Hudson USA," discernible after using the steel wool on the wood part.

Setting the pulley on the flat edge makes a rugged looking bookend. Also in the metal eye of the pulley you can use a cast-iron candle holder and decorate with ivy. The eye of the pulley was purposely made to swivel. To use a candle you will want the eye to hold in a horizontal position. To tighten the eye take rubber bands and wrap around the shaft end where it passes through the U iron. The eye will hold in a horizontal plane. See illustration.

Wheel Making Tools

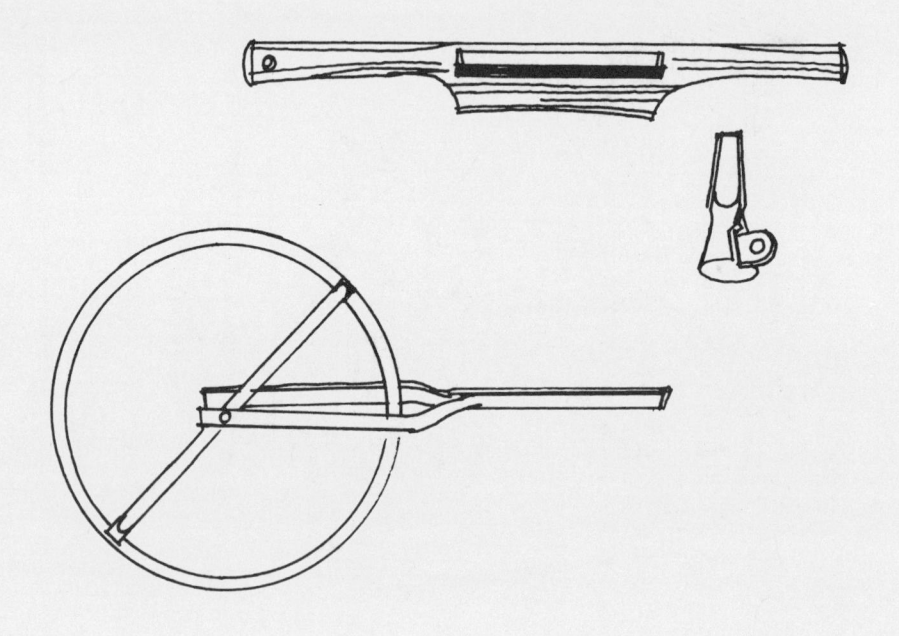

Years ago when a blacksmith made a "tire" of iron for a wagon or buggy wheel, the circumference of the wheel was found by the use of a "tire measuring wheel." The length determined was then used to cut the tire the exact size for the wheel. The one we used in this project was crudely made and quite old. In the early 1900s these were perfected with the measurement in inches shown on the rim of the wheel. Also an index hand was added which could be moved to indicate the stopping point in the measurement. This tool was soon nicknamed "the traveler."

The spokeshaver used is also of the early type dating back before the Civil War. It is simply a planing tool with a steel cutter blade, used with both hands. The depth of the cut made by the tool was increased by tapping the two "tines" or spikes that extended out from the ends of the cutting blade. Later models had thumb screws that fit over the tines which adjusted the blade by loosening or tightening the screws.

The spoke pointer was used to sharpen the ends of the spokes which fit into the wheel rim and hub. This was made to work in any standard brace.

How To

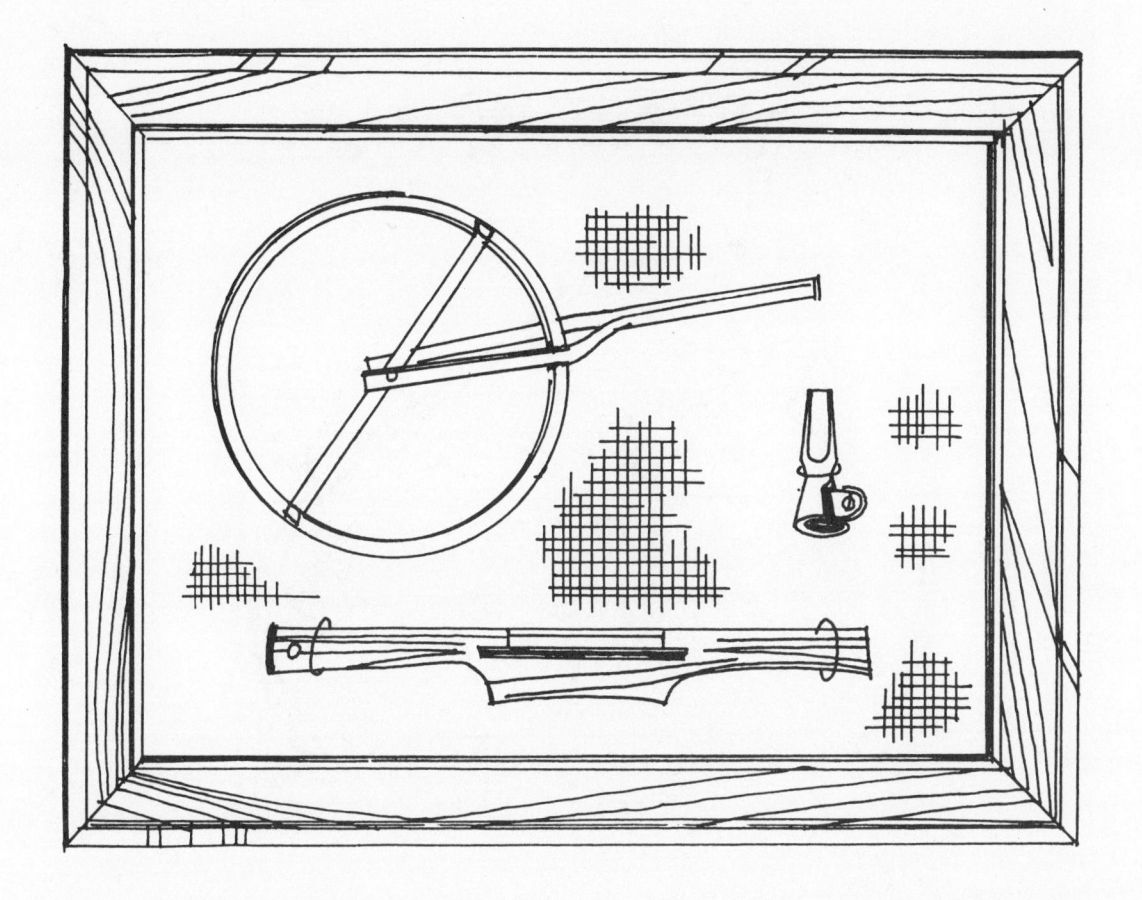

The old frame used was of oak and simply restained to keep the used look. The frame measures 12″ x 18″. Cut a piece of eighth to quarter inch plywood to fit in the frame and cover with contact burlap. Secure in frame and attach two saw-edge hangers to backside. The spokeshaver and spoke pointer are light weight and mounted with elastic banding. The "traveler" is secured with black wire by drilling small holes in the board and looping the wire around the metal wheel and handle.

Ice Tongs and Toy Ice Wagon

For those of us who were youngsters when the ice box was a familiar item in every kitchen, the sight of ice tongs probably brings back fond memories. Watching for the ice truck on a hot day was a favorite pastime. Diamond shape ice cards were provided by the ice company to be hung in the window or on the porch. These were printed with the figures 25, 50, 75, or 100 lbs. and were turned to the size piece of ice mother needed on any given day. The ice was carried on the truck in large scored blocks. When the ice pick was used to cut out a piece for delivery there were always several small slivers of ice for the eager gang of children waiting. Then the ice man would throw a burlap sack over his shoulder, and using the ice tongs, would hoist the cake of ice on his back to carry into the house.

Ice tongs were a familiar item in the earlier days too when ice was sawed from the lakes and rivers during the winter and stored for later use. Natural ice of this type was stored for commercial usage from about 1800. By the 1930s manufactured ice had for the most part replaced natural ice.

The toy ice wagon we used is a reproduction. Real ones that were made of cast-iron in the 1890-1910 era are available from antique dealers.

How To

The size of the board we used is 14" x 16". Stain as desired and nail two saw-edge hangers to the backside. The porcelain knob is then secured to the top center of the board. The shelf is made just big enough to hold the horse and wagon and measures 4" x 10". The brackets are 2½" x 2½". See page 162 for the shelf.

The ice tongs are placed so as to appear to be holding up the shelf, with the points at the very edge. Attach the tongs with black wire at the hand grip and also near the pointed ends. See illustration.

The horse drawn wagon was not secured to the shelf, but just rests there waiting for some little boy to play "ice man."

Stove Cover Lifter and Match Box

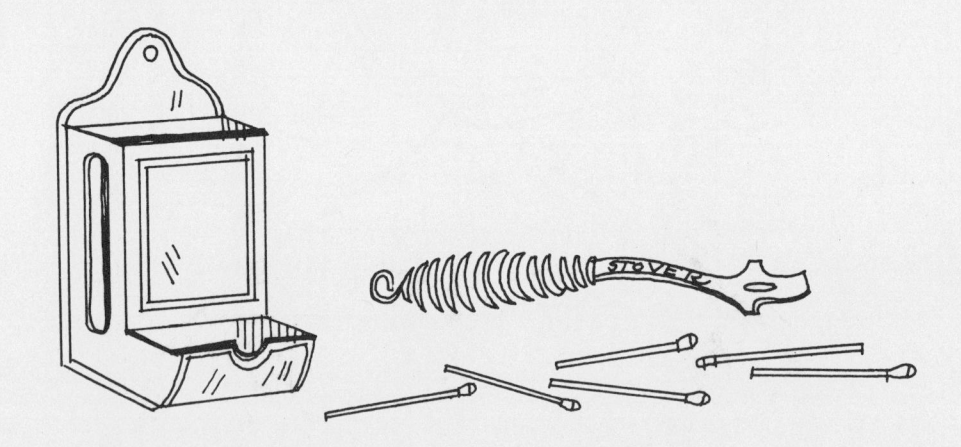

This type of match box is easily found. Although dating back prior to 1900, it was still in common use 50 years ago. Some of these have advertising on the front side. If in fair condition this should be left "as is." The one we used was plain and needed painting. Flat black was used to fit in with the lifter and candle cup.

The lifter handle for a stove lid or cover is from a kitchen range that burned coal or wood. These lifters were made in many different sizes and shapes. The one used for this plaque has a heavy wire spiral handle. It was designed to grip easily with the hand and to absorb as little heat as possible from the stove lid. The spiral effect works particularly well for design purposes in the candle arrangement. Some lifters were made with a metal part to fit into the lid and a wood handle. These were the best for a "cool" handle, but if left on the lid for any period of time, there was danger of scorching the wood.

How To

The board for this plaque measures 11" x 11". Stain the board and then attach a saw-edge hanger on backside. Next use a white porcelain knob at the center top of the board. We used an old brass knob to attach the match box and give contrast to the white one at the top. The lifter is attached to the board in two places, using black wire. The cast-iron candle holder is secured with a screw through the backside of the board. Insert a short white candle and the piece is ready to display.

"Patent" Medicine Bottle

In the early 1900s "Patent" medicine was widely advertised, usually with amazing claims. We found an old postcard offering a "liberal trial offer" for one dollar and with a 25 day free trial period. It even offers to send two boxes on trial for the same price of one dollar per box if both husband and wife are ailing.

Using this card along with a small bottle of Dr. Porter's antiseptic healing oil, plus a pair of old tinted reading glasses, makes an unusual conversation piece on a shelf or side table. The bottle of healing oil has a cork stopper and a looped wire pull for the cork. The label states that it's for cuts, burns, itch, corns, etc. It also makes the interesting claim that "it's for man or beast."

If someone you are fond of is of retirement age, this would be a real "fun" gift at a party.

How To

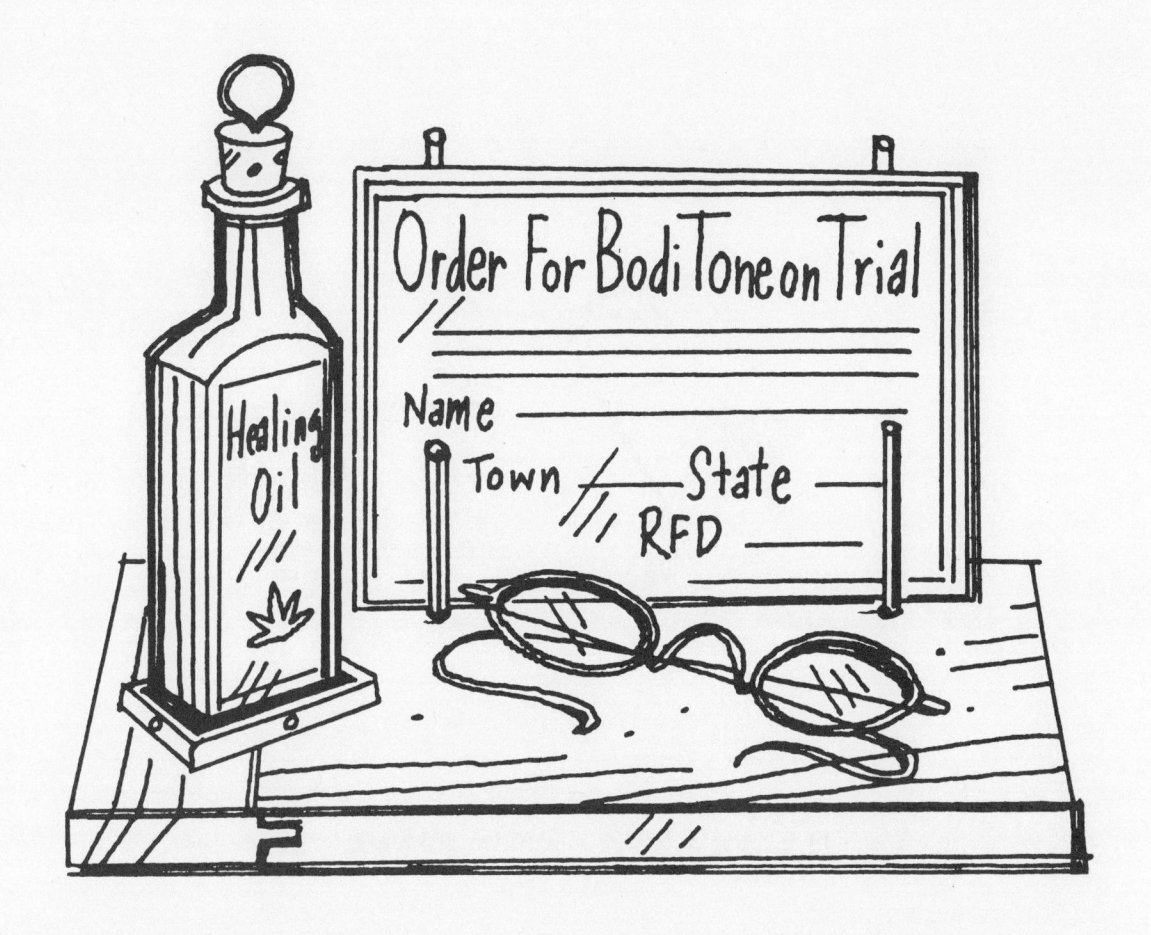

Use a scrap piece of cutting board 3" x 8". One inch from the backside of the top of the board drill two eighth inch holes at a slight back slant. Then a half inch forward of these two holes drill two more at the same slant. In the back holes insert 4" length rods and in the forward holes insert 2" rods. This is to hold the postcard. The bottom of the small bottle of medicine is glued to the board. If desired put a small wooden frame (one-fourth inch thickness) around the bottle for looks and sturdiness. The glasses are laid on the board with the ear pieces through small eyelets screwed into the board.

The "Show Off" Shelf

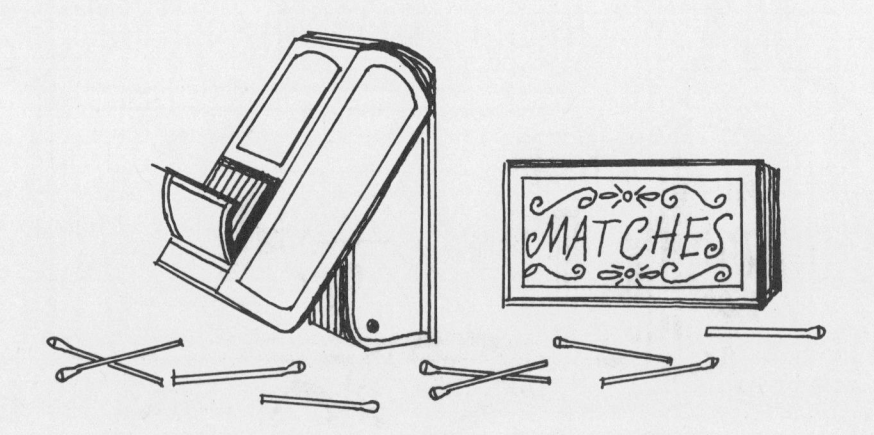

Nearly everyone has something precious, rare or unique. Such items should be displayed for one's own enjoyment and for the pleasure of friends.

Our rare item is a match box holder made from one piece of tin and with a closed top. The rarity of the box is that it loads at the bottom instead of the open top as with most match dispensers. It is so constructed that the rounded top acts as a spring and the box is opened by pushing on the bottom of the box. It opens to take a full box of wood matches. This holder was nickel plated but in such bad condition that we sprayed it black.

To give added charm to this match box, we placed a small piece of styrofoam in the take out slot and then stuck in several wood matches to show. See illustration.

How To

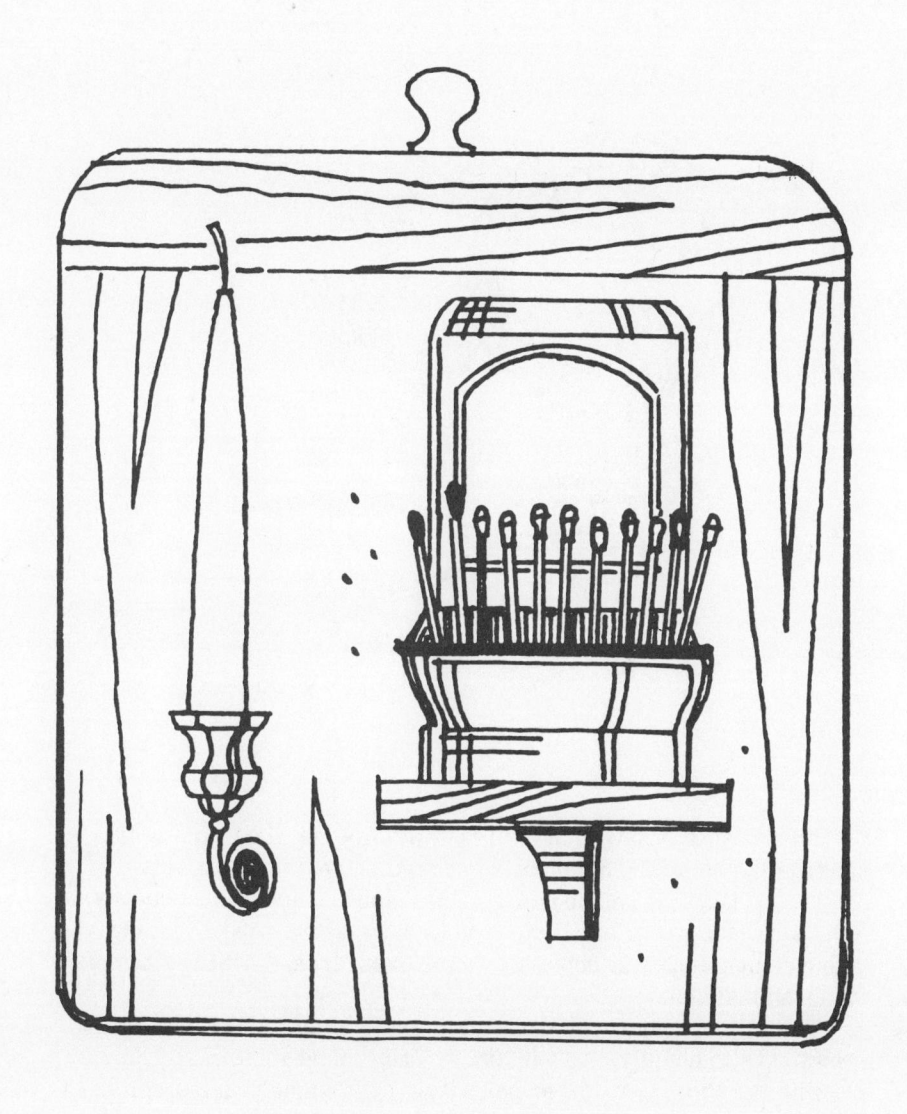

This shelf is easy to make following the procedure shown on page 162. The cutting board we used measures 8″ x 10″ and the shelf size is 2½″ x 3″, with the supporting bracket 2″ x 2″. Make your display to fit your particular "show off" piece.

A cast-iron candle holder is also part of this plaque and easily attached with a screw through the backside of the board. One should never have to look for a match to light this candle.

Vanity Hand Mirror and Curling Iron

This decor fits in well in either the bathroom or bedroom. Many of these "ebonized" hand mirrors were of good quality, made of select woods and finished to give the appearance of real ebony. The real ebony is a hard, heavy and very durable wood having a dark or black natural color. It comes from trees in the tropics of Asia and Africa.

The mirrors were sold separately or in a set with a brush and comb. Occasionally one will find a "ring hand mirror" which is similiar to the one we used but with a short handle and a hole of about one inch diameter at the end. These were made as an all-purpose mirror to hang or hold as the lady desired.

The curling irons are readily available in many different sizes. We suggest one 7" to 8" in length to fit in well with the mirror. The irons are made of polished steel and with various types of wood handles such as oak or rosewood. The latter wood is of a dark red or purplish color and obtained from various tropical trees. You may find some of the wood handles a little scorched from use as it was a common practice to heat the iron in a lamp chimney.

How To

This makes a rather long piece. The board should be about 8" x 19". We suggest you stain the board for contrast with the mirror. Then add the mirror. Then add the saw-edge holder and the white knob.

Next make the shelf which measures 4" x 8". Before attaching the shelf, drill a hole out a half inch from the board to hold the curling iron. A quarter inch drill will probably do the trick and make the hole just large enough so the steel end will fit in snugly. You may want to first drill a hole in a scrap piece of wood to determine the exact size to hold the iron properly. Attach the shelf as on page 162 except use only one shelf bracket and position it in the center of shelf.

On the backside of the mirror handle, drill two eighth inch holes (be careful not to drill all the way through) and use two dowel rods three-quarters inch long and glue into mirror handle. Position mirror on board and mark for holes to be drilled to receive dowel rods. Mount plaque on wall and add accessories to shelf.

Hand Mirror and Graniteware Soap Dish

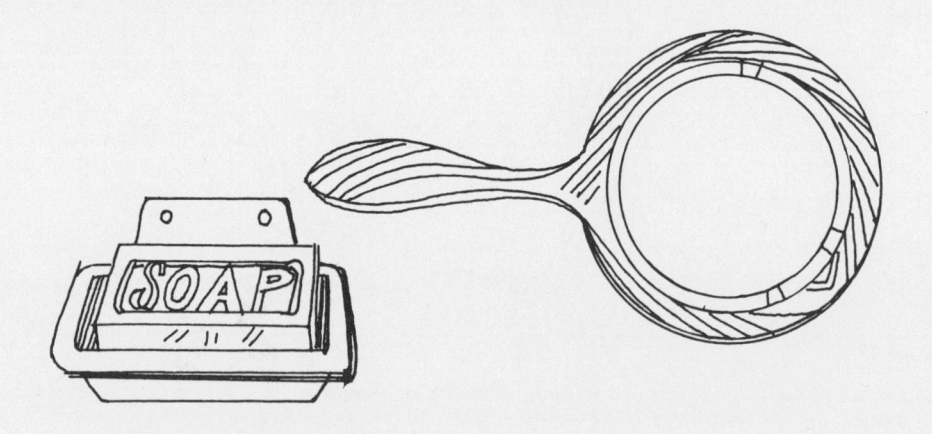

Graniteware soap dishes are fairly plentiful. The choice ones are white with a "drain grate." This is a top drain piece which fits into the soap dish and is removable. Most of the soap dishes are of a shallow one-piece variety. Often the grate has been lost. There are one or two holes at the back of these soap dishes which were used in bygone days to fasten the dish to the wall near the sink or washbowl.

How To

We used a bread board 10" wide and 16" long. After preparing the board, stain and drill a hole in the center top edge for the porcelain knob. Nail a saw-edge holder to the backside. The soap dish is attached, using small white knobs, one or two, depending on the holes provided.

To make the towel rack, use two 1" round wooden balls. Drill an eighth inch wide hole in the center of the knobs and another hole at a 90 degree angle. Cut two eighth inch dowel rods in 2" lengths. Insert one in each knob and glue. Then cut a rod 8" long and glue ends into the knobs. Place this on the board to position for drilling receptive holes. Stain the knob and rods and then glue the rods into the board. Leave a space of at least one inch for the towel to pass through. Use small decorative soap in the dish.

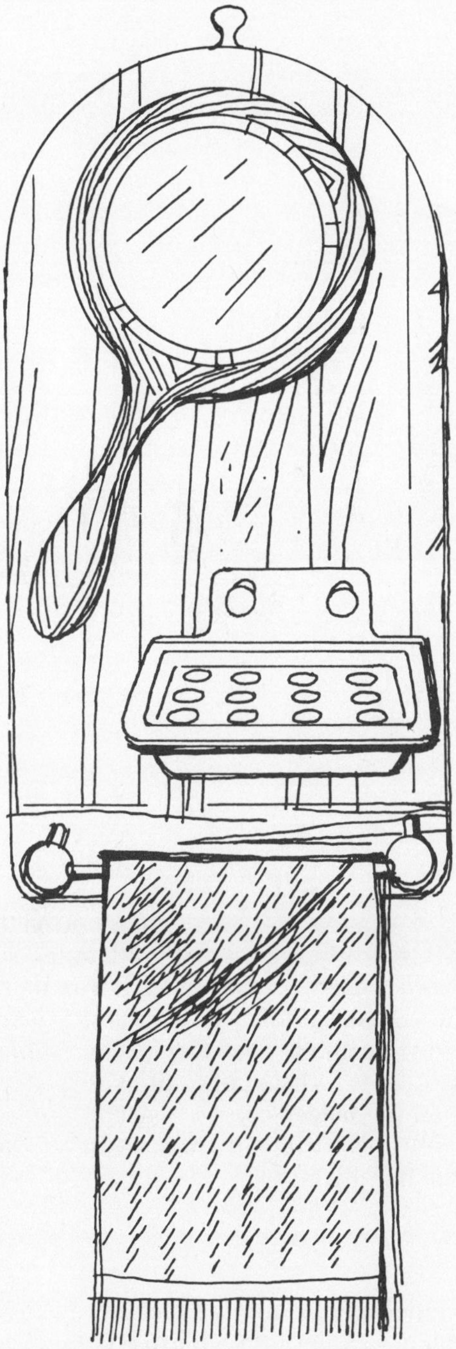

Old Hand Mirror with Wire Soap Holder

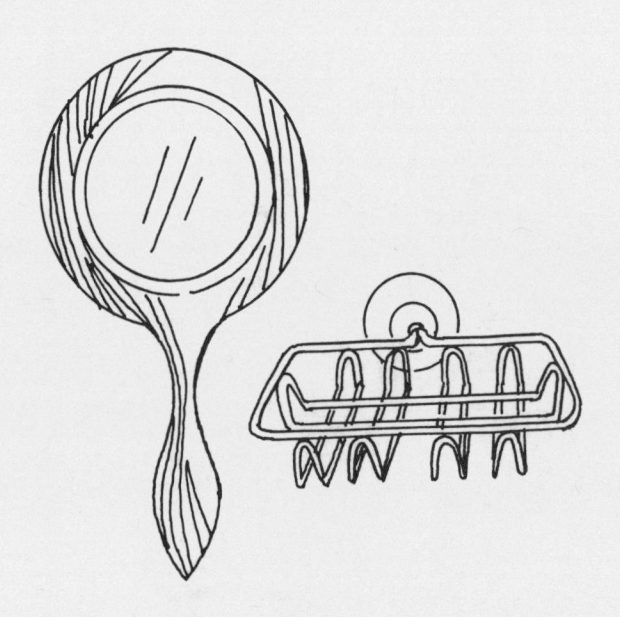

The wire type soap holder was usually mounted on the wall back of the sink so that any drippings would fall into the sink or drainboard area. Some of these were made with a wire loop on the back to fit over the rim of the bathtub. If one wanted to be really economical, there was a combination soap holder available with detachable U-shaped bands. These bands fit over the rim of the tub, and when removed the holder could be mounted as a wall piece. I am sure you will find variations from the styles mentioned as people were most inventive.

How To

Another attractive way to combine the use of an old hand mirror and soap holder is shown in the illustration. The board measures 10" x 16". Stain the board and attach saw-edge holder and white knob. Next attach the soap holder using the regular mounting holes provided. We made a small wood box to fit inside the holder. This was filled with styrofoam and covered with moss. Artificial ivy is used as a background for the flower arrangement which features velvet forget-me-nots and lilies of the valley. Fernery and star flowers are also added to complement the arrangement.

To finish the project attach the hand mirror by drilling two holes about 2" apart and an eighth inch in diameter in the backside of the mirror handle. Then cut two pieces of dowel rod three-quarters inch in length to glue on the mirror handle. Position mirror on the board and mark to drill the holes for the dowel rods. After drilling holes, attach the mirror and you are ready to admire your work.

Pipe and Tobacco Can

Advertising in the late 1800s often referred to tobacco prepared for pipe or cigarette as "the weed," with such engaging terms as "if you have the habit of the weed" or "if you like the weed," you will prefer such and such tobacco. The phrase was so commonly used for tobacco as to become a part of the dictionary definition of the "weed."

Rosewood and apple wood were used to make the bowls for many of the pipes. The size and shape of the bowl varied considerably as they do today. The mouth piece for the pipe was usually made of hard rubber. The fancier pipes might also have a nickel plated hinged cover to keep the ashes from spilling and to keep the pipe puffing even in the rain.

The old tobacco tins are still plentiful, with price varying according to brand, age, and condition.

How To

The "pipe" used for this plaque was of wood and originally a decoration on the front of the arm rest of an old Morris chair. One or two real pipes can be used with a similar effect as in illustration. For this project a pine board 6" x 17" was used instead of cutting board. It was rounded at both ends. Paint or stain the board. Attach the tobacco can with small nails just below the opening. Next the pipe can be secured with elastic banding. Just above the bowl, drill holes about a quarter inch apart on each side of the pipe. Insert black elastic banding and tie on backside of board.

Fill the old tobacco can with greenery and star flowers and the piece is finished.

Butter Paddle and Tea Strainer

The butter paddle was used to "work" the butter after it was produced in the family churn. The churning process took up to half an hour to separate the butter from the buttermilk. Simply stated, the churning process "kicked out" the butterfat from the cream, resulting in globs of butter, and the by-product left was buttermilk and cottage cheese. The wood butter paddle was used to further knead or form the butter, mostly to remove any excess milk remaining in the butter.

The old tea strainer as pictured in the illustration is of the type that was used to make a full pot of tea and measures about 2″ across the top. You will probably find these with the top and chain attached. Only the bottom part is needed to make the nest for the bird.

How To

We suggest the use of barn wood for this piece to make an interesting contrast to the natural color of the butter paddle. Use a rectangular board 7" x 14". First nail on the saw-edge holder and then attach the paddle with two small finishing nails or brads.

One small nail should be sufficient to attach the tea strainer to the paddle. Nail at the top inside rim of the strainer. Using excelsior make the nest and add a small feathered bird.

To attach the star flowers, we first used scotch tape on the stems and covered the tape with an old piece of leather nailed to the board with copper finishing nails. The leather can be from horse harness, old watch band, or any other source. It should measure ½" to 1" wide and 1" to 1½" long. Bring greenery from the backside of the paddle up and around the handle.

Broken Butter Paddle

The old paddle we found, made from Buckeye wood, was of fine quality but had a clean break with half the "paddle" part missing. This made it perfect for a decorative piece.

How To

First you will need a piece of cutting board about 6" x 17". Round the two ends as in illustration. Stain or paint the board and nail two saw-edge hangers to the back of board. Into the broken part of the paddle drill two eighth inch holes a half inch deep. Then cut two dowel rods 1" long, insert and glue into paddle. Place on board and mark for drilling holes to receive dowel rods. Attach and glue.

Use artificial red cherries and fernery to "fill" the paddle. A nice piece for the dining area!

Old 1750 Pistol with Book

The old pistol (sometimes referred to as a "horse pistol") dating back to 1750 or before is the focal point for this display. Many other old items instead of a pistol can be used to display with a book if desired.

The book used was printed in the late 1800s, and has a story from the year 1745 about the volunteer soldiers from the Colonies who joined the English to fight the French. The book is opened to a picture having the same type of pistol as that used in the frame. The circular brass piece, with an eagle embossed and holding the top of the book is from a military uniform of the 1850s.

How To

We used an old thin frame 1½" wide and measuring 18" x 27". After staining it, attach two hangers to backside of the frame. Use quarter inch plywood for the board to fit inside the frame. Next cut burlap (we used dark gold contact type) to size and apply to board. It is then ready to nail into frame.

At this point it is well to position the pistol and book in the frame. Make the wooden "clips" as shown in illustration.

These clips are small but easily cut by marking the pattern for each on the edge of a half inch thick board measuring 3″ x 12″. The illustration shows half of the board and the sequence of the steps for making the cuts with saw. After making the clips, drill an eighth inch hole to a depth of a quarter inch as indicated and glue in dowel rod, letting it extend three-eighths inch from the clip. Before attaching, stain the clips same as frame. Position book and drill receptive holes for wooden clips and glue on board.

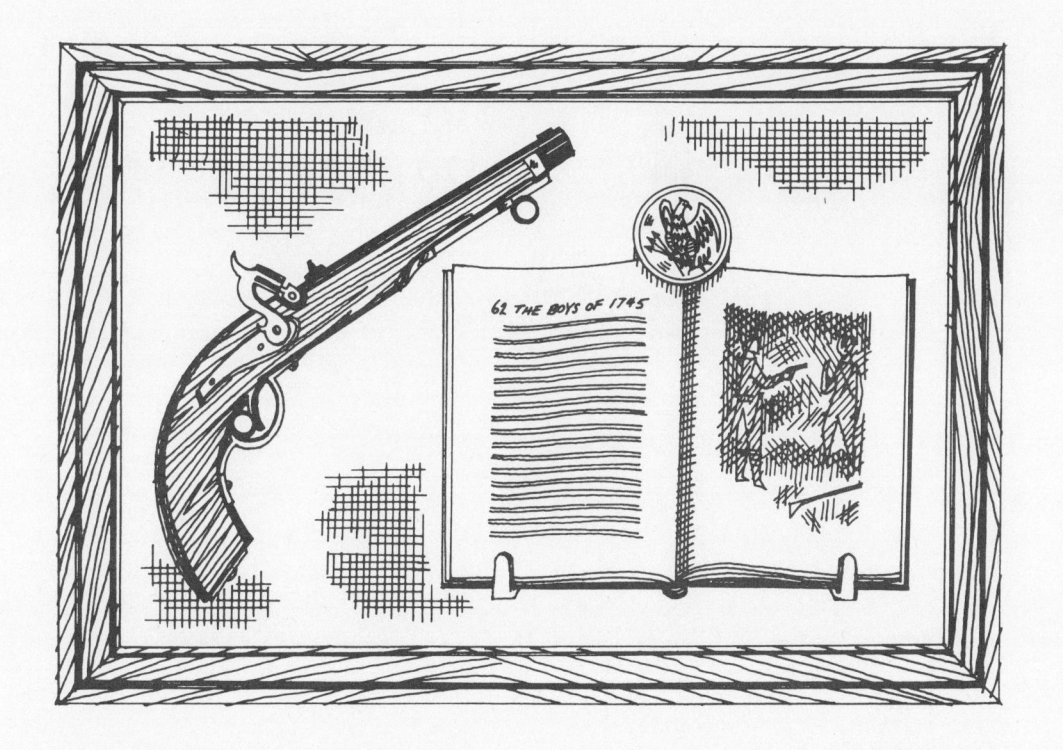

The circular brass piece is held out from the board by using a 1″ square of quarter inch plywood. It must be of a size to fit between ''hooks'' on the backside of the brass piece. Attach this small piece of wood to the board with glue or use a dowel rod. The brass circular is mounted so that about a quarter inch extends over the book. These pieces usually have hooks on the back, and through the hooks as illustrated we looped elastic banding. Then drill holes in the board to permit passing through and tying the banding. By mounting in this way the brass piece can be raised to take off the book for examination.

To mount the pistol, use quarter inch dowel rod as shown in the illustration.

Details of wood clips and eagle mounting are on next page (98).

Wood Clips

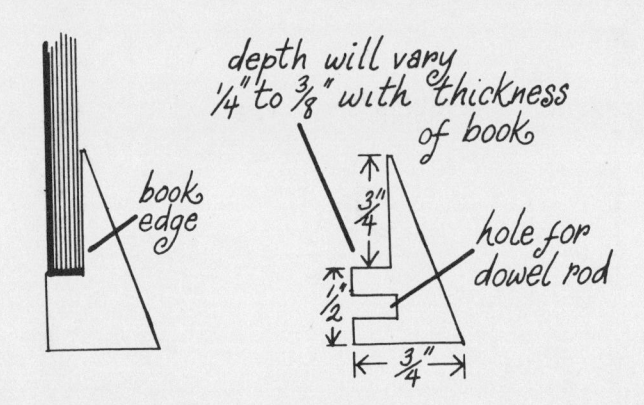

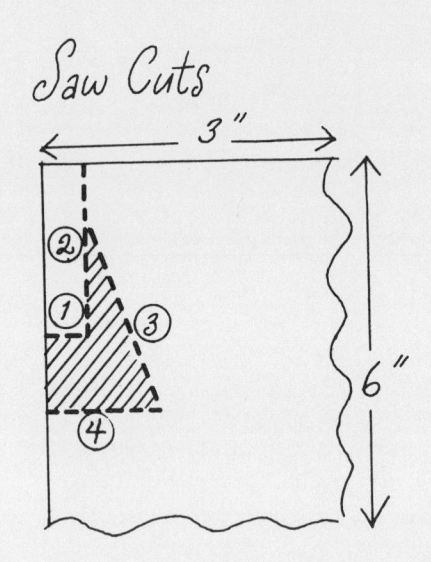

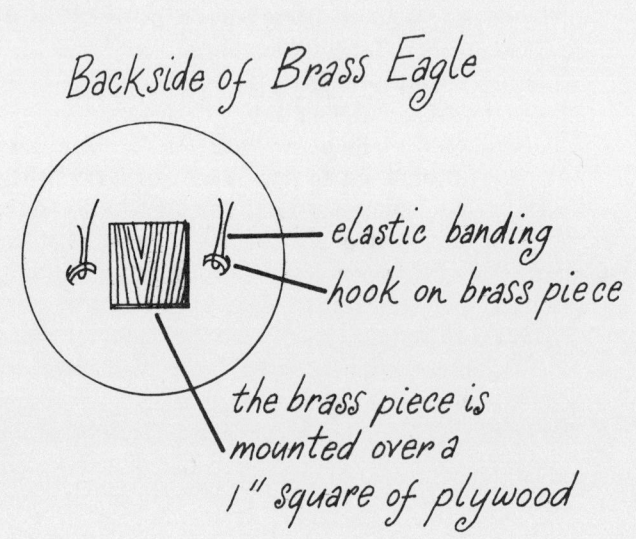

book edge

depth will vary 1/4" to 3/8" with thickness of book

3/4"

1/2"

3/4"

hole for dowel rod

Saw Cuts

3"

6"

①②③④

Backside of Brass Eagle

elastic banding
hook on brass piece

the brass piece is mounted over a 1" square of plywood

Enamelware Funnels

Enamelware funnels are most attractive when mounted on small cutting boards. They varied in size and shape and had many kitchen uses.

Long ago household supplies were purchased or stored in bulk form and in large quantities to last for several months. The funnel was an aid in pouring liquid materials into a smaller container. These old funnels have interesting shapes and handles as well as an attractive enamelware finish of gray, gray-white, or milk white. The funnels are hard to drill a hole through, but it is worth doing so the mounting can be done with the nandle free from the board.

How To

A board 7" x 8" is usually large enough for these kitchen funnels. Nail the saw-edge hanger to the backside of the board, then drill a hole in top center of the board for the white knob. Drill a hole in the upper edge of the funnel and then nail the funnel in place. Fill the funnel with flowers or greenery and perch the bird on the edge.

This plaque can be functional as a key or pot holder if desired. First spray three hooks with flat black paint, then attach these 1" from the bottom of the board.

Sewing Machine Drawer and Old Sewing Items

Many of the sewing machines dating back to the early 1900s have been discarded, but fortunately most of the drawers have been salvaged. Machines had at least two or four drawers. Many models had six. Usually the drawers were covered with veneer, and quite a few had fancy "pulls" of ornate metal, sometimes plated with nickel. Some of these drawers are rounded on the ends and make a nice planter for artificial greenery.

For a companion piece, we include a plaque with an old "egg darner" and a metal thread and needle holder. This latter item will hold six spools of thread and has a needle cushion in the middle. Sometimes these were made with two tiers to hold more spools of thread and were for the more energetic seamstress. In place of this metal thread holder you could well use other old sewing items. Quite often you will find a variety of things still in the old machine drawers.

When I showed the old "egg darner" to a dear neighbor, she mentioned that when she was a girl they didn't have one of the wooden egg darners but substitute instead a gourd of about the same size when mending holes in socks, etc.

How To

If you find a drawer with the veneer in good shape you may want to use it "as is." In our case we decided to use flat black over the veneer. By doing this and going over it lightly with fine steel wool, we achieved a grainy leather appearance. Before finishing the drawer it has to be cut in half lengthwise to give the proper depth when hung on the wall. After cutting the drawer, nail a piece of three-eighths wood for the backside and then attach two saw-edge hangers to the plywood for hanging. The pulls we had were ornate but small, so we used two pulls for better balance. The drawer was filled with greenery and a large partridge looking for a nesting place.

The bread board used for the plaque was cut 8″ x 10″. The shelf is 3″ x 3½″ and with a 2″ x 2″ bracket. See page 162 for shelf detail. To hang the piece nail a saw-edge holder to the backside top. Also a white knob in the center of the top edge of the board complements this piece.

Drill an eighth inch hole in the "ball" part of the egg darner and insert a three-quarter inch piece of dowel rod. Place the darner on the board and mark to drill for the receptive dowel rod hole and mount. The handle will purposely be free from the board.

Flour Sifter and Wood Spoon

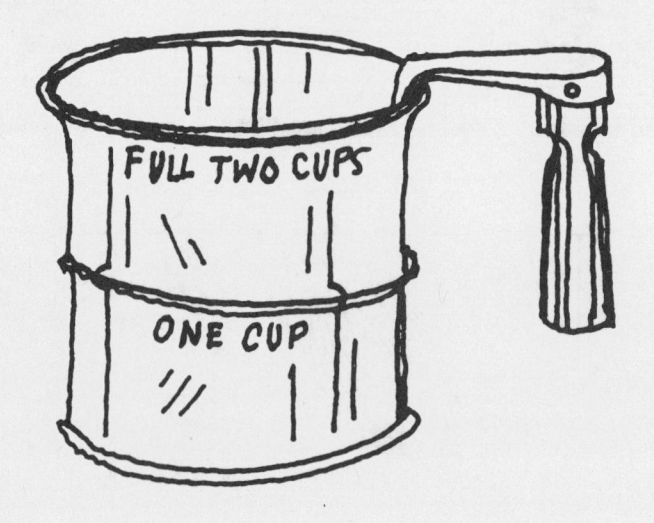

Years ago the small tin flour sifters were popular as give away advertising pieces by banks, hardware stores, lumber yards and feed stores. They were imprinted with the business name and slogan or message; such as, "When you sift it down, you'll find it pays to trade with The Smith Lumber Co."

If you have one of these, you may want to leave the printing intact. The one we used was plain and we painted it flat white. The wood handle was left natural.

How To

The cutting board measures 10″ x 12″. First attach the saw-edge holder and also the white knob. Then place the sifter so the handle stands out from the board about an inch. Nail the sifter at the top back rim and also at the bottom.

Now you are ready to add the wooden spoon. Drill eighth inch diameter holes into backside of the handle and just deep enough to glue in dowel rod. Cut two pieces of dowel rod three-quarter inch long and glue into spoon, position on board and drill holes for rods, attach and glue spoon.

We filled the sifter with mushrooms and pieces of wheat in the background.

Soap Saver

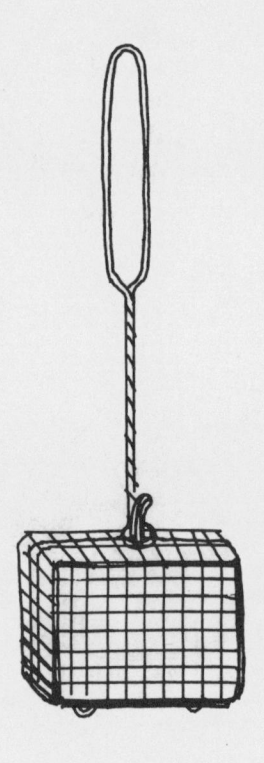

Ask grandma and she can probably tell you about using the "soap saver." It's a small rectangular, hinged wire basket with a 6" to 10" wire handle. The basket measures about 2" x 3" and 1" deep. Most of these have a wire ring that holds the basket closed when in an upright position.

When bars of soap became small, they were cut up and placed in the "soap saver," then swishing in the water made the suds. The soap saver was also handy to use for the scraps left over from the homemade "batches" of soap. Some of these we have found, still have soap caked on the wire and need a little brushing before painting flat black.

How To

Stain board as desired and attach saw-edge hanger. Open the basket and wire the bottom to the top so that it will stay open at a 90 degree angle (see illustration). The wire will be covered with a flower arrangement. Next drill a hole 2" fom the top of board for white knob. Let handle hang on knob and attach basket to board with screw. Fill "basket" with styrofoam covered with moss, then add greenery and flowers. This item makes an unusual piece for bath or kitchen.

Spring Balance Hand Scales

The spring balance scales were designed for personal or home use and many have the wording "not for legal use" on the face of the scale. These vary in size with many being about 6" in total length. A 1" diameter ring at the top is for holding or hanging the scale. The body of the scale has a metal housing around the spring and a brass face showing the weight in half pounds up to a total of 24 pounds or more. The hook at the bottom of the scale was for hanging the item to be weighed. A small tin pan with three chains supporting it was also at times attached to the hook to weigh small items. Most of these scales have a brass facing and clean up well to show the wording and numbers on the scale.

How To

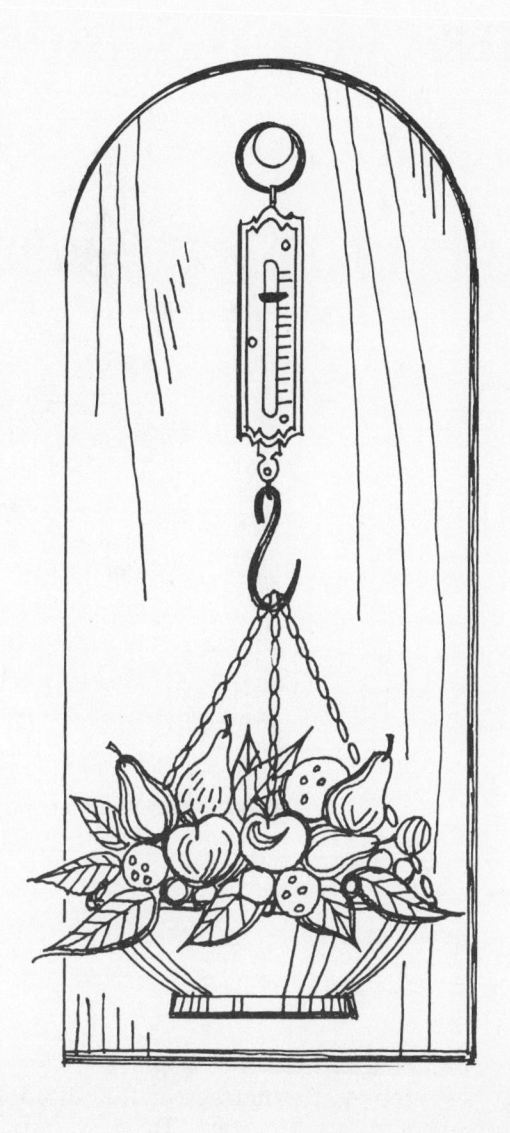

Select a small scale with total length of 6″ to 8″. The board should be about 8″ x 16″. Stain the board and nail on saw-edge holder and drill hole for the white knob and insert. Next, position the scale and bowl on the board to determine length of chain to use from bowl to scale hook. See illustration. Prepare the half wooden bowl. See page 162 for mounting to board. Before attaching bowl, drill a sixteenth inch hole on three places of rim to attach the chain with small black wire. After securing the bowl to board, attach the top of the scale ring to the board with knob. Then cut three chain lengths and secure to bowl and to scale hook. Fill bowl with vegetables or small fruit.

A delightful conversation piece for kitchen or dining area!

Biscuit Cutter

The biscuit cutter we used has the trademark "Rumford." This particular type has a removable tin insert in the bottom making it usable as a biscuit or doughnut cutter. These were used by the flour companies as advertising items.

This Rumford Company also put out a metal spoon designed to mix any batter using flour. If you're lucky to find one of these it could be included alongside the biscuit cutter.

How To

The cutter is attached in an upside down position on a bread board approximately 5" x 10" in size.

First stain the board as desired and attach saw-edge hanger to backside. Drill small hole for ivy stem (see illustration) back of the cutter to give appearance of growing from the board.

Make bird nest of excelsior and shape to fit top of cutter, spray nest with glue and let dry and insert. Place bird in nest. Attach ivy starting in hole behind cutter and arrange up and around nest.

Attach hooks to use for keys or pot holders. First spray hooks black if preferred.

Irish Cop Bank and Jail Key

We call this one the "keeper of the keys." It is made to display an old jail-house key and toy policeman bank. If you do not have the originals, these are still available at antique stores. Also reproductions of each have been made.

How To

The board is 7" x 12" and the shelf measures 2½" x 6½". After cutting these pieces to size, attach the shelf and bracket. See page 162 for full details. The bracket measure is 2" x 2". Stain shelf as desired and add saw-edge holder on back of board. Next spray flat black paint on five key hooks. (It's best to let these dry overnight.) Attach key hooks 1" from bottom edge of board.

To secure the jail key, use eighth inch black elastic banding to hold on board. Drill holes on each side of key for elastic and tie tightly on backside.

The cop will have holes in the bottom of each foot going up into the body. Insert an eighth inch dowel rod in each foot and drill holes in shelf to secure rods.

Carpenter Tools in Frame

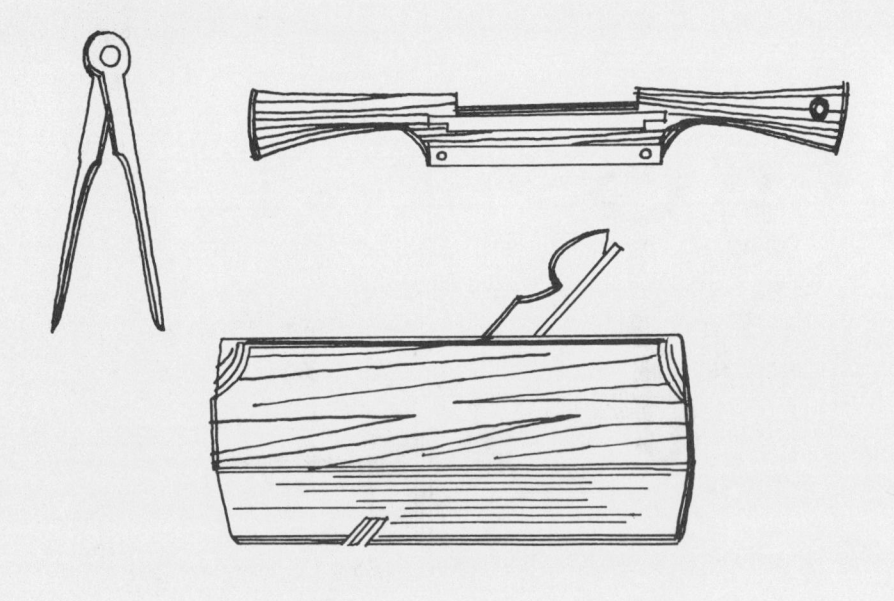

A variety of old carpenter tools can be used, with light weight and flat tools preferred. We used a spokeshaver, dating back to 1850, a wood plane (three-fourths inch total thickness) and also an old caliper.

The spokeshaver, as its name implies, was used to carve and shape the spokes for all kinds of wooden wheels. It was a much used tool in the 1850 to 1900 period. Many of these are found in good condition and of handsome hardwood.

The caliper appears to have been hand forged and crudely made. However, in those days it did the job of measuring the distance between two surfaces or points.

The wood plane is of the type used in the early 1900s and before by carpenters who were skilled in cabinetwork and fine detail finishing in home construction. Due to the different "cuts" needed for a molding in the making of cabinets and other trim, a skilled carpenter would possibly have as many as six to 12 planes in his tool box. Over the years the tradesmen identified the planes by the shape of the cutting blade and bottom of the plane. The plane shaved the wood by means of a steel blade which was held in place tightly by a hardwood wedge. Removing of the wedge allowed for raising or lowering the blade to adjust the cutting depths. Also from time to time the blades were removed for sharpening.

How To

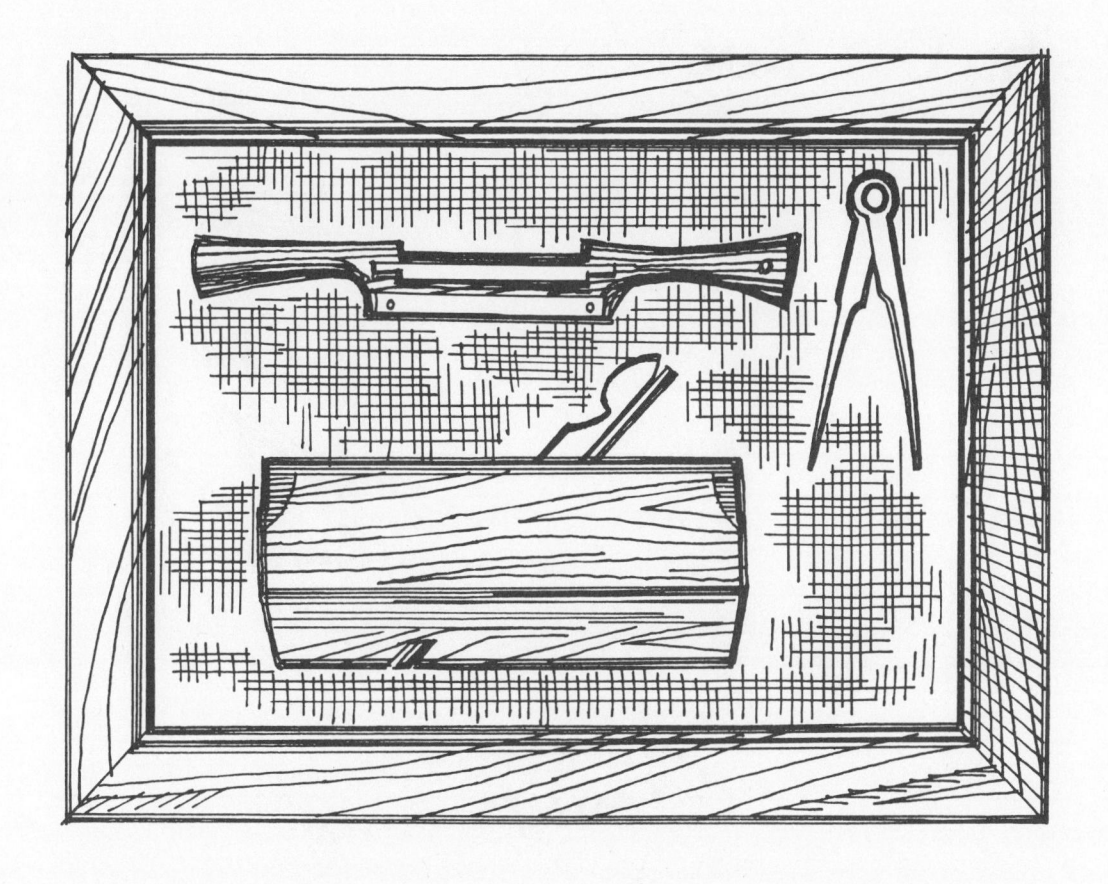

The old picture frame for this particular piece measured 15″ x 18″. Finish the frame as preferred. Attach two saw-edge hangers on backside of frame for hanging. Place these 2″ from each end of frame. This will allow the piece to hang evenly. Cut a piece of eighth or quarter inch plywood to fit inside frame and cover with contact burlap. Attach it to the frame and arrange tools.

Drill holes for inserting elastic banding to hold tools in frame. Drill slightly underneath the edge of the tools to conceal holes if possible. Put elastic around tools and through holes, pull tight and tie or staple elastic on backside. If a wide and heavy wood plane is used, a small shelf can be built in place of the elastic banding for support.

Lincoln Picture Drawer Using Old Bookend

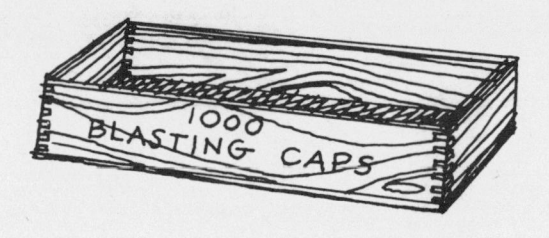

Here's a fun piece with a patriotic theme. First we found an old box with dovetailed corners. The stencil on the box was still readable indicating the original contents were dynamite blasting caps.

The Lincoln head is actually one part of a bookend set. It was a little deep for the drawer so the backside of the bookend was trimmed off.

For the flag we were fortunate to find a print in color of just the right size which was a cover on an old campaign booklet of a few years ago.

How To

The box was cut lengthwise to make a 10″ x 14″ rectangular "drawer" that is 2″ deep with the bottom attached. The depth of the drawer can be varied to retain any wording on the side. An old wooden drawer pull was attached to one end with a piece of dowel rod or with a screw. The drawer was then stained.

The cutting board which measures 16″ x 20″ was antiqued blue. You may obtain enough of a contrast by using stain. At this point attach two saw-edge holders to backside of drawer.

You are now ready to attach the drawer to the cutting board. Position the drawer on the board and secure with small nails which will be covered with the burlap. Measure the inside of the drawer and cut a piece of contact burlap to fit. We used a dark red color.

The next step is to drill a hole in the bottom of the bookend and secure with a screw through the drawer and into the bookend. Then cut about a 4″ x 5″ piece of plywood and decoupage the flag to it.

To mount the flag in the drawer, first nail in a 2″ x 2″ square of wood about a half inch thick. To this apply glue and place the backside of the flag on it. This gives the piece depth. Let glue dry overnight and the Lincoln piece is ready to put on the wall.

Enamelware Ladles and Dippers

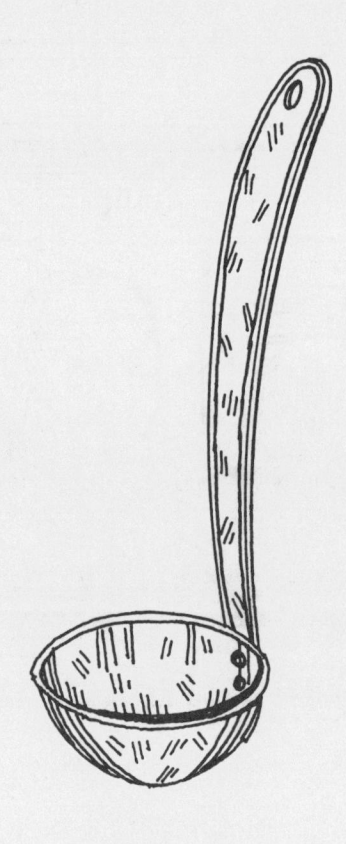

Although ladles and dippers are similiar in size and shape with the names being used interchangably, there is a functional difference. The ladle was used primarily in cooking to "dish out," so to speak, the semi-liquid food from the kettle. The ladle was usually more shallow and more rounded on the bottom than the dipper, with the handle at a more horizontal level. Also the dipper was of a cup like shape and was primarily thought of for drinking water.

When water hand pumps were outside the house, it was customary to have in the kitchen a bucket of drinking water and a dipper. If you were drinking after someone else and wanted to be a little sanitary, you would take a little water in the dipper, swish it around and throw it out before satisfying your own thirst. Such were the sanitary rules in the old days.

For a decorative piece, old ladles or dippers of the enamelware type are preferred, due to their natural beauty. Tin ones too are desirable, particularly those with wooden handles. This item seems to be a natural to mount on barn wood.

How To

Use a piece of barn wood 4" to 6" wide and about 5" longer than the length of the ladle. After nailing on the saw-edge holder, secure the ladle to the board at the top and also where the handle joins the cup. Drill holes on both sides of the handle and use wire to secure, tying on the backside.

Ladle handles are of many varieties. The one illustrated had a hole at the top of the handle for hanging. We used a porcelain knob to fasten the ladle and for decorative purposes. Some handles simply had a curved end for hanging. If yours is of this type it can be hooked over the top edge of the board.

The ladle can be filled with any type of decorative flowers. Ivy twined around the handle gives an added touch.

Comb and Brush Case with Vanity Mirror

Even before 1900 Junior (this applied to Dad too) had little excuse for not "slicking up" before dinner. Mom saw to it by having a handy comb and brush case near the water basin.

The basin would likely be located in the kitchen by the hand pump. The comb case was usually made of tinware in various shapes with the length 8" to 10" Some were quite ornate, in different colors, and occasionally with a small mirror in the center of the back. The case had one or two holes in the backside for easy hanging on the wall.

The "ebony" type hand vanity mirror was probably kept on the wash stand or dresser in Mother's room. It was considered a deluxe item for primping and for a side as well as a back view of the hair style.

How To

The board we used for this piece is 10″ x 12″ in size. Adjust this measurement to the size of the mirror and comb case. We do suggest you round off the top corners of the board to blend with the roundness of the mirror. Stain the board and attach the saw-edge holder to the top center backside. Also drill a hole for the white porcelain knob and insert.

The comb case is secured with one or two white knobs, depending on the number of holes already in the backside of the case for mounting. If necessary use small nails too, placing these so they will be covered by the greenery to be added later.

On the backside of many of the hand mirrors you will find a small metal ornate tab. This is held to the wood with a brad and easily removed with a pocket knife. Clean this piece with steel wool and attach to the handle on the mirror side.

To attach the hand mirror, first carefully drill two eighth inch diameter holes in the backside of the handle. Glue into these two half inch long dowel rods. Place the mirror on the board and mark where the rods make contact and drill receptive holes. Greenery is then placed in the comb case and the piece is ready to admire.

School Slate and Wooden Bowl

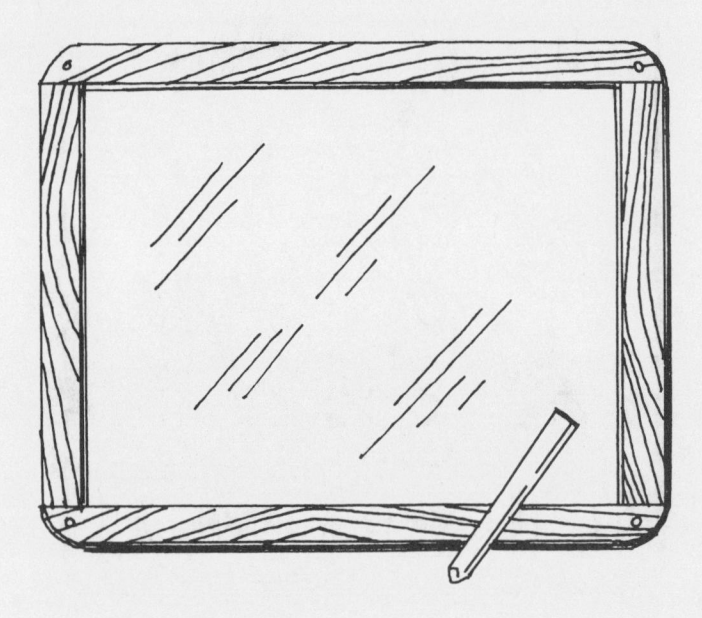

In many of the one-room school houses dating back to the middle of the 19th century, children used slates for their writing and arithmetic lessons. Those usually measured 8" x 10" or slightly larger. The slate was in a wooden frame, and quite often the wood part was edged with a brightly colored yarn-like material. Each child furnished his own slate and marker to use during the school day. A small piece of sheepskin was used to erase. After several erasures, the slate would need washing with water to be usable again. For this purpose a wooden bucket containing water and a piece of cloth was kept in front of the schoolmaster's desk.

Due to the lack of school books, the lessons in math and history were quite often presented by the teacher in song or rhyme for easy learning. Such lessons were written on the blackboard across the front of the room for all to see. A typical rhyme for a first grade class might read something like this:

2 pennies had Tom
His sister had 1
They gave them to me
And then I had 3
Thus you may see
1 and 2 make 3

Old slates vary in price according to age and condition. If you don't now possess one, the price can range from $2 to $10 dollars or more.

How To

The best size slate to use is about 8" x 10". Use a cutting board at least 1" wider than the slate. Also allow 1" space above the slate and 6" below to mount the wooden bowl. After finishing the bread board as desired, attach the saw-edge hanger to the backside and the white knob at the top. Then cut a wooden bowl (5" to 6" diameter) in half. See page 162 for detail. Stain or paint the bowl and attach to board.

Next, position the slate and attach with small finishing nails, or we prefer to use small dowel rods through the wood frame of the slate in each corner. Stain ends of dowel rod before pounding in flush.

Use excelsior or straw in the bowl and five or six plastic eggs. We wrote on our slate, "Eggs 26¢ per dozen," indicating the price years ago. This alone brings a lot of comments.

If desired you can use a 1" wood knob with dowel rod and attach alongside the slate as indicated in illustration. To this tie a string for a piece of chalk or slate marker.

School Slate with Shelf

We also made up a slate arrangement using a shelf instead of the half wood bowl. This might be preferred for decorating in the den or family room.

The shelf is made 3" wide and 10" long and is suitable for a number of small cherished items. If you have something special to display, first place the object on a board to determine the best size shelf to use. Take into consideration the "railing," which should be set in a half inch from the edge of the shelf. Our figures show a bashful boy with a gift for his fifth grade girl friend.

How To

Use a cutting board 1" wider than the slate. Cut the board to allow 1" above the slate and 6" below. Attach the slate to the board as in preceding illustration.

The board for the shelf should be 2" shorter in length than the width of the cutting board. Our board was 12" x 14" and the shelf 3" x 10". The shelf brackets are 2" x 2½".

The attachment of the shelf to the cutting board is shown on page 162. Before securing the shelf to the cutting board, make the railing. Use two wooden knobs of 1" diameter. From the illustration you can see that two holes are drilled in each knob at a 90 degree angle. Use an eighth inch drill and make the holes about a quarter inch deep. Cut two 1" dowel rods for the railing "posts" and one piece of rod 8" long for the rail. Glue these into knobs and position on shelf for drilling receptive holes. Stain shelf and railing before attaching to board.

Spigot with Old Tin Bucket

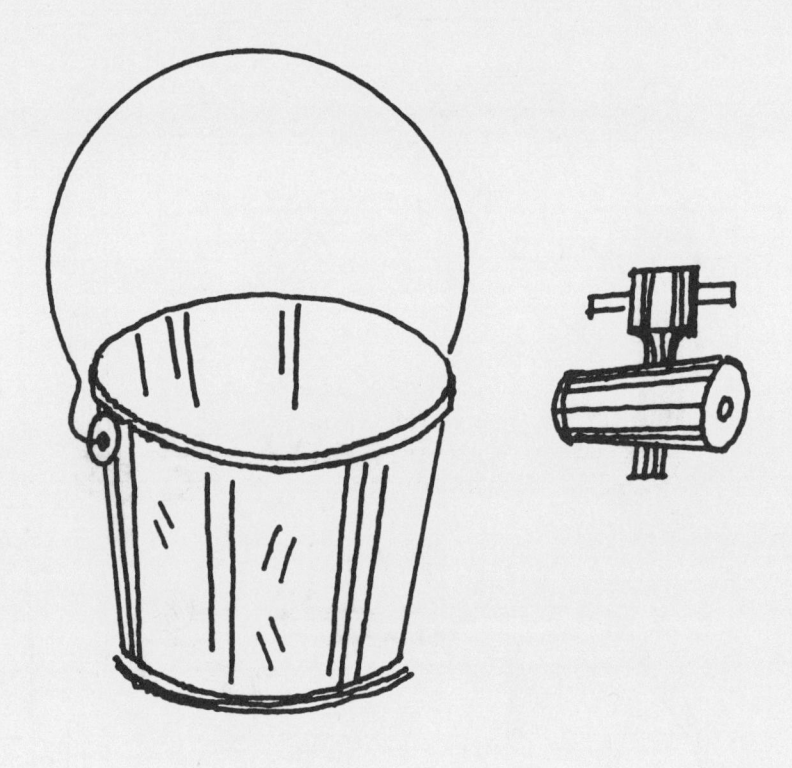

The theme for this piece is two little birds taking turns drinking from an old tin pail. These small tin pails or buckets are about 3½" high and with the same diameter at the top. Some we have seen contained peanut butter, mince meat, or maple butter, according to a paper label or printing on the pail.

Spigots had many uses in the old General Store as well as in the home. They were used to "tap" kegs and barrels for bulk liquid to measure out a quart, pint or whatever quantity was desired. Quite often the customer would supply his own container, a tin bucket or crockery type jug. This of course made the cost of the item a little less. For storage and convenience, water was sometimes pumped into barrels. The spigot was occasionally referred to as a water faucet.

How To

Weathered barn wood with a ragged top was used for this piece. The wood measures roughly 7" x 15". From the top of the board measure down 6" and mark for inserting the spigot. A small spigot 3" to 4" in length is preferred. To use a larger spigot, cut off the insert so it will not extend out more than 4". Next drill or saw a hole in the board to fit the spigot.

Attach the bucket about 3" below the spigot. Nail through the top rim edge only, using one or two small nails. Leave the wire handle free.

Drill a hole slightly below the bucket to receive the ivy end. Then arrange the ivy around one side of the bucket and up over the spigot. Small pieces of fernery are placed in the bucket. Attach the small bird to the edge of bucket. Use masking tape across the wire that extends from the bird's feet and stick to inside edge of bucket. The other bird is placed on board in upper right hand corner, waiting his turn to drink. Drill a small hole and secure the wire from birds feet in the board.

Wooden Spoon with Towel Rack

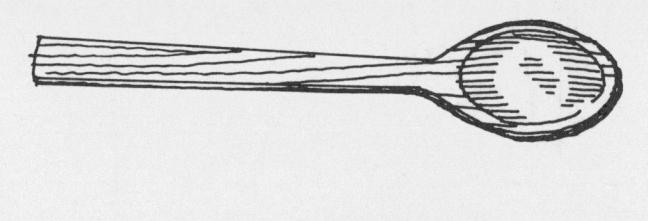

Wooden kitchen spoons date back even beyond pioneer days but are still found in most kitchen drawers. Many housewives still prefer the wooden spoon for making jelly, applesauce, mush and other items common on the farm years ago. Old ones stained and worn from use are readily available and give an added touch to kitchen plaques.

How To

As shown in the illustration, we used the conventional cutting board (9" x 12") with the half wooden bowl placed off center, then included a spoon and a towel rack.

To start this project, prepare the surface of the cutting board as desired. Then attach saw-edge hanger. If the board doesn't have a hole at the top, drill one and attach the white knob. Next drill two eighth inch holes in backside of spoon handle, being careful not to drill through—just deep enough to insert and glue in eighth inch dowel rod. Then place spoon with dowel rods protruding from holes on the cutting board and mark for receptive holes. Attach spoon to the board. Next attach half wood bowl as described on page 162.

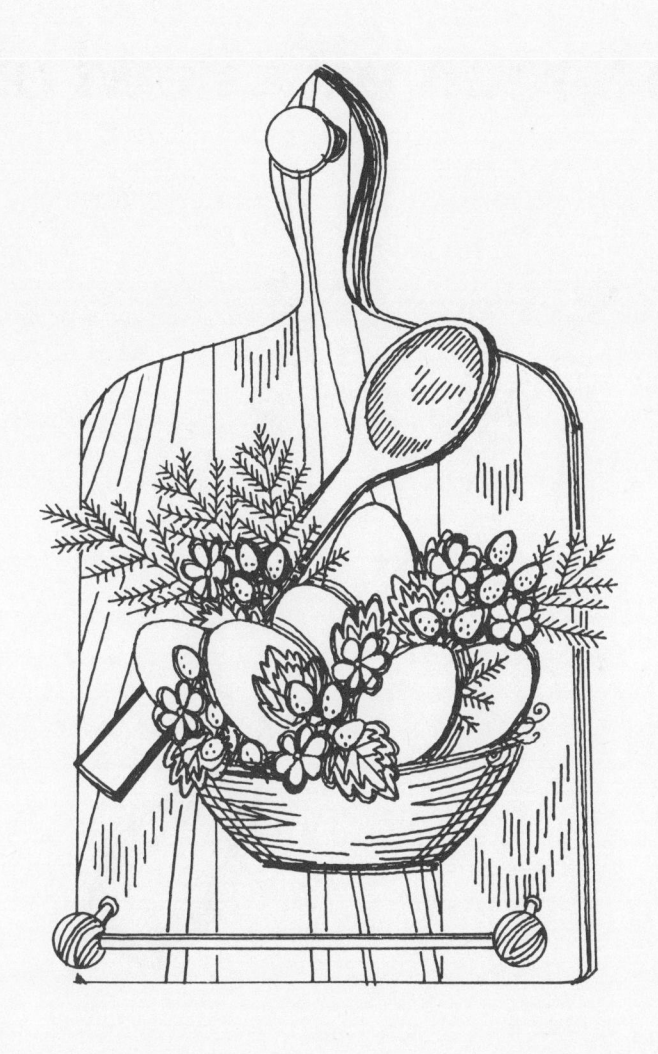

To make the towel holder, use two round wooden knobs 1" diameter and drill an eighth inch hole a quarter inch deep into center of the knob. Drill another hole at 90 degree angle to the first hole. Cut two pieces of dowel into 2" lengths and glue one into each knob. Next cut a piece of rod to an 8" length, insert and glue each end into a knob. Then the towel rack is ready to place on the bottom of the board and mark for drilling holes a half inch deep. Insert and glue the towel rack into the board. The towel rack could be omitted but the results are worth the time involved. We filled the bowl with eggs and strawberry picks.

Wooden Spoon with Bowl of Eggs

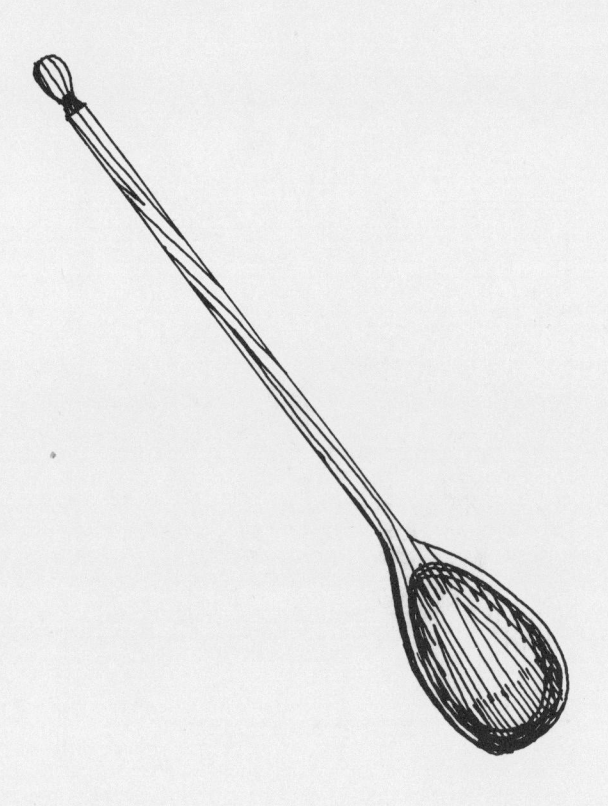

In the 1850s one might well find in the typical kitchen a wooden bowl used for holding eggs freshly gathered from the chicken nest. Quite likely the bowl would have been made from a "burl." This was a large lump or knot that grows on the trunk of many trees. The burl was particularly hard, and when carved and smoothed into a bowl shape it made a very beautiful as well as useful piece. Such bowls would sometimes be as much as 18" in diameter and 8" deep. This was an all-purpose storage and mixing bowl. The wooden bowl used for this display is not necessarily old in comparison and is of the salad type.

Wooden spoons were made in various sizes and handle length to meet a cooking need. Spoons were also occasionally made from cow horns. This was accomplished by cutting the horn in half, and applying heat to shape the horn into a crude spoon. It would then be trimmed with a knife and made smooth. Such a spoon would have been used for eating or dishing out the food.

How To

The barn wood used for this piece measures 8" x 15". After attaching the saw-edge holder, the next step is to cut and mount the half wooden bowl. See page 162 for detail. Then drill eighth inch holes in two different places on the backside of the spoon handle. Glue in two half inch dowel rods. Place on board and mark to drill for receptive holes. Secure with glue. A round wood ball or old drawer pull can be used for the bird perch.

Fill bowl with excelsior, plastic eggs and star flowers.

Kraut Box as Horse Stall

We found a very graceful old brass statue of a racing horse about 8" high and 10" long. It seemed appropriate to put the horse in a "stall." The slide box from a kraut board was in excellent shape and the horse stood in it just right, with his head held high. We stained the box to bring out the highlights of the grain and to emphasise the "multiple dovetail" corner construction. This strong construction was important as the box did not allow for any top or bottom. It's simply an open square about 3" deep. Plywood with burlap cover was used for the backing of this stall. A fancy metal ornament sets off the top of the box. This metal piece was used at one time to hold the tieback for a window drape.

How To

Measure the outside square of the box to determine the size to cut the piece of quarter inch plywood. Then attach a piece of contact burlap of the same size and of any color desired. We used dark red which contrasted nicely with the antique maple stain used for the box and with the brass horse. Stain the slide box before nailing the plywood on the backside. When nailing the plywood include the saw-edge hangers for mounting the piece on the wall. Next add the ornament on the top center of the box. Position the horse in the stall. The left hind leg of the horse should touch the burlap. At this point drill two small holes, to accommodate an elastic loop around the leg. This should be sufficient to hold the horse in the stall and really won't be noticeable.

Kraut Box as Chicken Nest

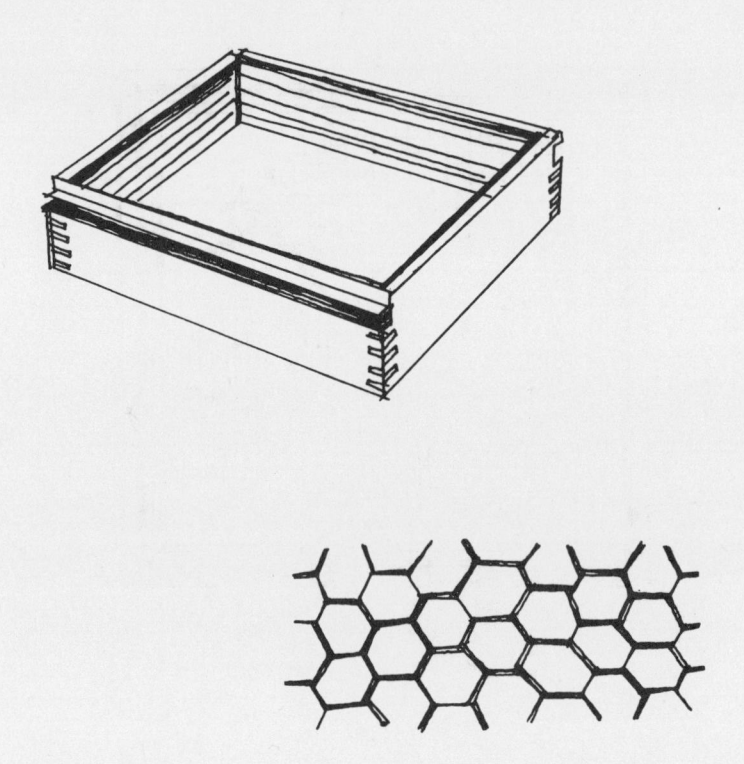

Most of the old kraut boards had a slide box to hold the cabbage head when shredding to make kraut. The boxes had a strip of wood along two sides to fit a groove running the length of each side of the kraut board. The box we had was found minus the kraut board. It was quite weathered and seemed most suitable to make a chicken nest.

The wire used to hold the straw in the nest was called "poultry netting." Today it is commonly known as chicken wire and still does the job to corral small chicks or other farm fowl. The netting is available in widths of one to eight feet and has many uses.

How To

A piece of barn wood measuring 9″ x 14″ was used as the backing. After cutting this board, attach saw-edge holder to backside. Drill eighth inch holes in two places on backside of box and insert dowel rods. Let these extend a half inch to go into the barn wood. Drill holes in barn wood and mount. Next take a piece of chicken wire and fit in the box to make the nest. Spray the wire black and then secure in box using small staples.

Fill the nest with excelsior or straw and add the plastic eggs. Place a few straw flowers in the back of the nest for color. An old wood drawer pull is centered on the top of the nest box. Also if desired add an inquisitive bird on the barn wood or nest wire.

Vegetable Grater

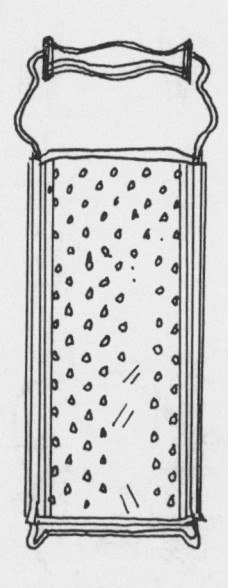

The old grater we found for this plaque measures 3" wide and 9" long and has a wooden handle. We understand these were made in about three different sizes, one larger and one smaller than the grater described. This grater has an open back. The grating part is supported by heavy wire down each side. This wire also forms the small "legs" at the bottom of the grater. It was advertised as a "radish grater" but was surely used also for other vegetables, roots, and nuts.

How To

The bread board used is 6" x 15". After cutting the board to size, stain and attach saw-edge holder. A white knob is added to the top edge of the board. Then center the grater on the board and drill a small hole on each side of the bottom right hand "leg." Secure with back wire twisting the two ends together on backside. Do the same at the top left side of the grater where the wire for the handle meets the tin part of the grater.

Make a very small nest from excelsior and spray with glue, then place in top of grater below handle a small bird. Drill a hole for the ivy stem at the edge of grater, insert and then fasten end on backside with staple.

Hooks for keys or pot holders are sprayed flat black and then attached at the bottom of board to complete the project.

Ice Cream Dipper and Sundae Dish

As early as the 1890s families enjoyed the delight of homemade ice cream. The hand-cranked freezer was a cherished possession. The soft ice cream made a real treat for a hot Sunday afternoon. The freezers were made in various sizes to yield two quarts up to two gallons of ice cream at one cranking. The cream couldn't be kept for a long time and usually was consumed at one sitting. This pleased the kids.

The ice cream dipper as we know it today was originally called a "disher." It was made in various sizes to yield four to ten dishes from a quart of ice cream. The dipper dating back prior to 1900 was made from heavy tin or combination of tin and iron. Inside the dipper was a metal V. A half turn of the knob which was attached to the V at the bottom would loosen the ice cream from the sides to make a perfect "dip." As with many of the early utensils, the dipper was made in many different styles.

A much used item at the early drug store fountain was the brass "sundae dish." These were still in use in some areas as late as the 1940s. A heavy conical white paper was inserted in the brass dish to hold the ice cream and the topping. After the delicacy was consumed, the paper was disposed of and no dish washing was necessary.

Both of these pieces are found at antique stores, shows, and flea markets, with the dipper being the more plentiful of the two.

How To

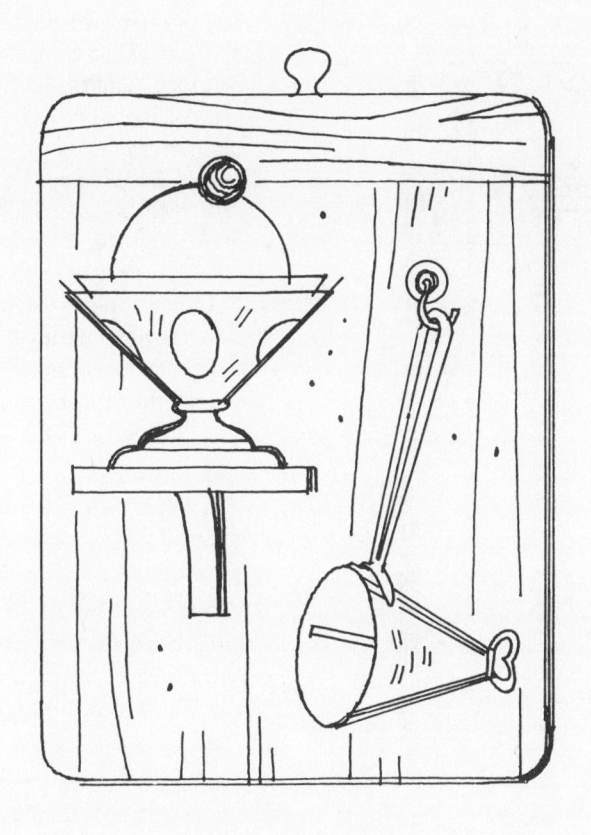

For this plaque, the board should be about 9″ x 12″ in size. Finish as desired, attach saw-edge hanger to backside and white knob at top of board. The shelf to hold the sundae dish measures 4″ x 4″ and detail for attaching is on page 162. Mount the shelf 6″ from the top of the board and 1″ from the left side. The shelf support is 2″ x 3″. With a little practice you can cut a piece of white paper to fit the dish. Also add a styrofoam ball with an artificial cherry stuck on top. You can simulate chocolate too if desired. It looks almost good enough to eat! The dipper is hung from a brass hook so it can be easily removed to show your friends, or if you have an ice cream freezer, you may even want to use this old "disher" when serving your guests.

Recipe Booklets

In addition to such advertising "giveaways" as biscuit cutters and mixing spoons, the Baking Powder Co.s also gave away helpful booklets with cooking recipes and kitchen hints. During this period of the early 1900's the cooking booklets were also published and distributed by some stove manufacters as well as food extract houses. Several of these booklets have colorful covers showing the lady of the house in the kitchen and "costumed" of course in the dress style of that period.

The recipes for making breads, pastries, meat, cheese and vegetable dishes as well as household hints for "those days" are of interest and the booklets are nice reminders of one phase of the life style of yesteryear. In one pamphlet dating back to 1911, we found a hand written recipe on a small piece of paper for that all time favorite "chocolate fudge."

Fudge

two cups sugar
two heaping teaspoons cocoa
butter size of hickory nut
enough milk to dissolve
Let boil till forms a ball when dropped in water.

Booklets we have seen were put out by Royal Baking Powder, Swans Down Cake Flour, K. C. Baking Powder, Town Crier Flour, Rumford Baking Co., Walter Baker & Co. and a Range Manufacturing Co. This information was often passed out by the grocery stores as a courtesy and usually the proprietor's name is found stamped or imprinted on the back cover.

Some of the Booklets such as the "Rumford" were punched with a small hole in the upper left hand corner. This was for the purpose of tying a string through the hole so the booklet could be easily hung. A nail was driven in the wall near the preparation table or perhaps in the end of the kitchen cabinet. If you have occasion to buy an old cabinet at an auction, you may find a booklet for cooking still tucked away in one of the drawers.

HOW TO—Using wood spoon and bowl

The Rumford Booklet used for this plaque measures 5" x 7". The board was cut to a size of 8" x 16". After preparing the board, stain as desired and attach sawedge hanger to top backside. Also drill hole and insert white porcelain knob.

The wood clips are made as given on page 166. Note that we used the clips at the bottom of the booklet instead of at the sides of this eliminates the need for the small shelf. However, the booklet does have to be held in place at the top. Some of the booklets such as this Rumford one had a small hole in the upper left hand corner. This was done so a string could be looped through same to hang the booklets on a nail near the cooking area and it was always handy when needed. To add to the conversation about this piece, we used the hole in the booklet to hold it in place at the top of the plaque.

After clips are in place, position the booklet and make a mark through the hole on the board. Drill a 1/8" diameter hole 1/4" deep in the board. Then using a 3/8" diameter dowel piece, drill a 1/8" diameter hole in the end 1/4" deep and insert a piece of 1/8" dowel 3/4" long. Cut the 3/8" dowel piece 3/8" from the end. If you do not have the 3/8" size dowel just insert a 1/2" length of the 1/8" dowel which will do the job nicely. This dowel pin is stained and then used to hold the booklet in place.

The wood spoon is held on the board with elastic banding. Position spoon on board and drill 1/8" diameter holes on both sides of the handle and through the board. Put the elastic through holes and tie on backside. The 1/2 wooden bowl is secured as on page 162. Fill the bowl with plastic eggs of greenery and etc. as preferred.

HOW TO—With 2 cup flour sifter

This booklet put out by the Royal Baking Powder Co. in the early 1900's has a very attractive and colorful cover. It was referred to as "A Manual of Practical Recipes for Home Baking and Cooking."

The simulated bread board used is 10" x 13" in size. Two sawedge hangers are attached to the top backside one inch from each end of the board. Then drill a hole and insert the white porcelain knob. The board was stained a light honey color. The old two cup flour sifter used had a nice wood handle that was stained to contrast with the greenery. We painted the sifter flat white. A 1/8" diameter hole is drilled in the backside of the handle part that rests on the board and insert a dowel rod piece 3/4" long. Place sifter on board and mark to drill receptive hole for the dowel piece. At this point position the green leaf sprig and drill hole for stem behind the sifter. Then secure the greenery. Next place sifter on plaque with dowel in hole and work greenery around handle. Inside the sifter at the front edge (where the bird nest will cover) nail securely to board. Nest of excelsior is made and placed so about 1/2 of it will stick out of sifter. Place bird in nest as shown.

A small piece of masonite (or wood) 1/8" thick, 1/2" wide and as long as the width of the book is used as a "shelf" to hold same. Glue this in place. Directions for the wood clips to hold the booklet are the same as for the Bible on page 166. An ideal gift for a new bride.

137

HOW TO—Using old extract bottle and stove lifter

This book of "Tried Recipes" was published for a "Range" manufacturer that made stoves to burn coal or wood. The cover pictures the "Range" and children having a party with tea and biscuits. It seemed appropriate to use an old stove lid lifter and an old paper labled bottle of lemon extract to complete this kitchen piece.

The simulated bread board measures 10" x 13". Stain as desired and attach porcelain knob to top center. Also attach sawedge hanger to top backside. Then make the wood clips and shelf for the booklet as given for the first kitchen plaque. The extract bottle needs a small shelf too of masonite and then the bottle is secured around the neck with elastic banding. Drill 1/8" diameter holes on both sides of the neck of the bottle, insert banding and tie backside of board.

The stove lid lifter can be attached in a similar way with elastic banding at both ends of same or use black wire.

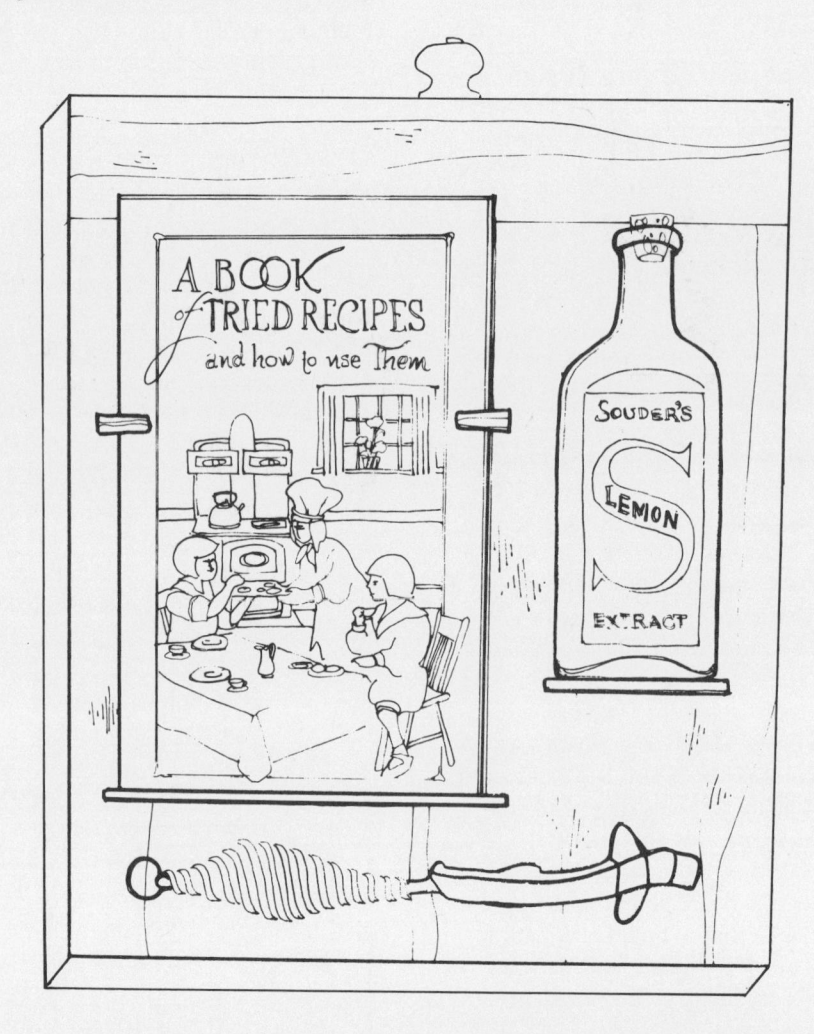

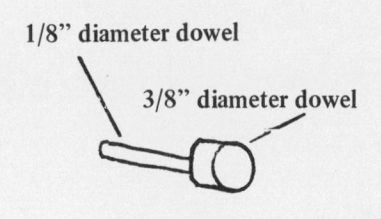

1/8" diameter dowel

3/8" diameter dowel

Dowel pin

Mincing Knives (chopping knives)

This kitchen item was familiar to the housewife dating back to the early 1800's. It was used to make the "mixings" for the mince pies and to prepare sausage and any other meat dish that was prepared from chopped rather than ground meat. As with many other tools and utensils the first one were of necessity made by the head of the house or the local blacksmith. Later in the 1890's the "mincing" knife of several shapes and sizes were available "factory made."

The mincing knife was made of cutlery steel and although not usually as sharp as a regular butcher knife, it would readily cut meat, vegetables and the like when used in a "chopping" fashion. In view of the manner in which the chopping knife was used, the ingredients were put in a wooden bowl or chopped on a bread board. The wooden bowl was one of the earliest kitchen utensils and the large old ones demand a good price in the antique market today. Many times you will find these with small cuts on the inward sides and bottom of the bowl caused by "chopping" with the mincing knofe. These wooden bowls were commonly found in the 1850's with diameters of 12 to 20 inches. Some of these containers made of wood were oblong being about 12" wide and 20" long and were called wooden trays.

The mincing knife illustrated was of the double blade type and with a wooden handle. There were several different types with some having single blade and made of all steel. These ranged in price from 3 to 6 cents each.

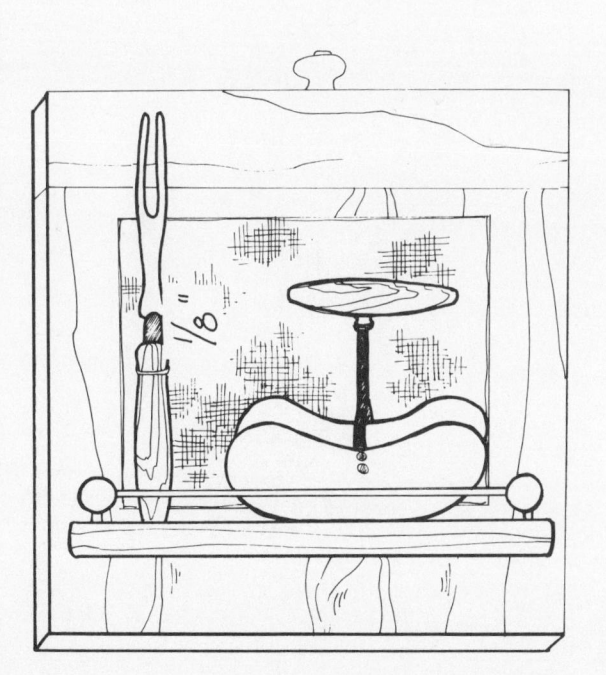

The wood handle on the mincing knife we purchased had been turned on a lathe (the lathe holding marks were visible on each end of the handle) and forced on the stem of the iron frame. This frame affair in turn was riveted to the two steel cutting blades. These were advertised in the early 1900's as having an enameled handle which was an appealing factor in those days as a relief from the plain wood finish.

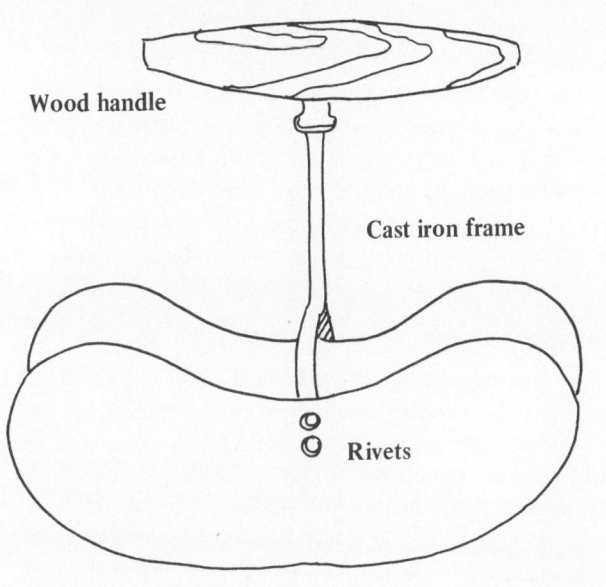

Wood handle

Cast iron frame

Rivets

2 cutting blades

HOW TO

First we pulled the wood handle off the shank and scraped it down to the bare wood. The handle was stained and replaced. Use steel wool to clean the cutting knives if necessary. As this piece with the double blades will stand upright by itself, we decided to display it on a shelf. The simulated cutting board used is 10" x 13". The shelf is 3" x 9". Detail for making shelf is on page 121. The wall plaque needed some contrasting color so we used a piece of gold burlap 6" x 8" in back of the mincing knife. Also an old 2 prong cooking fork was added and held in upright position using elastic banding.

Potato Mashers

The all wood potato masher dates back many, many years ago and could be bought at retail stores or through a catalogue into the early 1900's. Some of these were made from one solid piece of hard wood and make handsome display pieces. Other all wood potato mashers, very similar in appearance, were made with two separate pieces of wood, the "mall" or masher part and a handle. These were advertised as "driven handle" mashers to distinguish from the one piece item and cost about one-fourth less. The handle was driven into the masher part to make a tight fit. Another potato masher of this same general period was the heavy twisted wire type with wood handle.

The third type shown is more easily found and probably grandmother has one of these still in the drawer for her culinary tools. This masher with a hardwood handle and steel mashing head can be purchased at the usual antique sources. These are also called "potato ricers" and this name is found on the steel part of some of these items. As the potatoes are "pressed" with this culinary tool, the resulting product takes on a string like appearance having the diameter of a grain of rice. This model is used for our plaque and makes a nice place to put this item to rest and still be in sight. In this way you can remind yourself how fortunate it is to have "the electric" and that grandmother in those cherished yesteryear days had to use a bit of muscle to prepare the mashed potatoes.

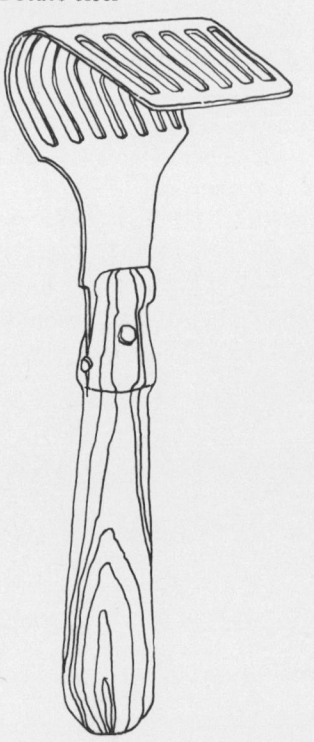

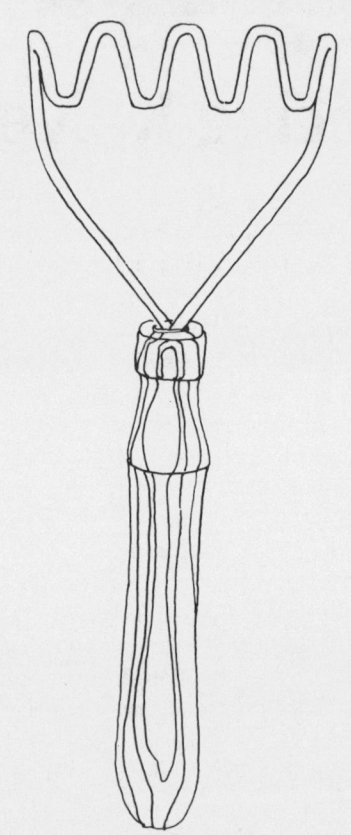

Heavy twisted wire type

All wood masher

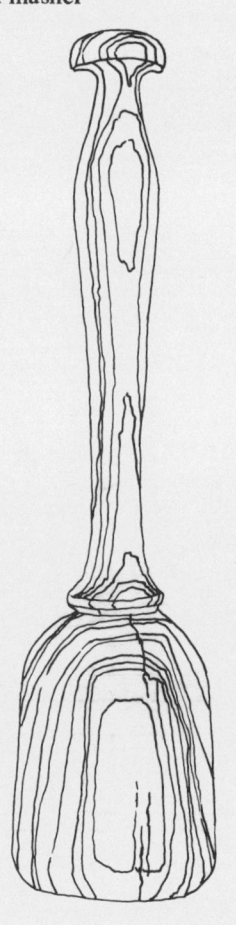

Potato ricer

HOW TO

The bread board used was cut to a 10" x 13" size. If you have to use a new board, one this size should be available at your local Craft shop.

A light stain was used namely, honey maple. After you have perfected the board and are ready to work with same, first attach the hangers on backside and drill a hole for the porcelain knob on top center. This will make it look as a real bread board. Position the potato masher and drill a small hole into the bread board by the side of the handle to insert the end of the greenery. The wire end is then stapled on the backside. Next drill a hole 1/4" diameter in the backside of the wood handle and near the end where it will rest against the bread board when laid flat. Glue into the handle a 1/4" dowel

HOW TO—Twisted wire masher with wood handle

The board used was cut to a size of 5" x 13". It was stained dark walnut to give a definite contrast to the light colored wood handle of the potato masher. Attach sawedge hanger to top backside of board and wood knob to center top edge of board. We painted the knob white.

Before securing the masher permanently, position it on the board and work greenery around the handle and up wire part. Hole for inserting stem end of greenery is drilled along side or back of the wood handle. Remove masher and staple greenery stem on backside of board. About one inch down from where the masher wire is inserted in the wood handle drill a 3/16" hole and also a hole 1" up from the bottom of the handle. Insert 1" dowel pieces and then place masher on board to mark for receptive holes. Secure masher to board and move greenery into place.

Make nest of excelsior and position in "V" opening in masher and add bird to nest. One inch up from bottom edge of board, attach three hooks for hanging keys or pot holders. Paint hooks black.

piece 1" long. Again position the masher on board and drill receptive hole for same. Put glue in the hole and secure masher. This one dowel piece should hold the masher securely on the board, however if desired attach metal part to board with small wire through hole in masher.

While the glue is drying, cut off just the tip of 3 plastic mushrooms so the top will lay flush against the board. See below. Also drill a 1/8" hole in the side bottom of the mushroom and insert and glue a 3/4" piece of dowel. Position mushrooms on board and drill receptive holes. Put a little glue in each hole and secure the mushrooms. Next make a small nest and spray with glue. While still tacky, place in masher "opening" as you will have to shape it to fit same. Add the bird and eggs and stand back and admire your new kitchen plaque.

HOW TO—Masher with steel head

Use a bread board about 10" x 13" in size and use in a horizontal position as shown. Sawedge hangers are attached to backside and knob to end of board. Stain board to contrast with wood handle of potato masher. Drill two 1/8" diameter and 1/4" deep hole in side of masher handle that goes against board. (2" apart on handle) insert dowel rods to protrude 1/2". Place on board and mark for drilling receptive holes. Attach masher to board by glueing dowels into same. Make nest and attach with stickum. Glue the 1/2 bowl to board 2-1/2" from bottom and 1/2" from side of board. Cut a small piece of styrofoam and place in bowl to secure egg picks. Add eggs and other decorations as desired. Bowl mounting details is on page 162.

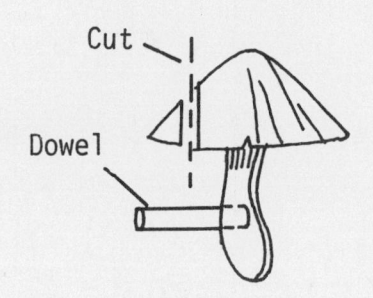

HELPFUL HINT—Mushrooms

When attaching mushrooms, cut off the top backside as shown. This gives a natural look when placed on board. In stem of mushroom drill 1/8" hole and insert 3/4" dowel piece. Place on plaque and drill receptive hole.

Patent Medicine

For man or beast

Liniment and healing oil were two of the popular patent medicines available in the late 1800's and into the 1930's. Bottles that contain these items are sought by collectors today. The directions on the paper labels, the closures used and the shape of the bottles make these old keepsakes of interest to about everyone.

One bottle we consider as our "prize" is triangular in shape and it declares on the label, "The genuine is always in triangular bottles." On one side of the triangle this bottle has a paper direction label "For Man" and on another side a label "For Beast." This was a liniment as well as an antiseptic.

The bottle pictured with a cork closure and the familiar wire ring to pull out same, contained "Healing oil" and specified that it was not a liniment but an antiseptic — surgical dressing.

Many of the quality liniments, healing oils and etc. were formulated by physician or veterinarian and often included the doctor's name on the label. This was true of "Sloans" liniment. Dr. Earl S. Sloan compounded this liniment about 1885 while working as a Veterinarian for

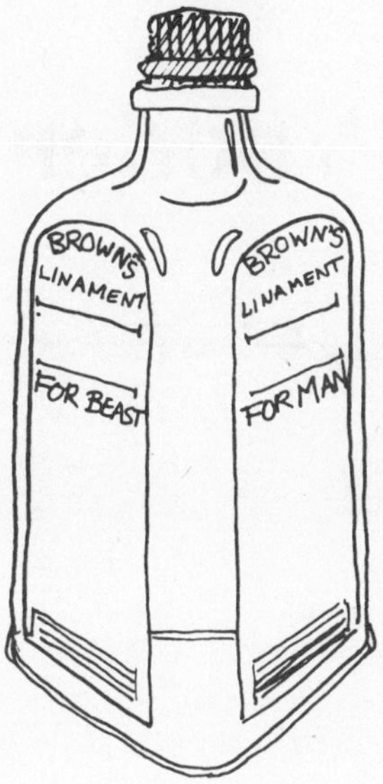

Sloan's liniment

Triangular bottle

the Street Car Co. of St. Louis.

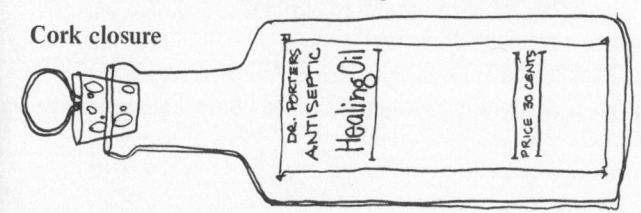

One guide to determine the age of bottles is the fact that metal screw type caps became available about 1930. Prior to that time cork inserts were used.

The bottle of old medicine we used for this plaque was found at a flea market and still in the original cardboard box. It's Dr. Boyd's Fever and Cough Cure for horses and cattle. The liquid contents are still in the bottle and sealed with a cork covered with wax. It is interesting that the paper label does not declare the ingredients used to make the medicine or the contents of the bottle in ounces. It does give these directions: "1 teaspoon every 30 minutes until relieved, then every hour. Not genuine unless bearing Dr. Boyd's portrait." This medicine also cured colic, loss of appetite and other diseases for a total of 15 in all. This item was sold through drug stores for fifty cents per bottle.

The "Pappy" bank is a reproduction of the cast iron bank dating back to the early 1800's. It's a comical figure about 5" tall and the toes are sticking out of the shoe of the left foot. The mule is not necessarily old but has that tired and stubborn look associated with most mules. It is made out of paper mache and 7" long.

Cork closure

HOW TO—Pappy and the mule

A bread board was cut to a size of 10" x 20". The left-over pieces were used to make the two shelves and the three wood brackets. The shelf to hold the bank and mule is 3" x 12" in size. The shelf for the bottle is 1-3/4" x 3-1/2". The larger shelf brackets are 1-3/4" x 2" in size and the one for the small shelf is 1-1/4" x 1-1/2". **Detail for attaching to the board is on page 162.**

Before attaching the two shelves and brackets, attach two sawedge hangers to the backside near the bottom backside of the board. Nail a plywood strip 1/4" thick, 1/2" wide and 18" long. This will "set-out" the bottom of the plaque so that the shelves will be level. Also insert the white porcelain knob in the left vertical end of the board. Stain the board as desired and the items are ready to place on same. If you want to secure the figures to the board, run small dowel rods up the feet leaving 1/4" extending to go into holes drilled in the shelf. For safekeeping the bottle could be glued to the shelf or use some kind of florist adhesive on the bottom.

Wooden Shipping Boxes

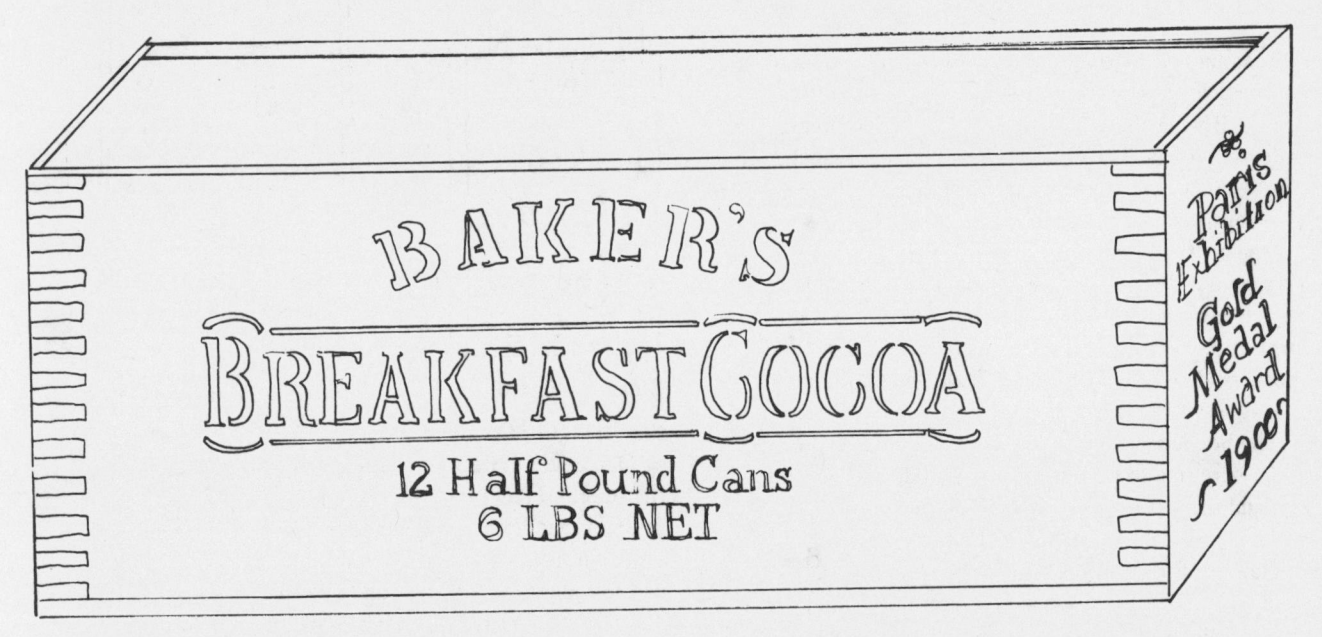

Old and small wooden shipping boxes make ideal planters

The old dovetailed cornered wood box sketched above was used by the Baker Co. to ship their tins of breakfast cocoa. Being of a nice size (approximately 6" x 10" and 4" deep) to store odds and ends, these boxes are often found when auctioneers are cleaning out an attic or basement of an old homestead preparing for a sale. Such boxes also seem to find their way to flea markets, antique shows and the like.

The back side of the "Baker" box shown was also stenciled and tells that this company was established in 1780 by Walter Baker, Dorchester, Mass. and that their breakfast cocoa won the Paris Exposition Gold Medal award in 1900. This company was one of the first to produce cocoa in the United States. They also made sweet and semi-sweet cocoa for cooking purposes.

Royal Brand Cocoa offered money-back guarantee

Another brand of cocoa familiar in the late 1800's was the "Royal" brand. This company was established in 1872 and also sold their item in half pound cans. They proudly advertised the guarantee "your money back if you want it" and also stated on the can "the grocer pays you the money, you keep the cocoa, only a good article can stand this test." The can we have is marked as selling for 25 cents and has a "pry-off round cap."

The other half of the Baker's Cocoa box, the backside that you cannot see, includes the famous Baker's trademark of "La Belle Chocolatier." A portrait of a young lady by Jean-Etienne Liotard and which is widely known throughout the world. The original portrait is today in the Dresden Gallery in Germany.

At one time the shells or hulls from the cocoa bean were sold to make a hot chocolate beverage. The shells were boiled in a mixture of water and milk for a period of time and then drained off to make a satisfying hot chocolate drink. A chocolate and cocoa recipe booklet published by the Walter Baker & Co. LTD in 1911 refers to the availability of "cocoa shells" and these were packed by them in "1 & 1/2 papers." It further describes the cocoa shells as being the thin outer covering of the bean and having a flavor similar to, but milder than, cocoa. Due to the low price of the shells, a pleasant and satisfying chocolate drink was affordable by about anyone. Today cocoa bean hulls are used as a ground cover, particularly for roses, and give off a very chocolatey aroma when first spread from the burlap bag.

This cocoa box is of a size (4" deep, 8" wide and 10" long) that lends itself well for a planter type plaque. In fact it can be cut in half so that both sides of the stenciling can be used. By using steel wool and two coats of light stain the "box" has a handsome, aged look. Eggs of course are associated with breakfast and it would seem appropriate to include these as part of this kitchen wall decor. For hanging in the dining area, a selection of artificial small fruit might be preferred. The old wooden spoon fits in quite well for the time element and may well have been used to beat the eggs to use in a pancake batter. The hand rotary mechanical egg beaters were not invented until the 1870's. The bread board used as a background for this piece of course was a most essential part of mother's kitchen tools in this era.

HOW TO—Wood box for planter and towel bar

For this plaque we used a small wood box without any stenciling and decorated same by attaching an old wood spoon to the front of the box. Part of the beauty of this piece is obtained by sanding the wood well and staining to perfection.

The bread board (if not available use pine or knotty pine wood 1" thick) was cut to a size of 10" x 13". The box used measured 10-1/2" in length and 3-1/2" wide and cut to a depth of 2-1/4". The size of the piece of course can vary depending on the box used but cut the bread board to allow the "box" to set in 3/4" from each side. Stain the pieces before putting together and use different stains so you will have a contrast between the bread board, box and spoon. Quite often we will find the spoons to be deeply colored and will not need stain for contrast. Attach 2 sawtooth holders to backside and also drill hole for knob and top of board.

The towel rod is made using two wooden balls about 7/8" to 1" in diameter. See page 163 for detail. Drill 1/4" holes in bottom of box 1" from outside edge to insert towel bar. Attach the box to backboard with small nails from backside of board. Drill 1/8" deep and 1/4" diameter holes in backside of wooden spoon and glue in 1/4" dowel pieces 3/4" length. Place on box front and mark for drilling receptive holes to secure.

To finish this piece, first fill the box with excelsior, then add eggs, a little greenery and some star flowers. Include too a bit of baby's breath to give a bit of frilliness. If you like birds, add a small nest of excelsior and a little partridge.

HOW TO—Bakers box

The bread board used measures 12" x 15". It was stained to contrast with the old Bakers box. Then add 2 sawedge hangers to the top backside. The front of the box used was cut to a 2" depth and was positioned on the board 1/2" up from the bottom. It is secured to the board using small finishing nails, through backside. Next drill a 1/8" hole in the backside of the spoon and handle and glue in 3/4" lengths of dowel rod. Place on the board so the spoon handle is partly in the box and drill receptive holes where dowel pieces touch and glue in place. The 1/2 wooden bowl was painted with dark brown acrylic to give further contrast to the piece. Attach bowl with top edge 4" from top of board. Detail for attaching on page 162. Greenery is placed in the box using styrofoam to secure. Eggs or artificial fruit go in the bowl and the piece is finished.

Silver Evening Purse and Vanity Mirror

Evening purse and vanity mirror.

Chatelaine bag.

Grandmother may still have in her keepsakes this dainty and elegant evening "bag."

The silver evening purse is just big enough to hold a fancy hanky and a few essentials for make-up. The purse was made of solid silver and is so stamped on the inside. The purse shown had a much worn silk lining indicating the mistress attended a number of social gatherings in her day. It measures a petite four and one-half inches long and the "pocket" is three inches deep. The chain is approximately 10" long.

The small steel beaded bags of the early 1900's were also popular and usually had a chamois skin lining. These were made with a silver plated frame and were considered dainty and stylish for this era. Other similar size ladies bags of this period include the "chatelaine", which was usually a beaded bag with a steel frame. To the middle of the chain for this purse was attached a very ornate hook so that the bag could hang from the ladies belt.

The word "chatelaine" is identified by Webster as a broach-like clasp or hook from which a watch, purse, etc., were suspended. A black silk belt with a chatelaine bag was the "go" in the gay 1890's. Belts were also made from calf skin, patent leather, satin and usually those black in color were the most popular. See illustration.

The old wooden vanity mirror goes back to the late 1800's and was finished with white enamel rather than the black ebony look of most of these mirrors. There is a small reed-like "ring" that fits over the mirror edge and holds it in place. The "ring" is cut at an angle on both ends and fits together to "lock in" the glass mirror. This is easily removed to take out the glass part of mirror for safe keeping if it is desired to do any refinishing to the wood frame of the mirror.

HOW TO—Using mirror frame

It is preferred to use an old frame with a semi-ornate look to hold the old purse and hand mirror. The one we used measures 13" x 14".

The first step is to do any refinishing work needed on the old frame selected. The size of the frame, of course, will depend somewhat on the size of the evening bag and hand mirror. Our frame of a 13" x 14" size measures 2" in depth. The depth of the frame from the outside edge to the "backboard" used, should be a minimum of 1". After the frame is completed, attach two sawedge hangers to the top backside of the frame. Then cut a piece of 1/4" to 3/8" plywood to fit into the frame. For the material to go over the plywood, we used red velvet contact paper. After this velvet is applied then use small finishing nails to secure the plywood in the frame. Place the purse and mirror on the velvet and position for proper balance. See illustration. Next, the mirror is prepared for mounting. In the backside of the handle and about 2" apart drill two 1/8" wide holes and be careful not to drill through to the frontside. Into the holes glue and insert 1/2" length dowel rods, 1/8" diameter. The mirror we used, due to age, had the enamel badly flaked. We removed the "ring" from around the edge of the mirror, which freed the glass and this was put aside for safe keeping. Then the front side of the wood mirror frame was sanded well and sprayed with antique white satin. After the paint has dried well (use at least two coats) go over lightly with four "O" steel wool to remove any shine and to give a used look. Next replace the glass and position the mirror on the velvet to mark for drilling receptive holes for the dowel rods. Secure mirror and then drill a small hole for the white porcelain knob from which the purse simply hangs. Due to the thinness of the backing board used in the frame, the threads on the knob should be cut to 1/4" so the shank will not protrude too far out on the backside.

To retain the dainty and old fashion look in this wall decor piece, we used baby's breath, pink velvet flowers and two pink roses in the purse opening. Make this arrangement as one piece tied together at the stems and position in the purse opening. By clasping the purse shut, the flowers will be held in tightly. If you have a keepsake fancy hanky of Granny's this could be included too with just a corner peeking out. This is a piece you can enjoy in about any room in the house. Particularly elegant for hallway entry or at end of hall in bedroom wing.

Finished piece using old picture frame.

HOW TO—Purse on Shelf

If you have an evening bag but not the mirror frame, here's an easy way to show off the purse on a small shelf. This smaller version also makes a nice piece for the bedroom. The size of the shelf is determined by the purse and the length of the chain.

The backboard for the shelf measures 6" x 10" and the shelf 2" x 5". Round the top of the board as indicated and attach the shelf 1" up from the bottom. Nail on from the backside and no brackets are used. (See page 162). Attach sawedge hanger to top backside. Stain the board as desired. We used walnut to make a pronounced contrast for the purse and flower arrangement against the shelf. Place the purse on the shelf and stretch out the chain to determine placement of knob to hold the purse. We used a white porcelain knob. The flower arrangement is placed in the purse along with the "hanky" and it's ready to hang.

Some of the small metal beaded bags will hang quite flat against the shelf. As shown in the drawing using this type of purse, the shelf was made 2-1/2" deep and 4" wide so an old fancy perfume bottle could be included. For this particular plaque the backboard is 5" x 12" and the single bracket 2" x 2". See page 162 for shelf detail.

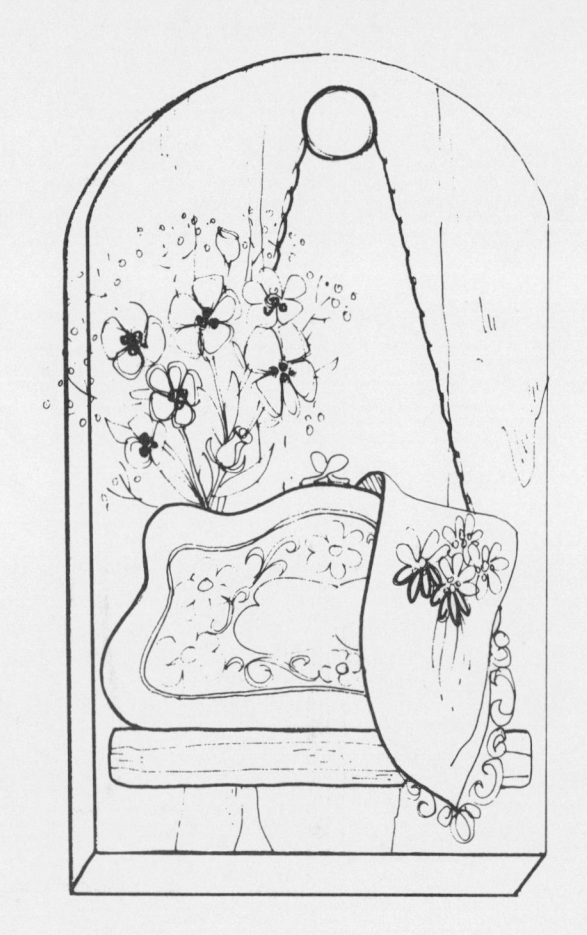

More Ideas Using Old Kitchen Utensils

All of these plaques call for a board of about 10" x 13" in size. Directions below assume you have first prepared board as per page 5.

Flour Sifter

Directions:
1. Place sifter at slight downward angle and 1" from side and 2" from top of board.
2. Before attaching sifter, drill hole behind same for end of greenery and staple in place.
3. Next nail the sifter to board inside front and at back rim.
4. Place nest of excelsior and small bird in sifter opening.
5. Bowl is glued to board 1-1/2" from side and bottom. Fill with eggs, etc., as desired.

Thumb Sugar Scoop

Directions:
1. Place Scoop on board 1" from side and 2" from bottom. Behind scoop position and attach 3 strands of wheat stapling to board.
2. Then nail scoop in place. Nest will hide nail heads. Make excelsior nest and put this in bottom of scoop with stickum and add bird.
3. Bowl is glued in place 1" from bottom and 1-1/2" from side of board. Fill with eggs, etc.

Tin Mixing Spoon "Rumford 1908"

Directions:
1. Place spoon at an angle as indicated. Arrange mixture of wheat and straw flowers and secure stems to board with staples to be covered by spoon handle. Then drill holes to attach spoon with wire or elastic banding.
2. The bowl is glued in place 3" from bottom and 1" from side of board. Fill with eggs and greenery.

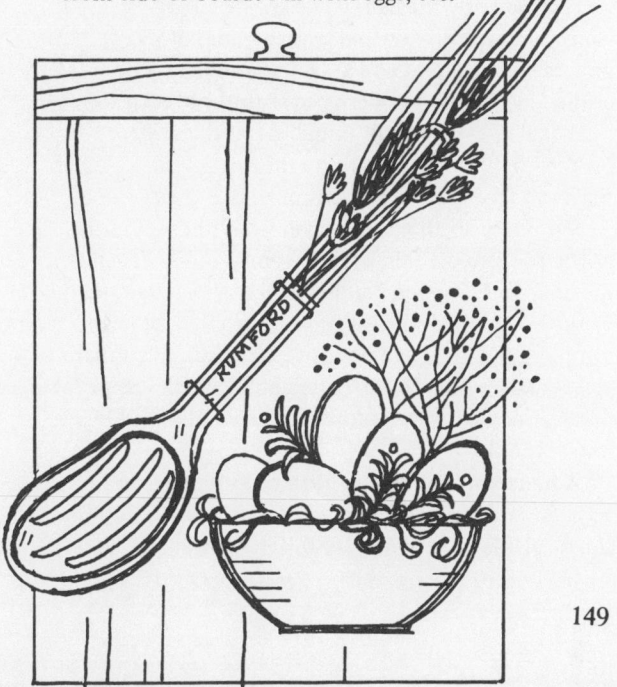

Old Milk Bottles

A "Cream Top" bottle is shown here with its small spoon, made to fit into the bulbous top part of the bottle. The larger skimmer, an earlier device, was used by farmers' wives in skimming cream from raw milk so that the cream could be churned into butter.

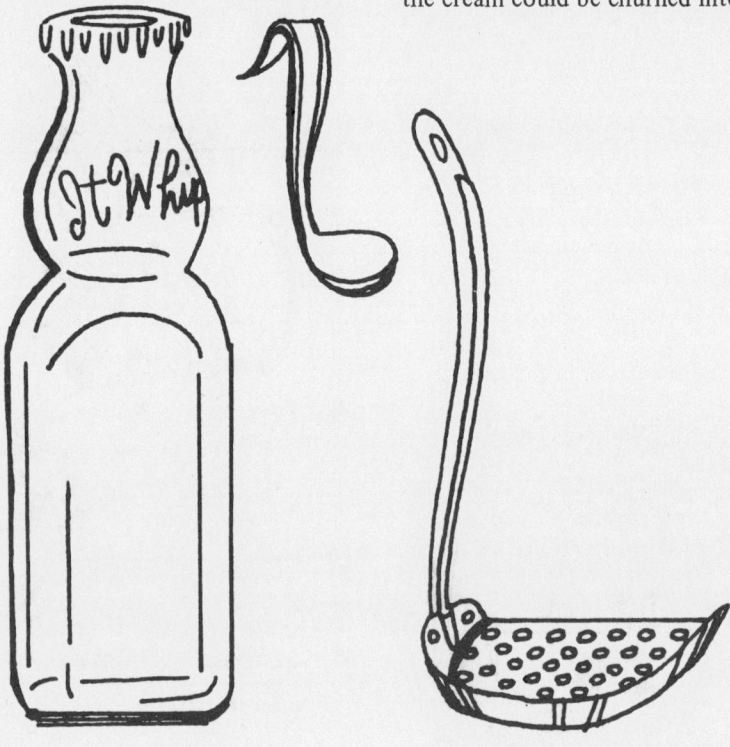

Dipper-like spoon 'reserves' cream for dad's cereal

The patented bottle illustrated above is called the "cream top." The purpose for the special design was to allow the cream to be poured off the top of the milk without mixing with same. A special spoon as illustrated was provided by the dairy. The spoon carried the trade name "cream top" too and was patented in 1924. In 32 ounces of raw milk there are approximately 4 ounces of cream. The bottle was designed with the special top to hold exactly 4 ounces of liquid. After the pasteurized "whole" milk was poured into the bottle and sealed at the dairy, the 4 ounces of cream would rise to the top.

For use in the home the spoon was inserted in the bottle to "seal off" the cream from the milk. Then by pressing on the spoon handle, which curved over the lip of the bottle, with the forefinger one could hold the bottle in one hand and pour off the cream for father's cereal and coffee. To further emphasize richness of the cream, the bottle at the top had the words "It Whips" molded in the glass.

A housewife in the mid-19th century wouldn't recognize this old milk bottle, as glass bottles for milk were not available until about 1880. Likewise her Great-granddaughter, after 1950, wouldn't recognize the design of this bottle with the crimped neck as being a storage place for the cream. Such bottles were discontinued after homogenized milk became popular in the 1940s. Homogenization is a manufacturing process whereby the whole milk is forced through a tiny opening under great pressure which breaks up the fat globules. In this way the "cream" is suspended throughout the milk evenly and it no longer rises to the top. By this method each ounce of the milk has the same cream (butterfat) content.

History tells us that dairy cattle were raised for milking purposes as far back as 6,000 years ago. Since colonial times the family cow was essential and looked upon with great favor as the supplier for the precious milk commodity. If one family had an excess of milk, it could readily be bartered to neighbors. As cities became larger and more numerous, laws were passed prohibiting the pasturing of cows inside the city limits. Therefore, around the 1850s it was a good source of income for farmers to have a small dairy farm and supply milk to the city folks. Later dairy plants developed to process the fresh milk and this was the beginning of a major industry in our country.

HOW TO—Decorative kitchen plaque

As both milk and eggs are considered essential to breakfast, we displayed, with the bottle and "cream top" spoon, a bowl of eggs, fresh from the nest. In fact, these are so "cackling" fresh that the excelsior from the nest is still in the bowl. A delightful conversation piece for your country or modern kitchen.

The bread board was cut 14" x 14" and the shelf 3-1/2" x 13". If an old bread board is not available, use new wood and distress as desired. The quart milk bottle has a base measuring 3-1/4" in depth and fits nicely on this size shelf. After cutting the boards to size, sand and stain as desired. Then to the 14" x 14" piece, attach 2 sawedge holders at the top backside. Also drill hole for the white porcelain knob that goes on top of the board and insert same. Next attach the shelf 1" up from the bottom by nailing through from the backside. The brackets for the shelf are cut from scrap wood and measure 2-1/4" x 2-1/2". These are secured with glue on the top side of the shelf and 1/4" in from each edge (see illustration).

The old wooden bowl used was of a 5-1/2" diameter and we cut one edge off so that the bowl top extends 4" out from the bread board. Paint or stain the bowl and secure to shelf using small nails through the bottom. The bowl is filled with excelsior and then plastic eggs are added along with a bit of greenery and star flowers. The "cream top" spoon is secured with one loop of elastic banding through the board and tied in the back.

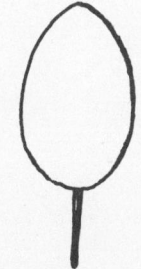

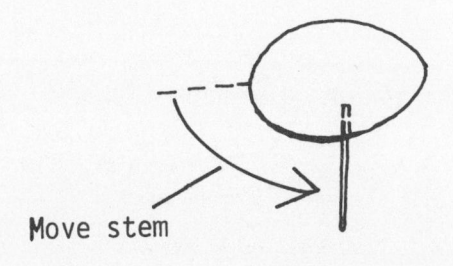

Move stem

HELPFUL HINT—Eggs

In an arrangement using plastic eggs, one or two of these should be laid flat in the bowl to look more natural. For this purpose, remove the stem from the end of the egg. Then with a nail, punch a hole in the middle of the egg and insert stem and put in arrangement. See illustrations.

Cream Skimmers

An early device used by housewives in skimming cream from raw milk so that the cream could be churned into butter.

HISTORY

Prior to 1880 and until bottled milk took hold in the early 1900's, a common sight in the cities was the milk wagon. People took their own pails to the "milkman" and he measured the amount needed from a large tank or milk cans. The milk was then poured by the housewife into a crock or some other shallow container so that the cream would quickly rise to the top and could be skimmed off easily.

Milk, as it comes from the cow either procured by hand or milking machine, is called raw milk. Such milk contains butterfat which is in the form of such tiny "globules" that the naked eye can't see. After the milk stands, the lightweight globules of milk fat rise to the top and this is the cream.

The cream was removed from the top of the milk with an assist from a tin skimmer and these were made in a variety of shapes. Normally this is a slightly concave tin piece having sieve-like holes (to let the milk go through, yet to retain the cream) and made with a short or long handle to remove the cream. As a quantity of cream was accumulated it was churned into butter and provided the by-products of cottage cheese and buttermilk.

History tells us that dairy cattle were raised for milking purposes as far back as 6,000 years ago. Since colonial times the family cow was essential and looked upon with great favor as the supplier for the precious milk commodity. If one family had an excess of milk, it could readily be bartered to neighbors. As cities became larger and more numerous, laws were passed prohibiting the pasturing of cows inside the city limits. Therefore, around the 1850's it was a good source of income for farmers to have a small dairy farm and supply milk to the city folks. Later dairy plants developed to process the fresh milk and this was the beginning of a major industry in our country.

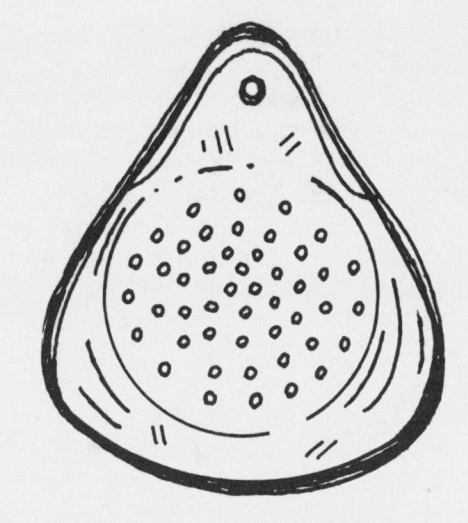

Tin-fan shape skimmer

Enamelware skimmer

HOW TO—Round enamelware skimmer makes "shelf" for corn husk doll

This old round enamelware skimmer is white and with a black handle (also enamelware) perpendicular to the round "skimming" part of the utensil. The total length was 10" and we mounted this piece on barnwood measuring 7" x 14". First attach a sawedge hanger to the middle top backside. Then drill a small hole in handle at the top to secure with a piece of wire through same and the board. Where the round part of the skimmer touches the board, drill another small hole in the edge of the skimmer and attach with wire or small nail.

About 3" up from the "shelf" drill a small hole to insert end of greenery stem and secure to backside of board. Let greenery wind around the skimmer handle. The 5" high cornhusk doll can be purchased from your favorite craft shop. It is attached by simply using a finishing nail up through one of the holes in the skimmer and into the bottom of the doll.

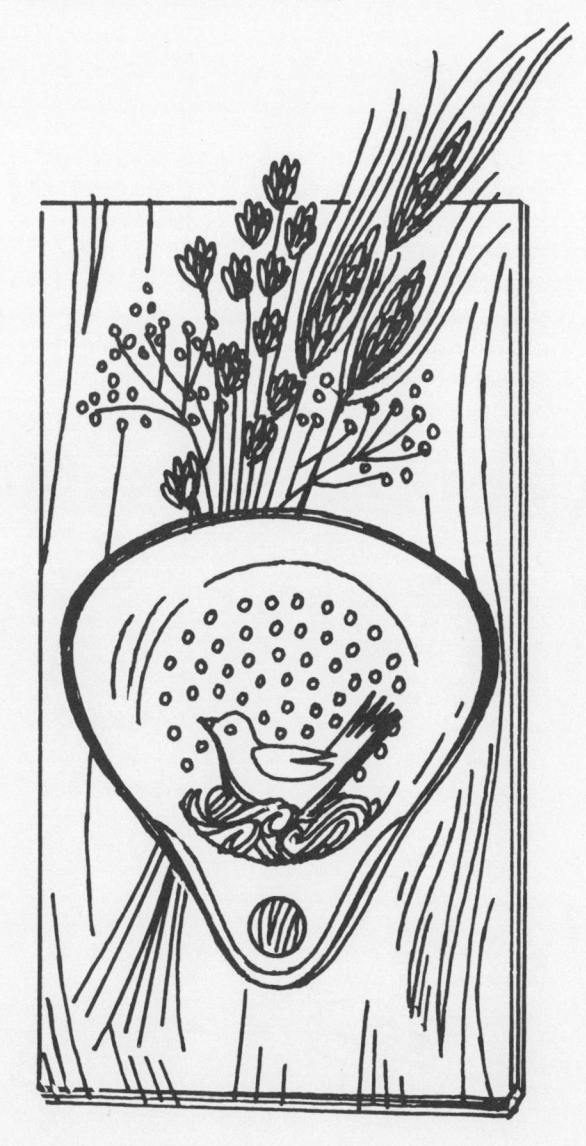

HOW TO—Fan-like shaped skimmer

This fan-like shaped skimmer is made of tin and is slightly concave. It was gripped in the hand at the narrow point and also has a nail hole in this area for hanging. A piece of barnwood 8" x 12" was used to mount the skimmer. First attach hanger to top backside. The flower arrangement of star flowers and wheat is made next as this attaches beneath the skimmer. Use masking tape around the stems where they will be hidden and secure with two small wire staples. Then place the skimmer on the wood and drill through the opening in the "handle" for knob. Next make a nest of excelsior and spray it heavily. After this has dried, attach nest with wire through two of the holes in the skimmer by drilling small holes into the wood. Draw tightly and add bird to nest.

Horse Curry Comb with Wooden Handle

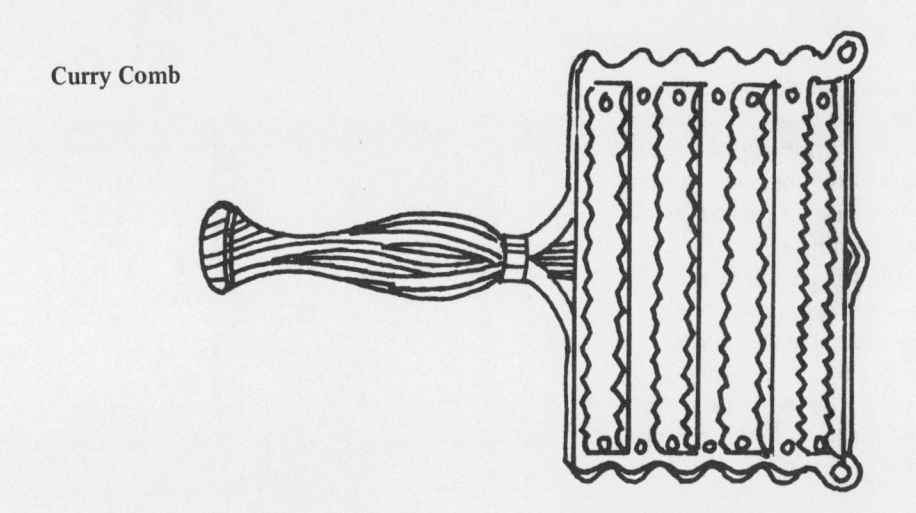

Curry Comb

Into the 1940's horses were still used considerably on the farm in the planting and harvesting of the crops. Early in the morning (about 6 AM) the farm hands started the day by grooming the horses before putting on the harness and collar. A curry comb and brush were used for this purpose. Manufacturers designed the curry comb in several ways but basically they are made with a frame of iron, tin or brass teeth, and with a wood or iron handle. The second item illustrated is a special comb for the horses mane having more course and rounded teeth than that used to "curry" the skin. It also has a hard rubber sweat cleaner at the top. Sometimes you will find the curry comb with a "mane" comb on the backside.

The curry comb was used to keep the skin clean and to loosen any grime that would accumulate from the previous days work in the field. The comb was held in one hand and a brush in the other to follow the path of the comb as the horse was groomed.

These old curry combs are still found in several different styles and many with handsome wood handles that make nice decorative pieces.

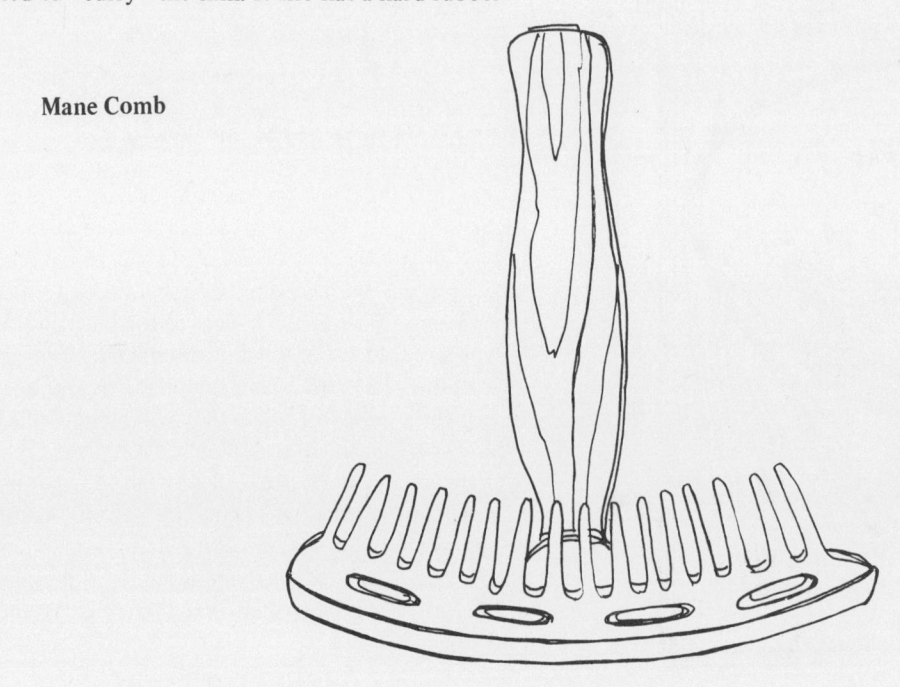

Mane Comb

HOW TO—Curry comb

Use a piece of barnwood approximately 8" x 10" and attach sawedge hanger to top backside. Then position the comb on board and arrange wheat and greenery. The decorative items are attached with staples and so the curry comb when mounted will cover same. If the metal part of the comb is rusted, spray with flat black paint, otherwise clean with steel wool. The handle should be sanded so that it will take stain to make a contrast with the metal part and also the barnwood. Sometimes there will be a "ring" of brass where the handle is attached to the iron part of the comb. Shine this with steel wool.

Attach the metal part of the curry comb to the barnwood using wire through holes in the comb and drilled holes in the wood. On top of the metal part of the comb and next to the handle tuck in a small nest of excelsior and include bird.

HOW TO—Mane comb

This mane comb had apparently been used a lot for the sweat cleaner was worn off and one curry "tooth" of the comb broken off. The wood handle cleaned well and was stained a light maple color which contrast well with the gray tone of the barnwood and the greenery. Mounted with the "teeth" out from the board it makes just enough shade and rain cover to entice the partridge bird to make a cozy nest.

Attach a hanger to the barnwood top backside (board size is 7" x 11'). Then drill a 3/16" diameter hole in side of handle that will be against the wood, and insert 3/4" length of dowel. Drill receptive hole in wood and secure. Along side the handle drill hole and insert greenery end and work greenery up through teeth of comb. The nest is only 2" in diameter and spray heavily with glue so it can be wired to board 1" up from bottom of handle. Add the bird and look for a place to hang your new creation.

Horse Saddles

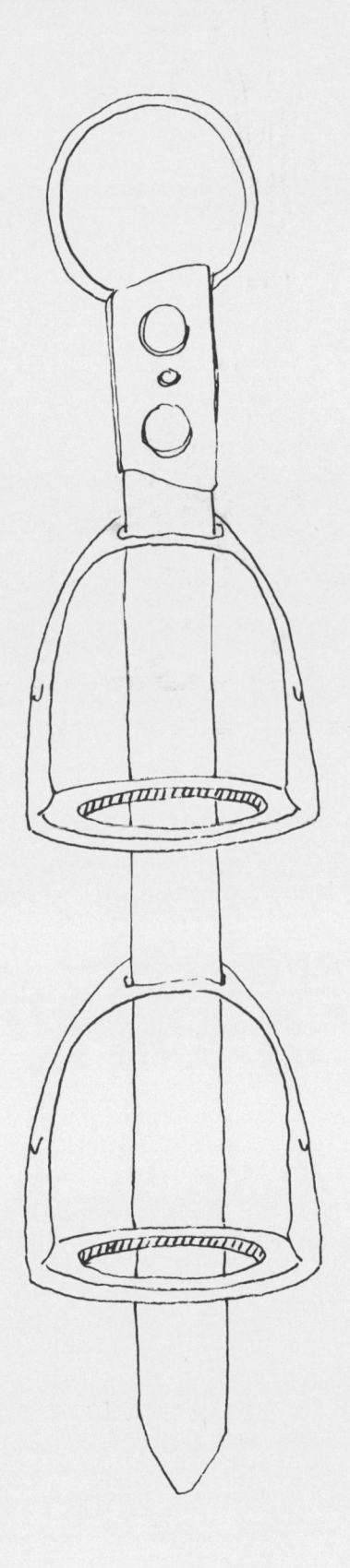

Sometimes at farm auctions, old saddles with leather torn and battered can be bought for a few dollars. Brass or wood stirrups may also be attached. When the saddles are stripped down to the bare wood, the result is an interesting and seldom seen saddle frame.

STORY

When Uncle John was a young boy, he cherished the horse saddle used by his grandfather and often when it was at rest over a saw horse, grandad would let him make believe he was riding away in the "wild blue yonder." When John was grown he inherited the old saddle as a keepsake but time had caused the leather to tear and wear away. The saddle was stripped to the wood and the stirrups of brass were still in good shape. To preserve the memories of the old saddle, it was decorated as shown and hung in the family room near the easy chair. (End of story)

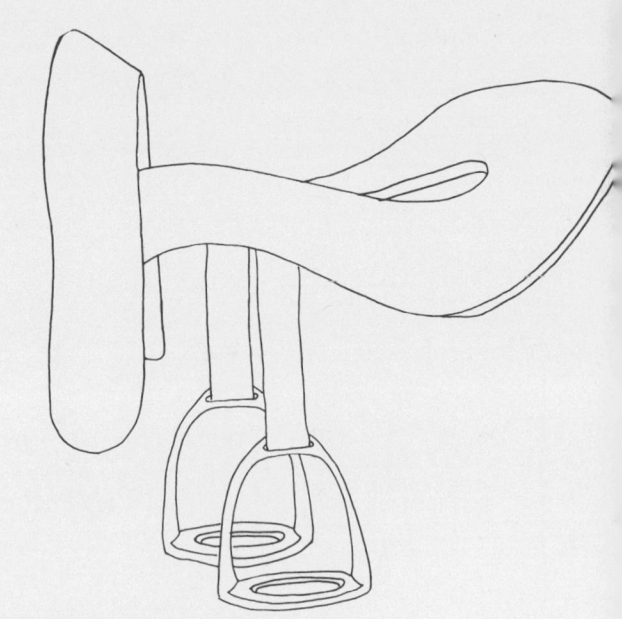

HELPFUL HINT—Greenery

When using artificial greenery such as ivy, drill a small hole in the board for the bottom stem. Staple same to the backside of the board. See drawing.

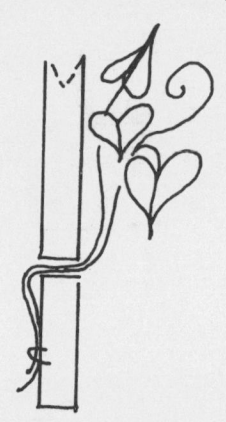

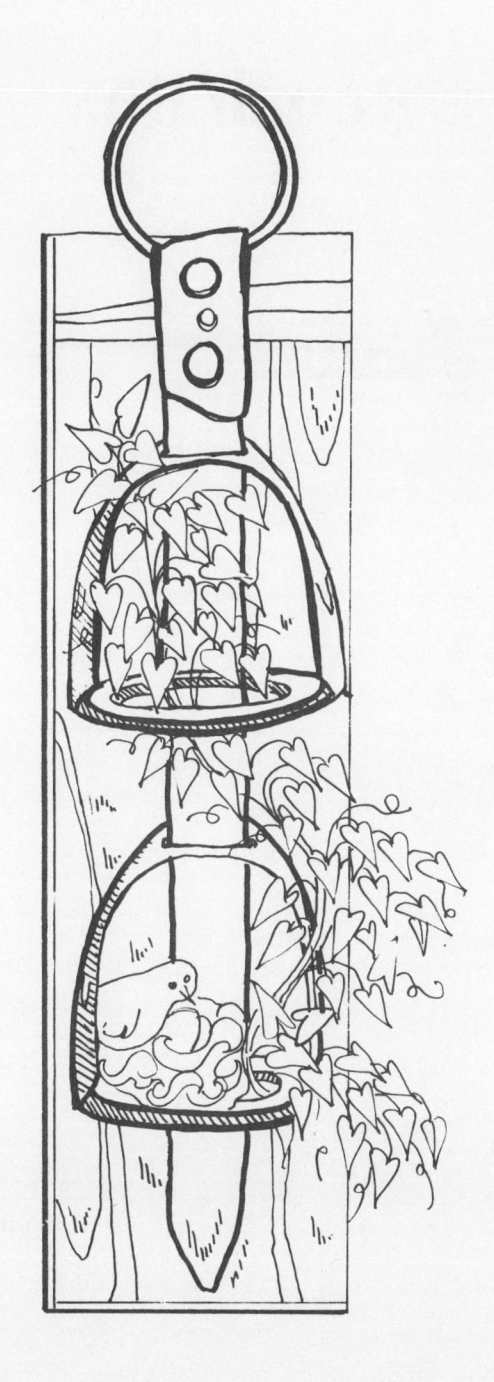

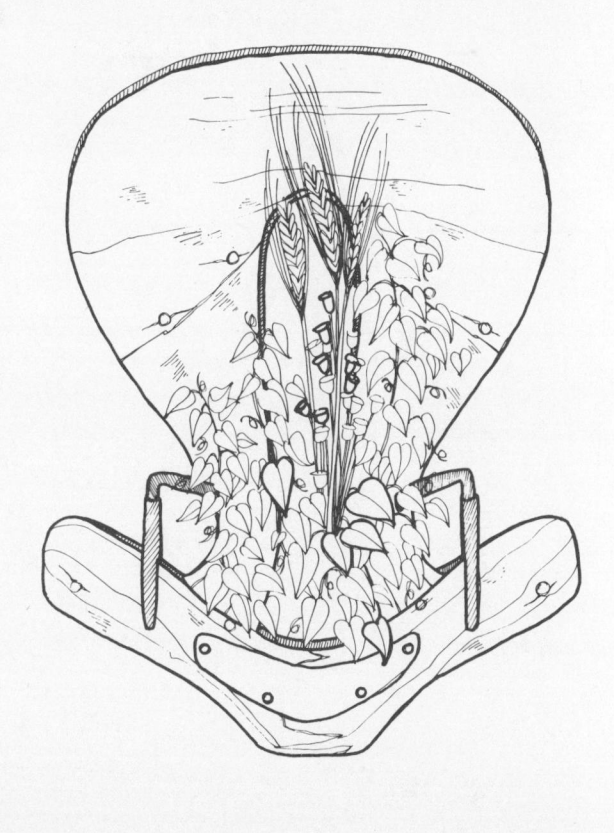

HOW TO

The old saddle that we "stripped" had a covering of burlap next to the leather, then a padding and finally another cover of burlap next to the wood. Pull all of this loose and also the many tacks that were used to hold the covering in place. At the wood joints on the saddle, metal was used to reinforce and strengthen same. Sand all saddle to perfection as desired and then paint flat black the metal part using masking tape and paper to cover the wood when spraying. Leave the wood natural.

Attach a wire to the backside of the saddle for hanging purposes. Fill the opening in the "seat" as shown with greenery, wheat and straw flowers. Hang on the wall and be ready for the "what's that" questions.

If you have stirrups and consider making a companion piece for the saddle, we suggest barnwood for the mounting board. We used a piece 6" x 16". Attach a sawedge hanger to the backside and then arrange items on board. A piece of old leather harness strap with a ring on the end was used to hold the stirrups to the barnwood and nail where needed. Then near one edge of the bottom stirrup drill a hole for the greenery stem and secure. Work the ivy up through the stirrups as preferred. We made a small nest of excelsior and placed this in one stirrup along with a bird.

157

1898 Shoe and Harness Repair Box

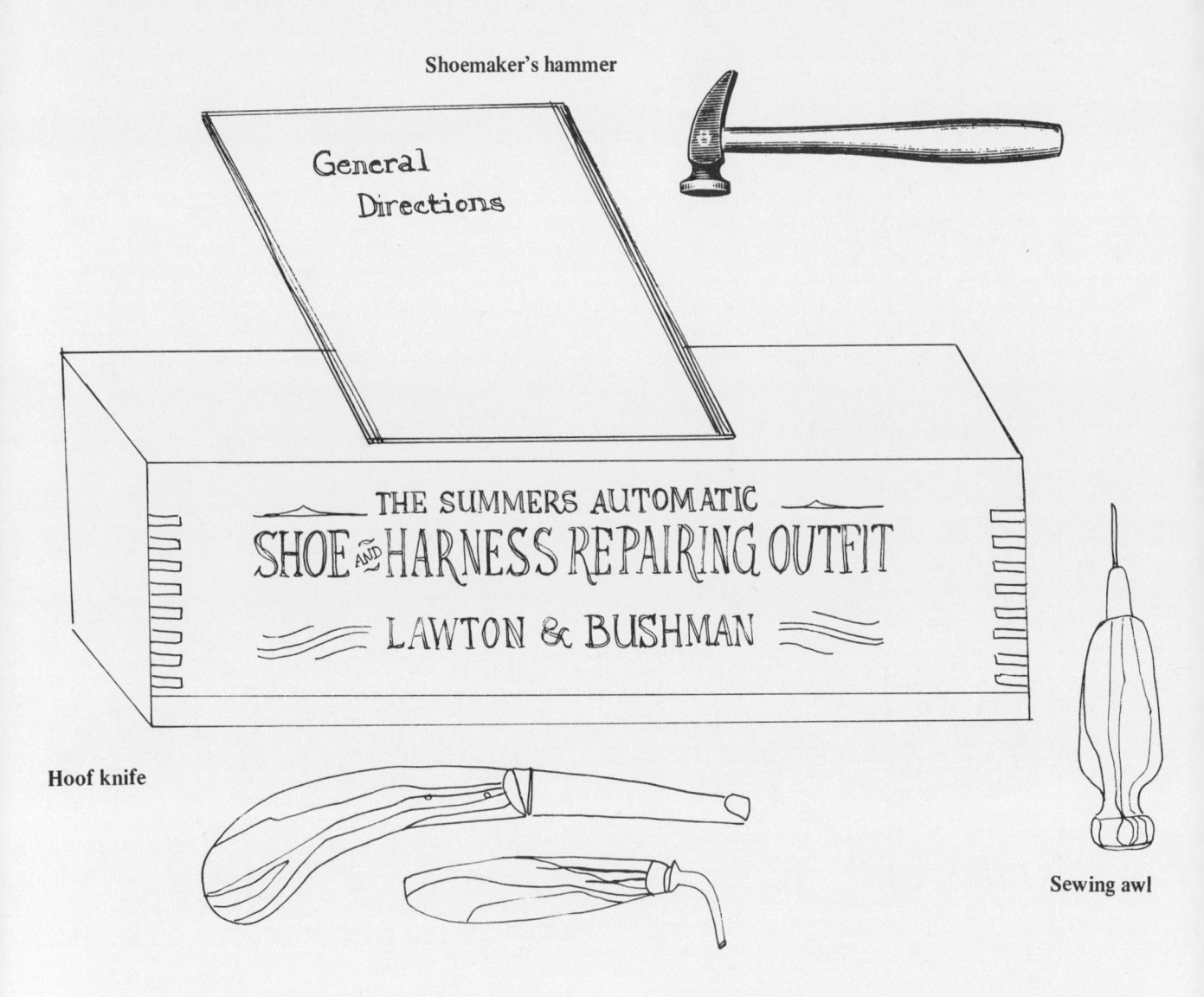

When horses were used primarily for all the heavy work on the farm, these animals were the farmer's "right hand" and even more. Keeping the leather harness in proper repair was essential and required certain tools. Some of these tools were likewise useful for keeping the family shoes in repair and served a dual purpose. Therefore, father of course being the all round handy man assumed the job of keeping the family shoes in repair too.

Enterprising manufacturers in the late 1800's promoted and sold a combination "Shoe and Harness Repairing Outfit." The tools were provided in a wooden box with identifying stenciling on the side. The one we found has this wording "The Summers Automatic Shoe and Harness Repairing Outfit — Patented, Jan. 4th, 1898 and Aug. 9th, 1898. Manufactured by Lawton and Bushman, Burlington, Wisconsin." The wooden box measures four inches deep and wide and 14 inches long.

Some of the tools included in the box were likely these. Three or more iron "lasts" of different size and an iron stand for the last, pegging awl, sewing awl, assorted awl needles, shoe maker hammer, steel knife, thread, wax, wooden shoe pegs, shoe nails, riveting machine and a box of rivets, harness clamp, heel plates and soles, other assorted items and of course a booklet of directions for using these various tools. Can you believe all this could be bought then for $1.50 to $2.00?

HOW TO

This arrangement should be pleasing to about any horse fancier and would make a grouping that could tie in with a picture of your favorite "mount." The old tool box lends an authentic antique touch. Any shoe or harness repair tools can be displayed above the box. The colorful mushrooms in different shades of brown, add color to the woodsy look.

The wooden repair box measured 4" wide on the inside. As the box was stamped on both sides, we cut it lengthwise down the middle so that one piece could be used for another purpose. The box is 14" long and we mounted it on a cutting board 12" x 18". At this point, attach sawedge hangers to the top backside of the board. Then the box is placed on the board 1" up from the bottom and of equal distance from each end. Fasten the box to the board temporarily with small finishing nails. Next from the backside of the cutting board, drill two 1/8" diameter holes into each end of the box. Secure by glueing in 1" lengths of dowel rod. The board and box are now ready to stain as desired. After this attach a white porcelain knob to the vertical right end of the board to give an authentic bread board look.

As the box, cutting board, and handles of the tools are wood, these have a tendency to blend together and need a contrast to make the piece attractive. For this purpose we used a 7" x 14" piece of burlap as the backing for the tools above the box. Green burlap was chosen but any color can be used to fit the other furnishings where the piece is to be displayed. After securing the contact burlap place the various tools in position and attach each with elastic banding. Drill a small hole close to the edge of each side of the tool, insert the banding, pull tight and tie on the backside of the board. As the last step for this piece, place styrofoam inside the box and fill with greenery or other decoration. We used mushrooms in this piece to give contrasting shades of brown and tan colors.

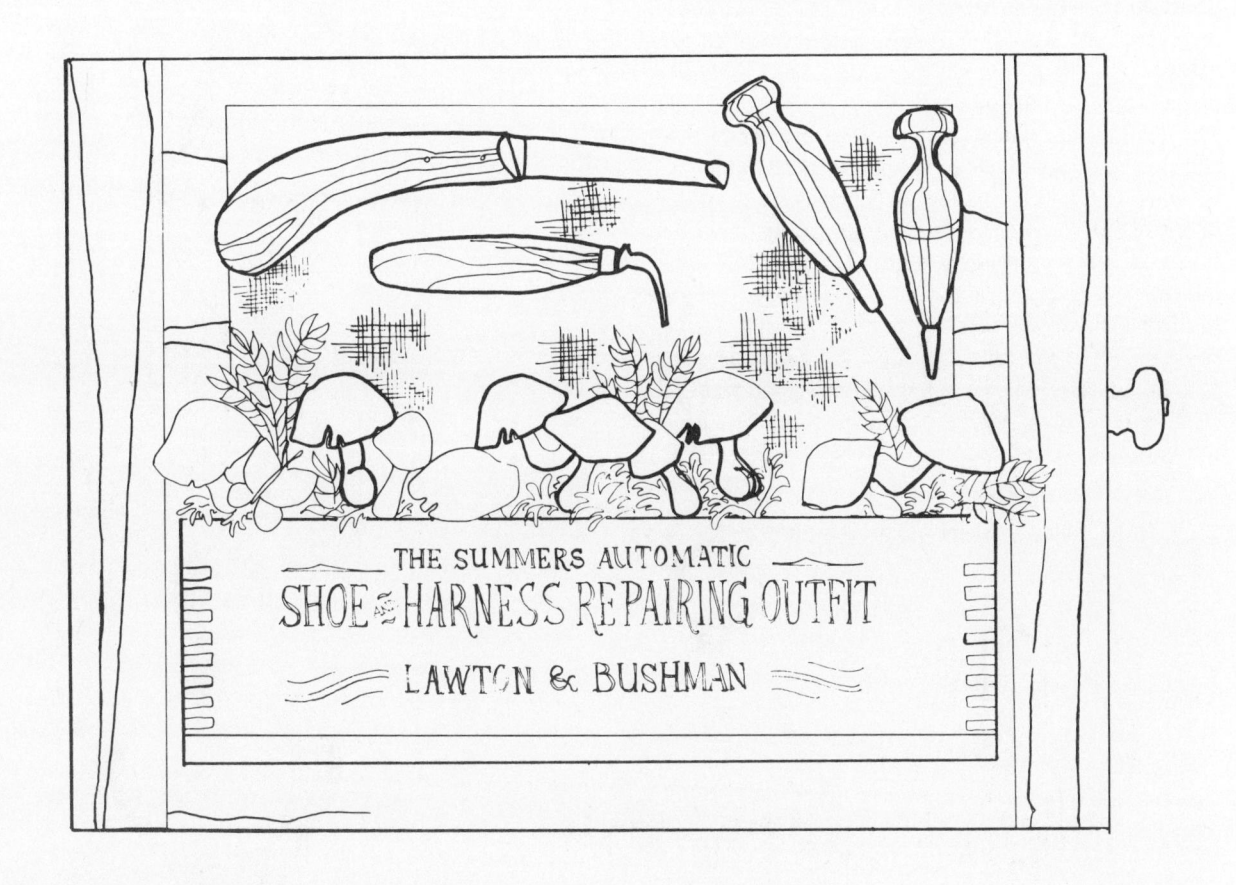

Hay Barn Pulleys of Yesteryear

Due to the heavy weight of old iron pulleys they make attractive and useful bookends.

In our book "It's Fun to Make Creations with Primitives" we included a detailed explanation as to how the wooden frame pulley was used on the farm for storing hay in the barn loft. The pulleys for most farm use were simply a grooved wooden wheel on a stationary axle held in a frame or block. When storing hay in the barn, which was the main use for the pulley, as many as three of these pulleys were put to use. The pulley attached to the hay fork was a "movable" pulley whereby the load of hay was suspended and therefore required a pulling force of only one-half the weight of the load. The amount of hay the fork would carry each time of course was such that a horse had to be used as the pulling force.

Some pulleys of this same era and which seem to be more plentiful were made with a frame entirely of iron and with a wooden wheel. Many of the cast iron frames or blocks have the makers name on the side. The two pulleys we use as a set for book ends are identified as "Meyers OK." The iron pin for holding the wheel of maple wood is round on one end and oval on the other. The holes in the "block" are patterned in the same way and this keeps the pin from turning when the pulley wheel revolved. Other pulleys of this type have a notch in one end of the pin that fits into the pulley frame and this too is for keeping the pin from turning while the pulley is being used. The purpose of this construction is to prevent the metal pin from turning against the iron frame which would cause friction and wear. This is an interesting feature of the pulleys that you will want to check when buying or looking at pulleys out of curiosity. Other pulleys of interest too have both the wheel and frame made of iron.

Parts of the pulley — wheel, frame and pin

Another differently designed pulley we found made with an iron frame and with wood wheel is known as the "Knot Passing Pulley." The eye or opening above the pulley wheel is two inches high which will allow a knot in the rope to pass through. Sometimes a rope would break and had to be tied or two rope lengths would be needed for a particular job.

Pulley in use position

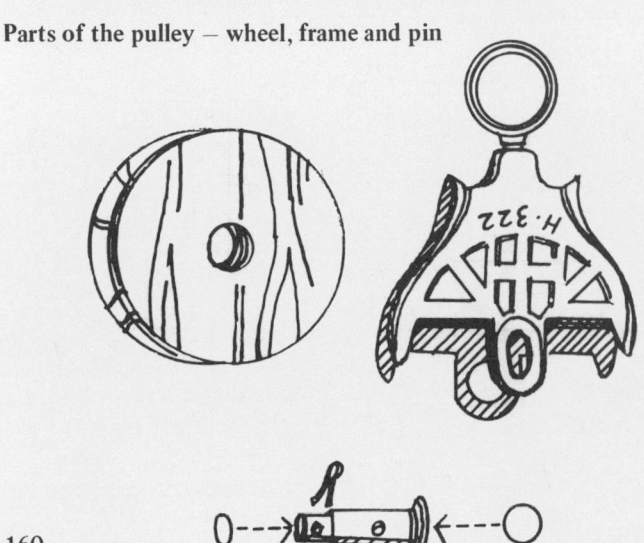

Knot passing pulley

Pulleys make rugged and handsome bookends

HOW TO

Usually you will find the iron blocks of the pulley to be somewhat rusted and the pulley wheel will need cleaning too. The iron frame of the pulley shown in the "use" position measures eight inches from the ring tip to the pin hole. The pulley wheel is 6" in diameter. Old pulleys have a rugged looking characteristic all their own and makes one visualize the stamina and heartiness of the farmer in years gone by.

To prepare the pulley for "cleanup" first take out the cotter key in the pin to remove the pulley wheel. Then wire brush the iron block and clean thoroughly. Spray the iron block with flat black which will give a nice contrast to the wood wheel. Also, spray the ends of the pulley pin and the cotter key. The pulley wheel should be sanded and then stained. We used antique maple for the stain. Allow the first coat to dry at least four hours. Then steel wool and apply a second coat, wipe off and dry for another four hours. Use steel wool once more and finish with a clear sealer. Reassemble the pulley and it's ready to use for bookends as shown or just as a handsome piece for display to use on a coffee table or shelf.

Shelving Construction

Shelving

When a shelf and brackets are a part of the display piece, these usually can be made from scrap pieces of cutting board or other suitable wood. When you have cut the shelf to size, position same on the board and mark lightly with a pencil. Make a straight line on the back of the board for a nail guide and drive two nails through the backside of board and into the shelf. Put glue on the two contact edges of the brackets and place in position. The brackets are normally 1/2" to 1" shorter than the width of the shelf. In some cases due to spacing, brackets are omitted.

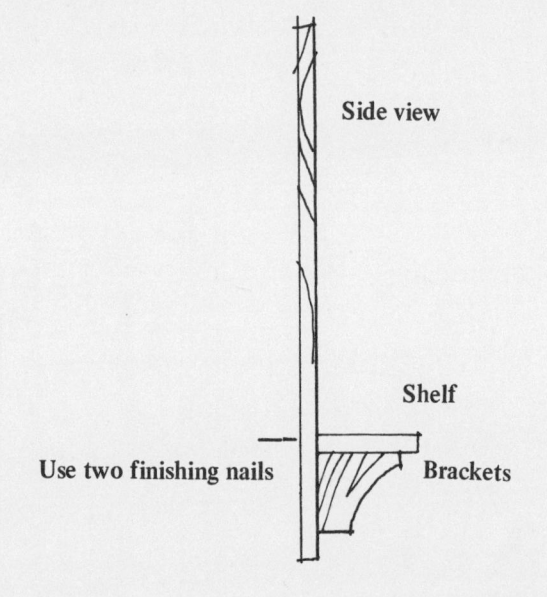

WOOD BOWL—5" to 6" diameter and cut in one-half

Leave the bowl natural, stain or paint. When using stain "test" inside the bowl for the shade desired as this area will be covered with decoration. Likewise test the stain on the backside of the board. After the bowl has been glued to the board and is dry, cut a piece of styrofoam to fit inside bowl and secure with stickum.

If the sawed edge of the bowl is not perfectly smooth, use dowel rods to attach to board. In the thick part of the bottom rim, drill two 3/16" holes as shown and 1/4" deep. Use dowel lengths of 3/4" and glue in holes. Then place bowl on board to mark for drilling receptive holes.

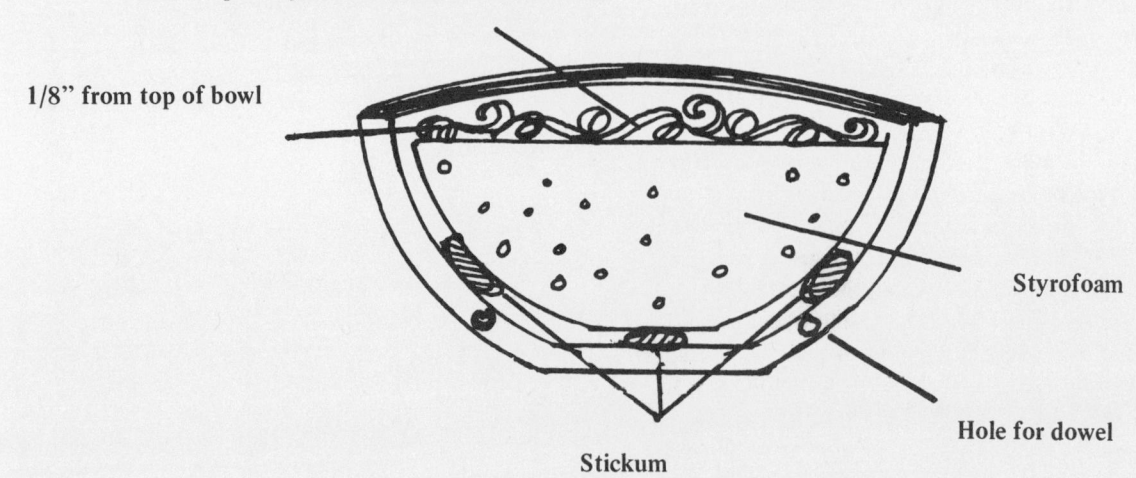

SHOW OFF SHELF—A unique shelf for general use

This shelf was made to hold any one of the canning jar lifters described on pages 176 and 177. However it is of a size that can be used to show off nicely many small keepsake items and is simple to make. The shelf shown measures 5" x 9" and was cut from a 1" thick board. Distress and sand the board as desired. Then two picture hooks are attached to the backside of the shelf board about 6" apart to hang the shelf on the wall. The picture hooks are attached by driving the "prongs" into the wood. It is suggested that a small nail be driven through the center hole in the hook after it is secured to be sure it holds well.

The wood brackets measuring 2-1/2" x 4" are cut from scrap wood, sanded and glued flush to the back edge of the shelf for support. The 4" side of the bracket is glued to the shelf leaving the 2-1/2" side to be the support against the wall when hung.

After the glue has dried, put a small finishing nail in each bracket, countersink and fill with plastic wood.

The last step is to drill 1/4" diameter holes in the top edge of each corner. Drill the holes about 1/2" in from the front and sides of shelf. Then attach 1" diameter wood knobs using pieces of 1/4" dowel. Stain the shelf and it is ready to use.

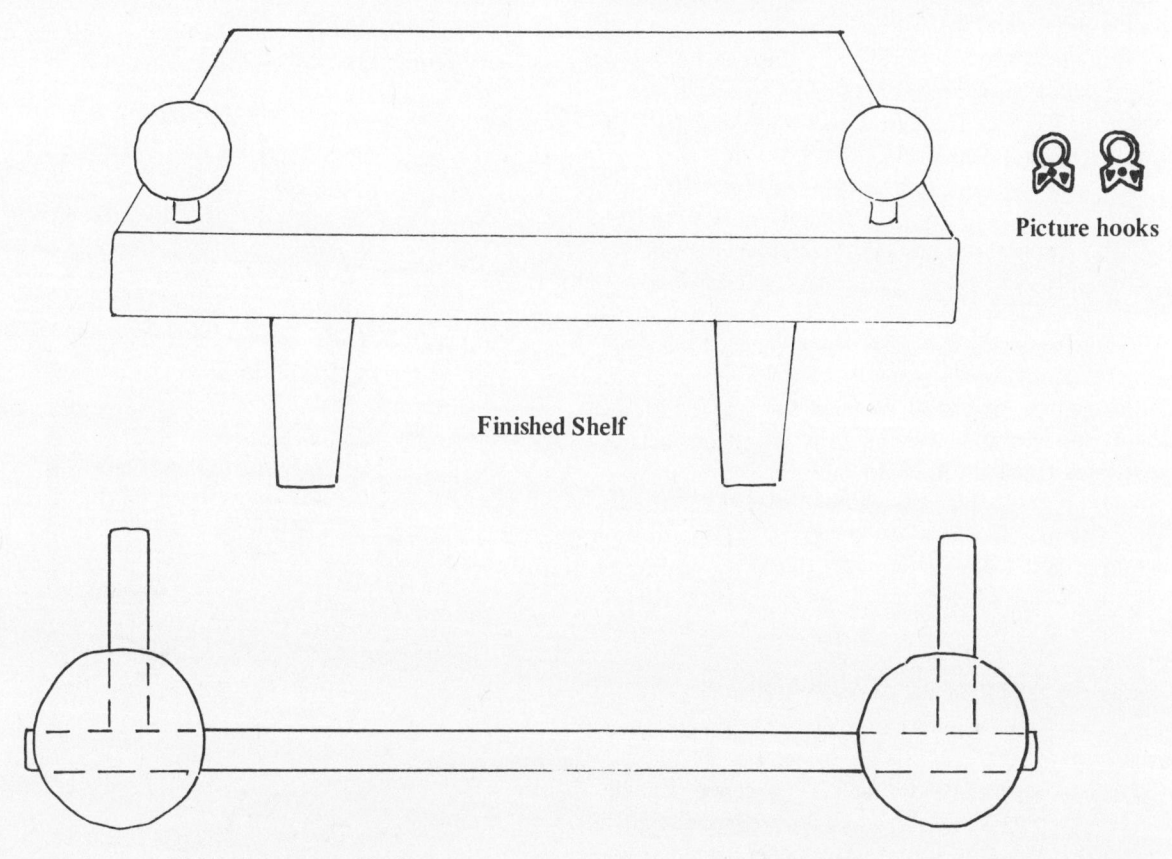

Picture hooks

Finished Shelf

1/4" holes in wood balls

TOWEL HOLDER

For a number of the wall plaques, we have created the use of a towel holder to enhance the attractiveness of the plaque and gives it a practical use too. The addition of the towel does mean an extra length to the entire piece of about 4" to 6". This is a factor to consider as usually one has an idea where the wall piece will be placed after it is made. It is for these reasons then that we give general information about the "towel holder" so that you may add it to about any one of these pieces illustrated and described in the booklet.

To make the towel bar, two wooden balls 3/4" to 1" in diameter are used along with 1/4" diameter dowel rod. The wood balls (beads) are available from most craft shops. Redrill the center hole to 1/4" diameter. Also in each ball drill a hole at a 90° angle to the center hole. See illustration. Cut 1/4" diameter dowel piece to length desired for towel bar and insert into center hole. Then use 2" lengths of dowel in the remaining holes to complete the towel holder. Position on plaque and drill 1/2" deep receptive holes and then glue in place.

Old Bible, Eyeglasses and Ink Bottle

"Keepsake" memory items of yesteryear.

In many families today there are still cherished small Bibles (probably tucked away in a drawer) that belonged to the grandparents or even farther back in the family history. Quite often the original owners name will be written inside the front cover along with the date purchased or when received as a gift. Old eyeglasses too were an item that seldom were discarded. These old "granny-type" glasses are of interest to all and bring back a certain nostalgia whenever seen.

The small Psalms of David book is leather bound and of the pocket size, measuring three by four inches and published in 1848. The Carter's ink bottle is dated 1897 and the eyeglasses are of the 1850-1900 vintage.

The drawings show several of the old interesting eye glasses that we have collected. What we refer to today as eyeglasses to improve the sight were more commonly known in the early days as spectacles. The "Riding Bow" spectacles were also known as "Hookbow." These were for the people that wore glasses most of the time as the "hook" like wire earpiece held the glasses in place more securely. Very small rounded wire was used for these spectacles and sometimes this was uncomfortable to the ear. One old pair we found had string wrapped around the ear loop part to ease the pressure on the ear. The "Temple" spectacles made with the straight temple ear piece were for those that used glasses for reading only or close work, and were designed for easy removal.

The "Pince-nez" which are eyeglasses clipped to the nose by the means of a spring type nose piece, were simply called "eyeglasses" in the bygone days to distinguish these from the spectacles. The frames were often made with hard rubber as well as steel. For the more expensive eyepieces, tin or nickel cases were provided for safe keeping. Cases also could be purchased separately and some of these were made of paper mache. A case with a hinged cover was used primarily for the "hook box" spectacles and many times the case for the straight temple type would have an open end. Silk cords and gold chains with a safety type in at one end were available for the eyeglasses (pince-nez) to let the eyepiece hang when not in use. Some of the chains were retractable into a small round flat like pin that attached to the lapel to hold the eyeglasses firmly when not being used. This is the type shown by the artist drawing and on the backside is the wording "Ketcham and McDougall, New York, pat. Feb. 24, 1903.

Quite often the glass cases were made from tin covered with leather on the outside and inside with velvet. One old case of this style we found which held the "pince-nez" style glasses, had a picture of two dear friends or sisters pasted inside the case. It is unfortunate that such an interesting "keepsake" was not passed on in this family.

Benjamin Franklin wore this type of old style spectacles described in this article. It is said that he invented the first bi-focal glasses when he needed an eye aid for seeing in the distance and a stronger power for reading. Franklin simply took both the reading and "distance" pair of glasses, cut the lens in half and glued one of each together to make the first bi-focals.

HOW TO

This makes a very handsome shelf to display precious items. The cast iron (but not old) candle holder gives an added touch that fits in well to the total creation and makes this piece an eye catcher. If a small Bible is not available you can use an old tin-type photo (as indicated on the next page) or just place keepsakes on this 3" x 7" shelf.

The backboard measures 9" high and 10" across and the top corners are slightly rounded. Sand the board well and then attach 2 sawedge hangers to the backside and the wood knob at the top. The shelf is 3" x 7" and again slightly rounded on the front edge. It is nailed to the backboard through the backside and up 2" from the bottom and 1/2" from the left side. The shelf bracket is 1-3/4" x 1-3/4" and simply glued in place. (Cut this from a piece of scrap wood.) The candle cup is screwed on from the backside and placed 3-1/2" from the bottom of board and 1" in from the side.

The shelf for supporting the Testament is made from a 1/2" wide strip of 1/8" thickness masonite and of a length the same as the open testament. The shelf is glued in position so that the top edge of the Bible is about 1/4" down from the top of the board. The wood clips to hold the Bible are made following the illustrations on page 166 Position Testament on the masonite "shelf" and drill receptive holes for the dowel rod part of the wood clip to fit into. The hole should be at the edge of the book and 1/3 distance down from the top and so the clips will extend over the edge of the pages. The wood clips do not have to be flush with the backboard and simply push dowel in the hole to a comfortable position to hold the pages securely. The clips can be turned to a vertical position to easily remove the Bible.

If desired, use this alternate mounting which eliminates the masonite shelf: (drawing below)

Drill small holes through board at top and bottom center edges of book for elastic banding to hold book against board. Then drill hole to position wood clips to secure Bible at the bottom edge.

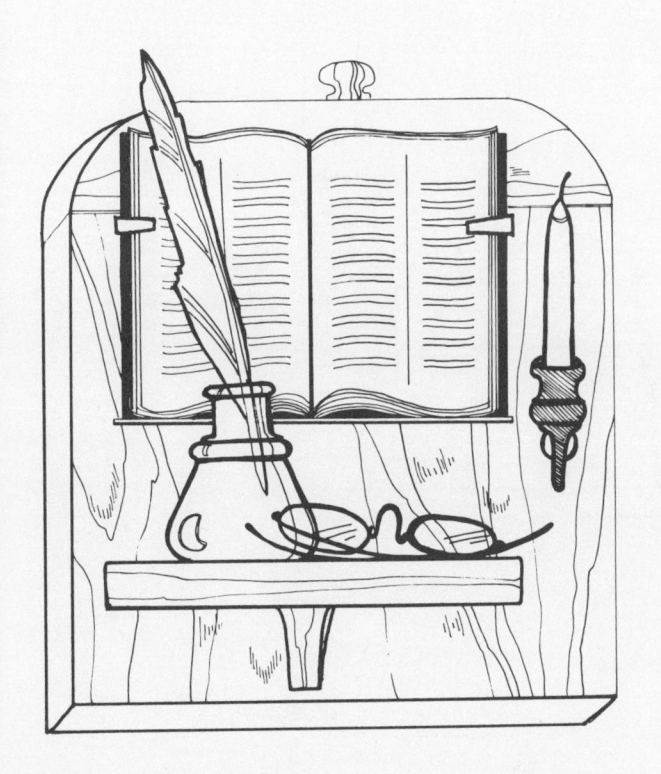

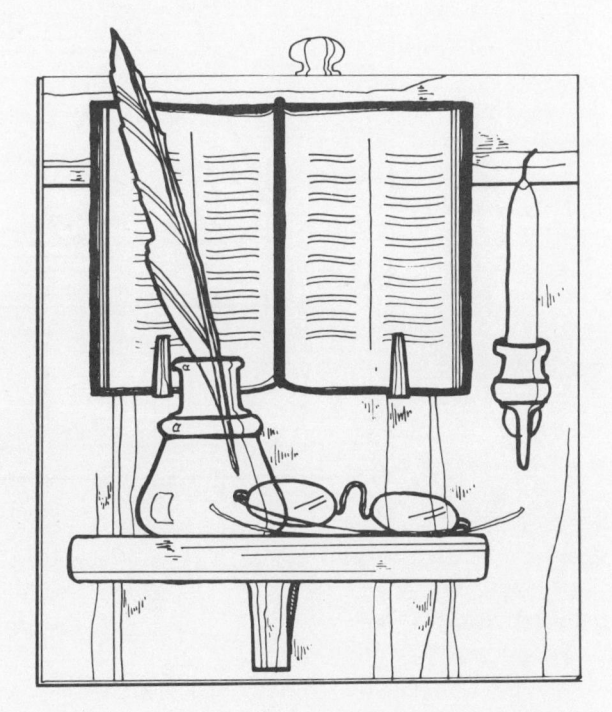

DIRECTIONS FOR USING TIN-TYPE PHOTOGRAPH OF YESTERYEAR IN PLACE OF BOOK.

Quite often these old Tin-type photos are found for a few dollars when the cover part of the frame is missing. If you like, remove the old Tin-type print and substitute a current picture with the old crinkly foil as a frame. The Tin-type is positioned on the board and centered over the shelf or to fit in with whatever you will display on the shelf. As when using a Bible, make the supporting shelf from 1/4" wide masonite and with a length 1/4" longer than the picture frame. To hold the picture at the top, make a wood clip as for the previous display piece. Drill a 1/8" diameter hole just above the picture frame and insert. You may want to shorten the wood clip so that it just covers the edge of the picture frame.

HOW TO—Wooden clips

On a piece of scrap wood 1" x 3" and about 4" long and at a right angle corner draw the diagram shown (illustration A). Then using a hacksaw cut down through the middle of the board (see illustration B) to a depth of 3/4". Next turn the board on its side and drill 1/8" diameter holes 1/4" deep. Then make the cuts on the diagram 1 through 4 and this will give you 2 wood clips of the same size. Glue 3/4" length dowel in each opening and after dry sand the clips to perfection.

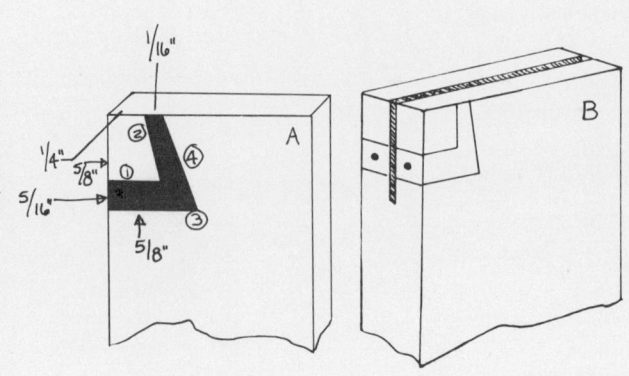

166

Simulated Handcuffs

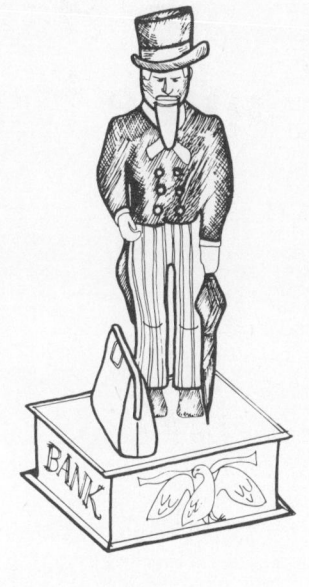

Here's how to show off horse bridle bits that may have sentimental value and also to create a conversation piece. The bits used are the twisted wire style and incidentally the most common and cheapest bits found at antique sources. By placing these in a proper position one at first glance get the impression that these are hand cuffs, particularly with the silent suggestion by the presence of the Irish cop. This latter item being a toy bank of the cast iron type made in sand molds and first produced in the early 1800's. These toy banks were cast in two pieces and attached together with a metal screw. The banks were made in the likeness of favorite people, animals or objects. Such "people" banks are 4 to 6 inches high and the animal banks 4 inches high and up to 16 inches in length.

These banks are said to be the forerunner of the mechanical banks which were introduced toward the end of the 18th century. The mechanical banks are unique having moving parts that causes the penny to be dropped or thrown into a slot. One bank that we had is called "Uncle Sam." You put a coin in his hand, press a button behind his umbrella and he not only tosses the coin into an opened carpet bag but also moves his whiskers in acknowledgement of your contribution.

Children are fascinated by these banks and are eager to put a penny in just to have the bank perform. It's easy to see why these banks were so popular when first invented and available for about $2.00. With these banks a child gets some entertainment when at the same time a penny is being saved. With the "still" bank only a dull clang is heard as a reward for being thrifty.

HOW TO

We made this arrangement as a "table piece" but if preferred the mounting could be used on a shelf. The board for the "platform" is 4" x 8". Stain and finish as desired, then cover the bottom of the board with contact burlap so that it will be smooth against any table top. Position the cop and "handcuffs" on the board as indicated in drawing and attach the bits with small black wire so these will stand up in the way desired. The policeman bank has hollow legs and a dowel piece is put up one of these, and then drill hole into board and insert to hold firmly.

Old castiron bank

Horse bridle bits

Old Vanity Hand Mirror and Candle Holder

Mother will appreciate the chance to take a quick look at her appearance when busily cooking for dinner guests.

HISTORY

Vanity hand mirrors are a yesteryear item that were made in many different styles. The vogue in the late 1800's was to have an ebony finished hand mirror to dress up the "Mrs." as well as to make the dressing table complete. The imported ebony wood with a shiny black finish made such mirrors about three times as costly as those made with American wood such as ash, cherry, maple or mahogany. This led to the imitation "ebonized" finish being used extensively and most of these old mirrors that have survived are of this type.

Many of the "ebonized" mirrors have an ornate sterling silver mounting on the backside of the mirror holder. The last one we used for a plaque had a very ornate butterfly in silver. These are attached with a small brad and can be removed and placed on the front side handle of the mirror if desired.

One of the interesting designs is the "Ring Mirror" illustrated. The large ring in the end of the handle allowed mother to primp and fix her face and then Father could hang the mirror on the wall by the ring and conveniently shave.

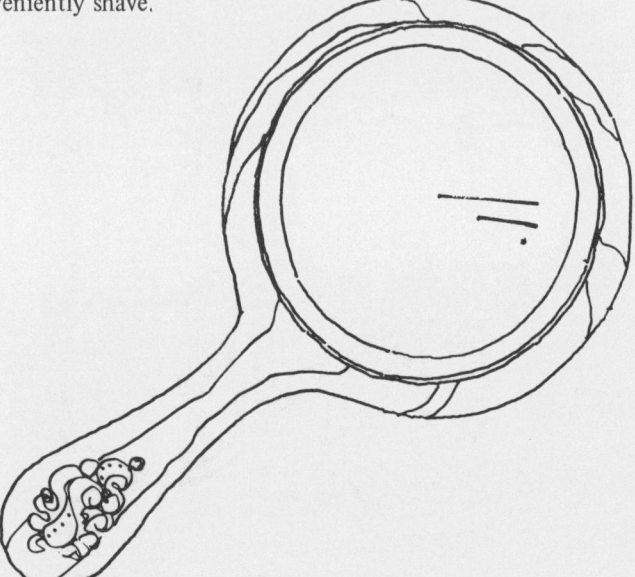

Ebonized "ring" mirror

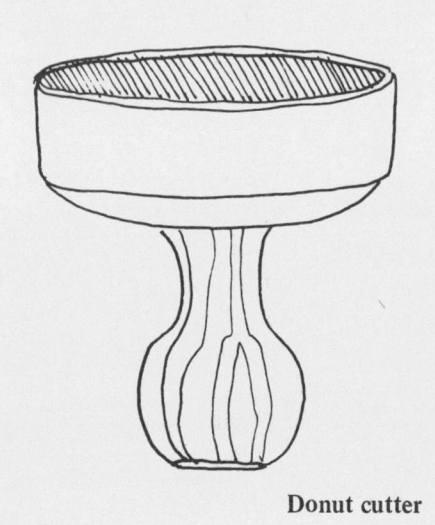

Donut cutter

HOW TO

We thought it appropriate to make this mirror plaque for the kitchen area as ladies do like to take a quick look wherever they are to be sure their hair, etc. looks just right. Anyone of the mirrors mentioned could be used for this plaque as long as it is small in size. The one we used measured 8-1/2" total length. The small bread board used measured 9" x 12".

First finish the board as desired and then attach 2 saw-tooth hangers to top backside. Then drill hole top center and secure small porcelain knob. To attach the mirror, first remove any ornate mounting from the backside and attach to handle front. Sometimes, and as was the case with the vanity mirror used for this plaque, the silver mounting will be too large to fit the handle. We put this one away for another use and made a small artificial flower arrangement to attach to the handle.

The reed like ring that holds the glass in place is removed and this releases the mirror. Put this aside and position the wood frame of the mirror in place. Secure with small nails through the middle of the circle where the glass normally fits. Next the doughnut cutter is placed as shown on the finished plaque. It is secured to the board with two small brads through the tin lip of the cutter edge. After all nailing is completed, replace the glass in the mirror frame and insert the "ring" to hold it in place.

We made a small arrangement of yellow rose buds for the mirror handle and these can be tied on with a ribbon if desired.

The piece is finished and now you can admire youself and the plaque.

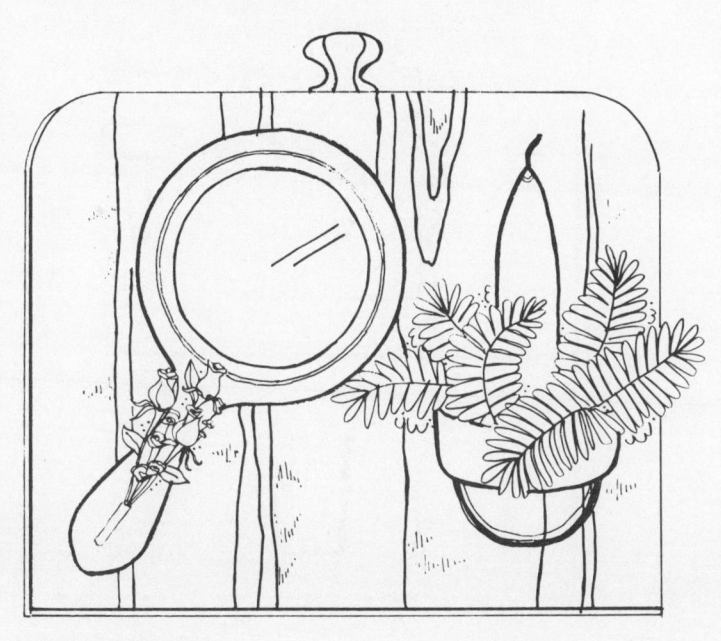

Vanity hand mirror as entry hall piece

For this piece the board is cut with a half circle top and is 8" wide and 16" long.

The shelf is 3" x 7" and the shelf brackets 1-3/4" x 2". See page 162 for shelf detail. Stain wood as desired and attach hanger to top backside. Attach mirror in same way as preceding piece. Use any suitable item for the shelf. We used an old "square" match safe and filled with a flower arrangement. To complete the piece add the cast-iron candle holder.

Mirror with ornate mounting moved to front of handle

OTHER POSSIBILITIES

If an old Vanity Mirror is not available, other items with mirror inserts can be used in place of same.

1. In some old job printing press advertising cuts, we found a rectangular frame with a copper scroll around the one inch thick wood frame. For the opening of 2" x 4" a small mirror was cut and "set in" 1/2" inside the frame. Dowel rods were inserted in the backside of the frame and then secured to the board.

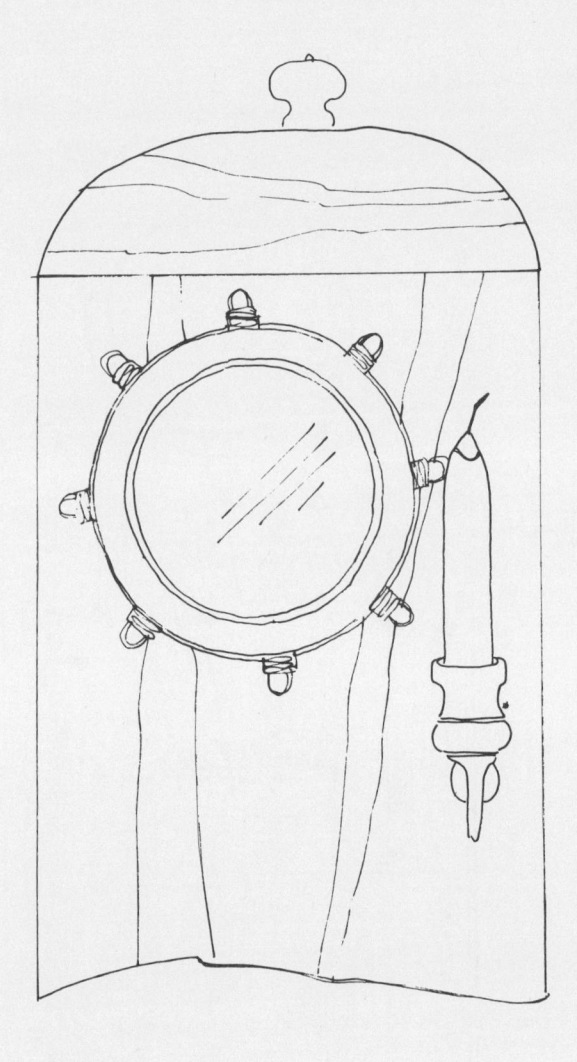

Job press frame with mirror insert used in place of vanity mirror.

2. At one time, ashtrays in the shape of a ship's wheel were made from composition material. We used a flat black spray on this piece and then had a mirror cut to fit. Drill small holes in part of ashtray that mirror will cover and attach to board with small nails. Then glue the mirror in place.

More Ideas Using Old Kitchen Utensils

All of these plaques call for a board of about 10" x 13" in size. Directions below assume you have first prepared board as per page 5.

Tin Cookie Cutter

Directions:
1. Place cutter 2-1/2" from top and 1" from edge of board. Drill 1/16" hole through board at the point and bottom of the heart.
2. Secure with elastic banding and drawing tightly attach to backside of board.
3. Fill opening with a small nest and add bird.
4. Place and glue bowl 1" from side and bottom of board and fill with eggs, bits of greenery and baby's breath.

Doughnut Cutter

Directions:
1. Position the cutter 2" from bottom and 1" from side of board. Attach with two small nails through inside of cutter and into board.
2. Inside the half circle made by the doughnut cutter handle, drill hole through board to insert end of greenery and secure on backside. Work greenery up through cutter and behind candle and fasten to board at top with staple concealed by greenery.
3. The bowl is glued on 2" from side and bottom of board.
4. Fill bowl with eggs and star flowers.

1890 Knife and Fork

Directions:
1. Bowl is glued to board 1/2" from bottom and centered.
2. Place knife and fork as desired (about 1" from edge of bowl).
3. Drill holes of 1/16" diameter (2) and 1/4" apart in two different places along the handles to insert elastic banding to make loops to hold knife and fork in place. Tie elastic on backside.
4. Add eggs and other flowers to bowl as desired.

Grandfather's Shaving Items

One of the first "safety razors" was the Durham-Duplex (see illustration). The handle and shape was patterned after the old style straight edge razor to make it easier for new users to like. In fact their advertising called the shape of the conventional safety razor today to be like a "garden hoe" and that only the Durham Duplex could give you the right diagonal stroke. This razor used removable blades which could be replaced when the edge became dull or for a time the blade could be sharpened with a stroop as with the straight edge razor. This particular make razor was patented in 1907 and was still being sold into the early 1930's.

In addition to the razor "Father" would also have a whetstone or leather stroop, shaving soap in a mug, shaving brush and possibly some kind of hair dressing. These were usually kept in some king of "toilet case" (medicine cabinet) on the wall and likely in the kitchen near the sink and water pump. The more popular and likely found items today handed down in the family are the razor, shaving mug, and brush and mirror.

The small holder shown with cut out sides, three rounded feet, and a handle was to hold the shaving mug. This item is brass plated.

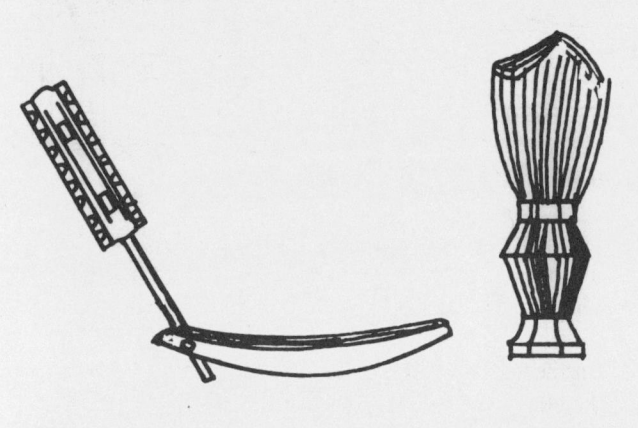

1903 safety razor

Shaving brush

Tin comb and brush holder

Shaving mug holder

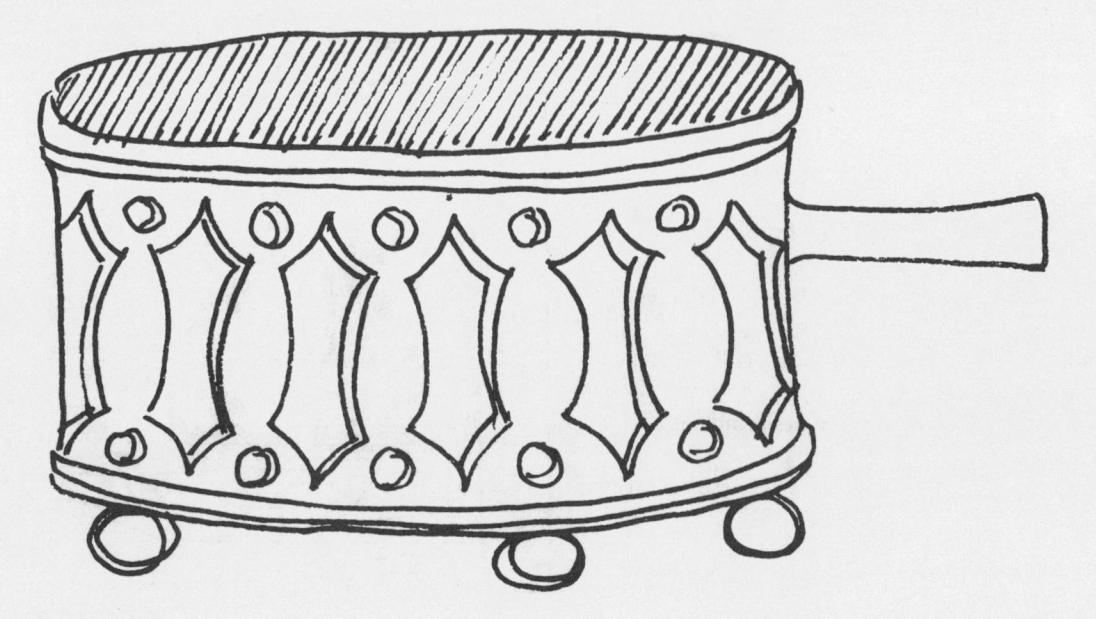

HOW TO

The first plaque shown displays an old comb and brush case along with Grandfather's razor and shaving brush. The comb cases are usually of tin and about eight inches wide. The board used is 10" wide and 16" long. We stained the board light maple after sanding and distressing same. Next attach sawedge hangers to top backside and drill hole for knob.

The shelf is 3" x 8" and is nailed on from the backside of the larger board. See page 162 for details but omit the supporting brackets. For additional support, use three nails and also glue the edge of shelf board before nailing. For the towel bar we suggest that you use the one described on page 163 instead of the one shown on this plaque.

Next the comb case is added using small nails and in a place that will be covered by the decoration. Place the shaving brush and razor on the shelf and your elegant piece is finished to hang in the bathroom.

HOW TO—Using shaving mirror

For the other plaque shown we used as the focal point an old shaving mirror with the stand made from tin. The board is 8" x 15" in size and slightly rounded at the top. Distress and stain the board, shelf and brackets as desired before assembling. The shelf is 3" x 7" and the brackets 2" x 2-1/2". Detail on page 162. Next attach a sawedge hanger to backside of board and a knob at top center of same. Use small finishing nails to attach the mirror around the edge. A small piece of masonite 1/2" x 4" was used to make a shelf for the razor and this is simply glued in place. The shaving brush is positioned and the shaving mug holder was filled with styrofoam to make the flower decoration.

A most delightful as well as unusual conversation piece for the bathroom.

173

Bathroom Fixtures of Early 1900's

Old tumbler and soap holder

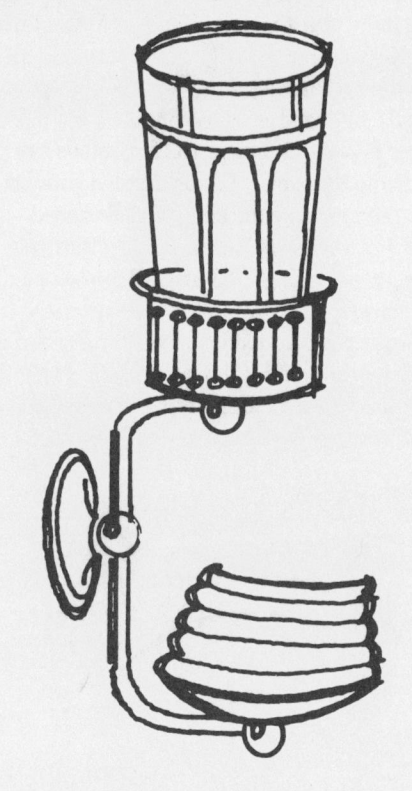

Old tin bath tub

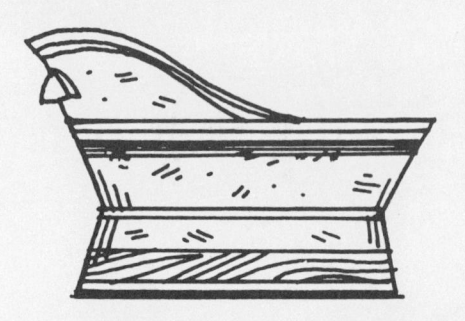

Cast iron bath tub

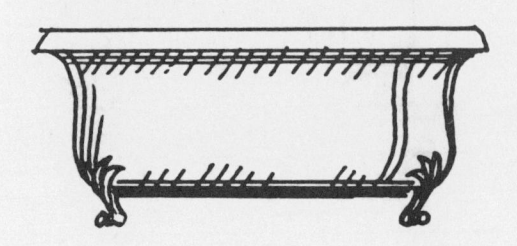

Bathroom wall fixtures of fifty to seventy-five years ago, may not be very romantic but are of interest as well as the "tubs" of that era. The old fixture illustrated above is a combination tumbler and soap holder. It is made of brass and with a nickel coating. The "Walls" of the tumbler holder are thin with an attractive cut out design and with a rolled lip around the top.

The soap holder part is of a sea shell pattern and the whole piece has rather graceful lines. Long ago soap holders were also called soap cups. Some of you no doubt will remember the tumbler holder which also provided a hanging place for each one in the families toothbrush. Other special bathroom fixtures of this time which attached to the wall were a match box holder, hooks for robe and razor strap, cigar holder, and various shapes and sizes of soap dishes. Many of these were made of solid brass.

Bathtubs of this era had their own particular charm too. In fact, some of the tin portable tubs are being reproduced today and used as a decorative piece to hold pillows and other items. Tubs then were either of the light weight type made from tin, and usually with a wood platform under the tin bottom, or of the "permanently placed" type made from steel or iron. These tubs of the steel variety had interestingly designed cast iron legs.

Some of the light weight tin tubs (20 to 30 pounds) had a drain opening near the bottom for the waste water. Most all of the steel tubs had the disposal drain and could be purchased with the connections and faucets for hot and cold water. It's quite likely however that the hot water, at least in the early days was heated on the range and "poured" into the tub. The tubs made of steel were usually heavily enameled on the inside for looks and smoothness. These tubs weighed 200 to 300 lbs.

The tin portable tubs were available in many different shapes and sizes from those for an infant to one an adult could stretch out in fairly comfortable. Other of the tin tubs were of a size whereby the person had to sit down in the tub with legs out or were used for the purpose of a sponge or "plunge" bath.

HOW TO

The size of the bread board to use will depend somewhat on the items to be mounted. For the tumbler holder and lamp, we used a board size of 10" x 12" and this worked out just right. The top corners of the board were slightly rounded as indicated, then sand the board to perfection desired. Two sawedge hangers are nailed to the top backside of the board and also a strip of wood 1/8" thick, 1/2" wide and 8" long to the bottom backside. The foregoing is essential for the wall plaque to be vertical and secure to the wall. After staining the board, drill a hole in the top center and insert a white porcelain knob. Next make the shelf for the lamp which is approximately 2-1/2" x 2-1/2". This is stained and then nailed to the board from the backside and 5" up from the bottom. Then make a 1-1/2" x 2" wood bracket, stain and attach under shelf with glue.

The tumbler holder was sprayed with quick drying gold paint and then antiqued with burnt umber. It was then attached using brass screws through the existing holes in same. Next we used two 1" wooden balls and a dowel rod for the towel rack attached to the bottom of the plaque. First drill an 1/8" wide hole into the center of each knob and another hole at a 90° angle. See page 15. Using 1/8" diameter dowel rod cut 2 pieces 2" in length. Insert one in each knob and glue. Then of the same size dowel cut a 7" length and insert in knobs to form towel bar. Position on board and mark to drill receptive holes and attach.

A small piece of styrofoam was cut to size covered with moss and secured in the tumbler opening. It was then filled with greenery and cloth flowers of varied colors. We suggest a small bar of soap for the "dish."

For the shelf at the side, we used a favorite aunt's small antique kerosene lamp. The lamp gives a nice touch and can be lighted for a soft glow in the bathroom. You may have other dainty and old items such as an old flowered glass keepsake tumbler to use on the shelf that would be more suitable for your wall decor.

Decorative wall piece

Old Canning Jar Lifters

An important item of yesteryear in the canning process to lift the jars of fruit or vegetables from scalding hot water to cool.

HISTORY

Single jar lifters were made in a number of ways with all having the same purpose of handling the hot jars without burning the hands. The "Handy-maid" lifter illustrated was easy to use being a double wire affair riveted together and with handles of wood. It is manipulated somewhat on the principle of using hand pliers. The bottom part of the lifter grips the outside lid thread and holds tightly when the top wooden handles were pressed together. These lifters can still be purchased today.

The jar lifter with a single wood handle and with a wire pull ring is also seen at Antique shows and the like. These are not as easy to manipulate as the "Handy-Maid" but are quite adequate for doing the intended job. The wire running through the middle of this piece to form the ring pull straddles the wood handle. By pushing the ring down against the handle, this causes the two one-quarter circle metal grips to tighten against the jar lid. It is detached by pulling the ring up.

A more simple affair is the jar basket. The jar simply remains in the wire basket during the canning process and is lifted by the handle. There are a number of types of the individual jar baskets and some will even fold flat for easy storage. Other baskets are made to hold 4 to 8 jars and have one common handle. This latter type would be used in a large boiler.

Handy-maid sure-grip lifter

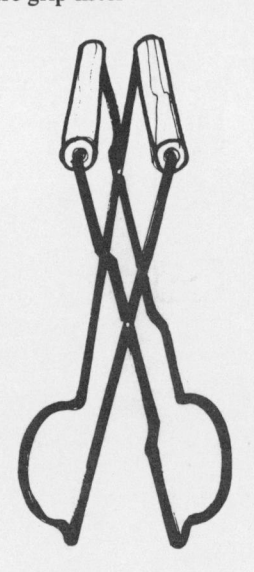

Basket type jar holder

1/2 pt. mason jar

HOW TO—Basket type jar holder

First simply spray the basket with flat black paint. To decorate the basket holder use a 1/4 or 1/2 pint jar. Cut a piece of styrofoam round and similar in size to the jar but smaller so that the styrofoam can be placed in the jar and moss stuffed down the sides. Use a piece of stickum to secure the styrofoam to the bottom of the jar. On top of the styrofoam use glue and cover with moss. Next use greenery, star flowers and the like to make an attractive decoration. Leave the handle in an upright position and hang or place on kitchen counter or shelf.

HOW TO—The wire pull ring lifter

First we used a half-pint jar and placed artificial crab apples inside and attached the lid. The wire part of the lifter was sprayed flat black and then the wood handle was sanded and stained. This was done to give contrast and improve the appearance of this piece against the greenery and bird nest.

Next place the "grips" on the jar lid and push ring down to clamp tightly, then from excelsior form a small nest and place on top of lid and around the wire part of the lifter and add a small bird. Wind greenery around the wire and up through the handle. You may already have a shelf or corner of your new decorative piece. We made a simple and attractive shelf from scrap material. See page 163 for details. Along side the lifter and jar we used an old time salt shaker from a set used on kitchen cabinets.

Jar lifter with wood handle and wire pull ring

HOW TO—The handy-maid lifter

First, fill the jar with miniature fruit or vegetables. To attach the "lifter" to the jar, unscrew the jar slightly and clamp the lifter against the glass threads and tighten the lid. Also wire together the two sides of the lifter. Ivy is intertwined from the nest and up through the wood handle as indicated.

Make the bird nest from excelsior and glue to the top of the jar lid. Include a couple of eggs and place bird on top of the lifter handles as shown to see if the eggs are at the boiling point.

Bee Smoker

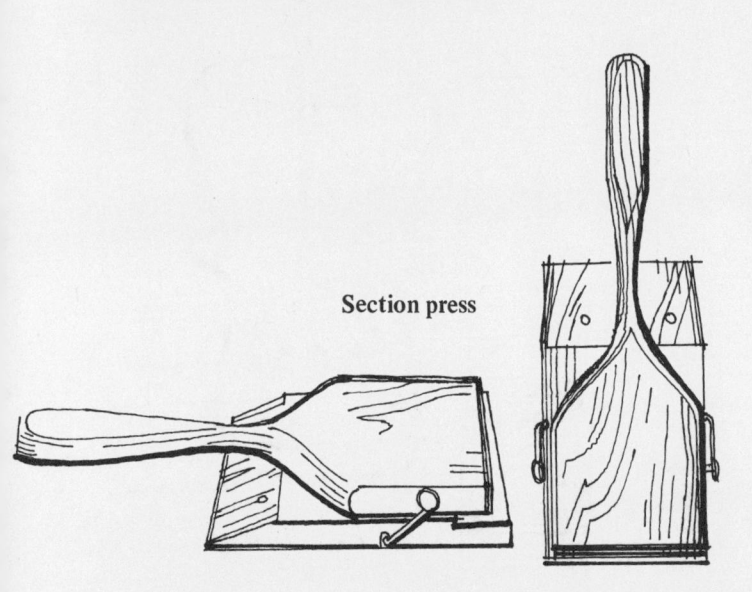

Bee smoker 1903

Section press

The industry of beekeeping dates back to 1850

The Bee Smoker shown has a patent date of 1903 and was manufactured by the A.I. Root Co. Similar smokers are still sold today and with very little change in construction detail. The diagram shown illustrates how the smoker works. A smoldering rag fire is started in the canister part of the smoker. An old gunny sack was often used as the fuel as it would smolder well. Then when smoke is needed the bellows is operated forcing air into the cylinder at the bottom of the canister, through the tin plate with air holes (which holds the rag above the bottom of the canister) and the air mixing with the smoke comes out the funnel-like spout, on the top.

The theory behind the use of smoke is that the smell of it makes the bees feel that they are going to have to vacate the hive. Because of this they are urged to fill their stomach with honey before leaving. The bees in this state become dormant and therefore not in a position to sting while the honey is being procured by the beekeeper. The beekeeper has to be careful not to over saturate the bees with the smoke as this can cause them to regurgitate the honey they have eaten and then the bee would become angry and likely use the stinger.

When approaching the beehives experienced beekeepers take their time and with slow movements so as not to disturb the bees normal habits around the hive. Usually when working with the bees, a type of wire screen or heavy cloth veil is worn over a hat and tied around the neck to protect the face. Also it is wise to tie the clothing at the pant leg and wrists to prevent a surprise sting inside the clothing. Heavy leather gloves are worn by some to protect the hands while others find the gloves too awkward and prefer to risk any sting on the hands.

The industry of beekeeping is also called "apiculture" and it started commercially after 1850. Mr. A. I. Root was one of the prominent early founders of this industry and the first edition of his beekeeping encyclopedia "ABC of Bee Culture" was available in 1877. At the time Mr. Root started this business, (1869) he was operating a jewelry manufacturing company in Medina, Ohio. After reading a book on beekeeping equipment by Mr. Langstroth, a Congregational minister who had invented the modern movable frame beehive, Mr. Root recognized the advantages of this new hive and started his beekeeping with it. The actual manufacture and sale of bee supplies was started in the jewelry facilities. Beehives, extractors, smokers and honey were among the early products. The company like most other successful businesses, had its beginning in a small way and then grew and grew. Large facilities were established in Medina, San Antonio, Texas and Council Bluffs, Iowa. Today this company is still very successful in the "bee business" and also a very major supplier of beeswax candles.

In working with keepsake and primitive items, we try to retain the original appearance and not change the item in any way. Sometimes broken or damaged pieces can be used to an advantage as with this Bee Smoker. Due to age the leather "bellows" had ripped apart and exposed the inside. Because of this we were able to purchase the smoker for one-half the original price. The canister part was used to hold a flower arrangement and we included a "non stinging bee" (artificial), and the wooden part of the bellows for the shelf arrangement.

On the backside of the wood part of the bellows, the stenciling was still readable with this information "A. I. Root Co., Medina, Ohio, BeeKeeper Supplies." Also pictured was their trademark and honeybees going to different kinds of blossoms to find honey. Many people today do not recognize a bee smoker or its function. A draftsman's type diagram showing how the smoker works is included as part of this interesting wall decor.

Another piece we picked up at a flea market, and didn't know what it was at the time turned out to be a "section press." It is used to put together the dovetail cornered boxes that were sometimes put in the bee hives for the bees to fill the honey in, rather than the thin long "hangers." We used it on the shelf made from one piece of the bellows.

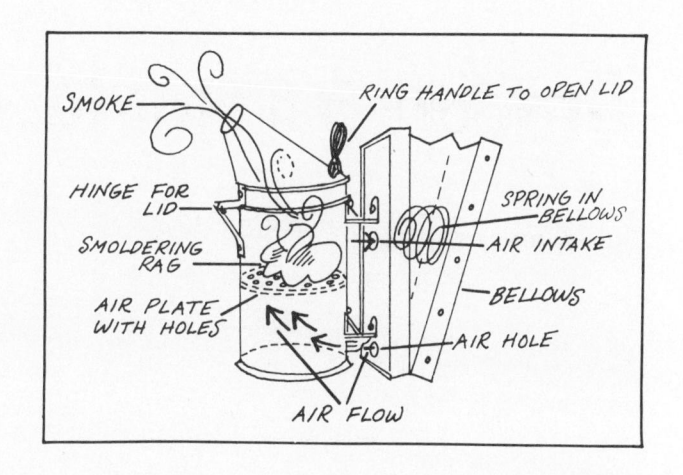

How it works

HOW TO

This arrangement was made on a board 15" x 16" in size. Stain the wood as desired and attach two sawedge hangers to backside. The one part of the bellows with the stenciled wording and design was attached to the top left hand side as indicated. The other bellows piece was used as a shelf for the "section press." Brackets 2" x 3" in size were used and detail for attaching is on page 162.

The cannister part of the Bee Smoker was sprayed flat black. Also the pin in lid hinge was removed to re-hang the lid in position shown. Attach the cannister to board through the metal pieces that heretofore held the bellows. Fill the Bee Smoker with greenery and flowers and the section press was placed on the shelf.

Grocery Bill Holder of the 1920's

Store bottle

Did you know that grocery stores in the past sold on credit? This was a practice in the 1920 era and also during this time mother could phone in her order for groceries and meat by 8 A.M. and have delivery to the door before the noon hour. The butcher would even throw in a meat bone for the dog on request. The credit arrangement wasn't particularly desired by grocery store management but in those days there was much more emphasis on service and convenience to the buyer than today. However, keeping track of the "grocery bill" was a chore for both parties concerned. The grocer hoped that the bill would be paid in full each week but particularly during the depression time it could accumulate for two or three. Some of the larger families in this length of time would have bills totaling twenty to twenty-five dollars. Today one trip to the super market for two bags of supplies will easily match this amount and you have to serve yourself, wait in line to check out and tip the boy that carries out your bags. Such are the advantages of progress.

In days gone by, when a credit sale for supplies was made the duplicate copy was given to the customer on delivery of the groceries. Sometimes bills would be lost by the customer or there would be some other reason to question the total due when it came time to pay. Because of this, some stores gave their accounts to keep at home a special "bill holder" with a wire spring affair to hold the bills. This holder had a metal backing and pasted to same was information for the purpose of the customer to keep an accurate accounting.

Likewise, such companies as McCaskey Registry made a special accounting and file system for the grocers record and occasionally are still found as special collectors items. These are small and compact in size and sat on the grocers counter. A drawer held cards with customers names which showed a cross reference by number to locate any bills outstanding. The spring clip that held the "bills" was similar to the one given the customer but there were about 18 to 24 of the clip affairs on each metal "sheet" in the file.

The store where we traded had the policy of giving a large bag of assorted candies when a two weeks or more large bill was paid. A neighbor family where I lived had such bills to earn this "reward" and occasionally I was asked to go along when the "pay-off" of candy was made. I can still see the grocer opening the candy case and filling the bag with a great assortment of goodies which included those delightful "jaw-breakers" in an assortment of colors and that still favorite with children of today, bubble gum.

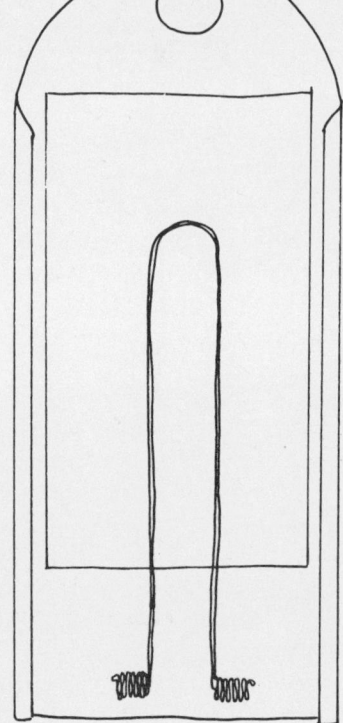

McCaskey Registry Co. Bill Holder

180

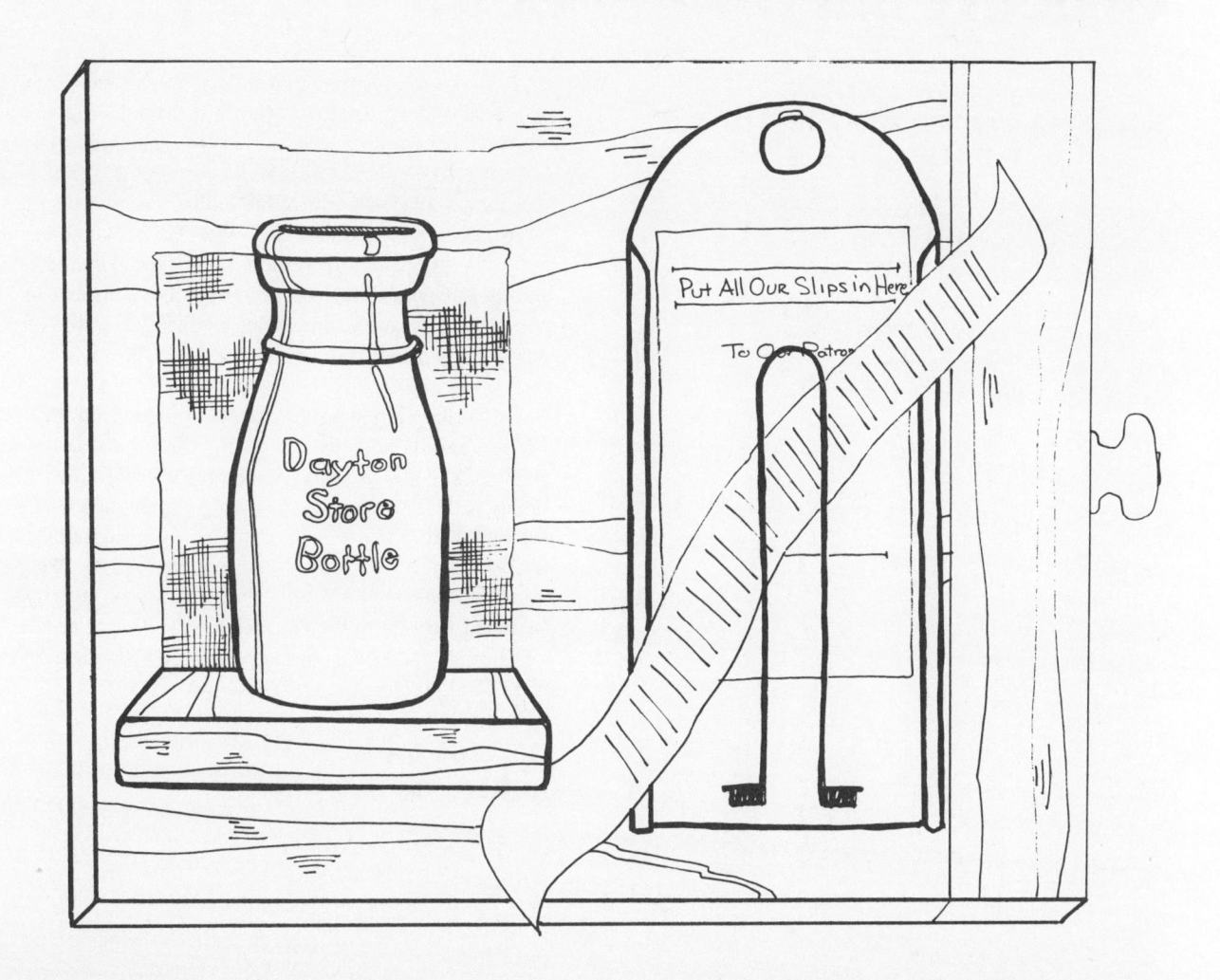

Services of early grocer included credit and delivery

HOW TO—Bill holder

This makes an ideal piece for the kitchen and the bill holder can be used as a message center for notes. Perhaps occasionally you will want to hang up an exceptionally large receipt for groceries for all the family to see. Another use for this piece would be to hold a recipe card while you are making a favorite pie or cake.

The old one half pint milk bottle illustrated on opposite page not only had the deposit price of 5 cents as part of the glass mold but also identified on the backside as a "store bottle." We assume this was necessary to keep separate the bottles used by the retail store from those used for delivery to the home by the Dairy. We used this bottle on the shelf and to make it show off better a small piece (5" x 5") of contact burlap was used behind same.

If there is a "sweet tooth" in the family, you might want to use an old (or new) small sugar scoop on the shelf filled with gum drops or the like.

The bread board used was cut to a rectangular size of 10" x 13". Attach two sawedge holders to the backside and sand as well as stain the board. Then attach a wooden drawer pull to the right vertical end. The information to "the patron" on the Bill Holder is paper pasted onto the metal. It's a good idea to give this a coat of varnish or some type of decoupage material to protect this finish. The holder measures 3-1/2" x 7-1/2".

To improve the appearance of the Bill Holder on the plaque, we first attached a 3/8" thick board that is 1" x 5" in size. This helps to set the Bill Holder out from the board and made it the focal point. Simply position and nail this board to the plaque. The Bill Holder has a hole at the top which had been used for hanging same in the kitchen. A porcelain white knob was placed in this. The threads need to be cut first to about 1/4", then attach with the nut. Then use small brads to attach the metal holder to the block of wood. The shelf for the bottle measures 3" x 5". See page 162 for attaching detail.

Rolling Pin and 'Friends'

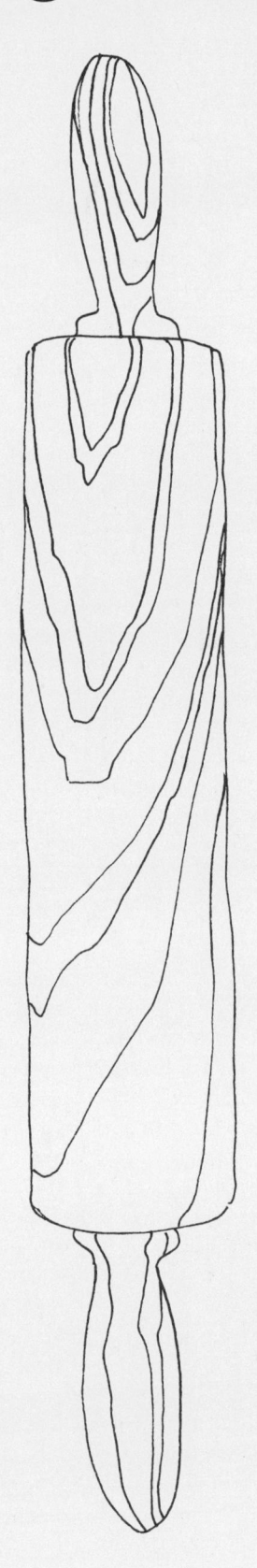

Those of us that remember the 1920-40 era, I'm sure will recall the comic strip "Maggie and Jiggs." Jiggs of course had a habit of sneaking out to play cards with the boys and when Maggie became aware of this, she was always standing by with rolling pin in hand to give Jiggs a reception he wouldn't soon forget. He sustained many a 'bop' on the head for his night out with his buddies whether he won or lost at the card game. Outside the comic strip of course the rolling pin belongs in the kitchen. There it is used to make delicious food to win a man's heart by the way of his stomach.

The rolling pin is one of the more ancient kitchen utensils and its origin will probably never be known. Some of the very old ones were hand carved rather than being made on a lathe. Being such a durable piece of kitchen ware, these are sometimes kept in the family dating back to great-great-grandmother. Such a "keepsake" is ideal for this plaque. The companion pieces we included with the rolling pin for this wall piece are the tin thumb scoop used for measuring flour or sugar and a can of baking powder.

HOW TO—Rolling pin vertical

The size of the board to use should be about 2" longer than the rolling pin. Our "pin" was 2" in diameter and 15" long. The board is 11" x 17".

First attach two sawedge hangers to the backside top of board and then stain the front side to contrast with the folling pin. Next drill hole and add white knob top center. The shelves used are 2-1/2" deep and 5" wide. The bottom shelf is up 4" from the bottom of board and 1/2" in from the side. The top shelf is 5" down from the top of bread board. See page 162 for detail. We omitted the brackets.

The small shelf to support the weight of the rolling pin is 2-1/2" wide and in a circular pattern as shown. Attach to left side of board and up 3/4" from bottom and 1" in from side. Nail through back of board into shelf.

Place rolling pin in position and drill 1/8" diameter holes on each side of handle for elastic banding to hold pin against board. Place your keepsakes on the shelves and it is ready to hang.

HOW TO—Rolling pin horizontal

The bread board used is 9" x 16". Some rolling pins are quite long and if the handles extend over the edge of the board an inch or so that is all right. If you have to purchase an old Rolling Pin for this plaque, try to buy one with a diameter of 2" x 2-1/2" and a length not over 15". After the board is cut to size, finished and stained, attach two sawedge holders to the top edge backside. Next drill a hole for the white porcelain knob and insert.

Two "brackets" are then cut to hold the rolling pin. See drawing and read directions carefully before cutting.

Shelf for rolling pin 2-1/2" wide

We used scrap material for the brackets and suggest you first make a pattern to follow. So that you can hold the board firmly while using the sabre saw, it should be at least 12" long and preferably 16". We can not give you exact measurements for the bracket "hole" as this will vary with the particular rolling pin used.

The distance from the straight edge of the bracket and the edge of the "hole" must be 1/4" wider than the diameter of the rolling pin so the towel will pass through easily. The "hole" should be 1" deep and 1/4" wider than the handle where it will rest on the bracket. Most handles are tapered and it should rest comfortably in the bracket at its smallest diameter part.

After you have cut the rounded part of the first bracket and the hole for the handle, it is well to sand the edge, otherwise you will have a very small piece of wood to hold and sand. The same applies to the second bracket cut.

After the brackets are finished, position these on the board one inch up from the bottom and lay the rolling pin in the bracket. When brackets are in position correctly, make a light pencil line on the bread board along the edge of each bracket as a guide when these are secured. Glue the brackets to the board and after dry nail the brackets to the board from the backside. The next step is to cut a shelf 3" wide and 2" shorter than the length of the bread board. It has to be positioned so the rolling pin can lift out of the brackets. Also you will note that the wood supports for the shelf are placed on the top of the shelf rather than below. This is for looks and to easily remove the pin. The brackets are 2" x 2". Detail for attaching the shelf and brackets is on page 162.

Use any small kitchen type keepsake items on the shelf. Miniature loaf of real bread would be ideal for the shelf. These are made in a size down to 2" x 2" x 3" long. A friend that contributed this item tells us that the dough with a preservative added was made in the conventional way and formed into a tiny loaf. It was then baked for 24 hours at 224°. After cooling, the bread is shellacked and will keep indefinitely.

Old Mirror Frame

These can be put to use to make elegant hallway or bathroom decorative pieces by "framing" collectibles of the late 1800's.

Small wall mirrors were commonly found years ago handing over the wash stand or perhaps even over the kitchen sink. The frame around the glass mirror was usually of wood measuring about 15" x 20" in overall size and the width of the "frame" was 2 to 3". Some of these were ornate with clusters of flowers made out of a composition or carved wood to adorn the frame at the two bottom corners and the top center. Usually the glass in the older mirrors has been broken but the wood frames are still available and were seldom thrown away.

Along with the mirror at the washing center one would likely find a comb and brush holder on the wall. These are of tin and about 8" in length with the opening for the comb and brush 2" wide and deep. On the front of the holder in raised lettering will be the words "Comb & Brush" or "Combcase." Many of these holders were nickel plated when originally made but you will find them with about any color today as people quite often painted these to blend in with the wall.

Early usage of these items date back at least a hundred years ago including the hand mirror which was usually considered mother's private property and likely kept in the wash stand drawer along with other items. The hand mirror could be purchased separately or in a "set" including a comb and brush. The comb was usually made of celluloid, aluminum or hard rubber. The brush would have a handle and backing made of ebony wood, rose wood, or black composition material. Many of the brushes had a silver mounting on the backside to enhance its beauty. The set illustrated is made of celluloid.

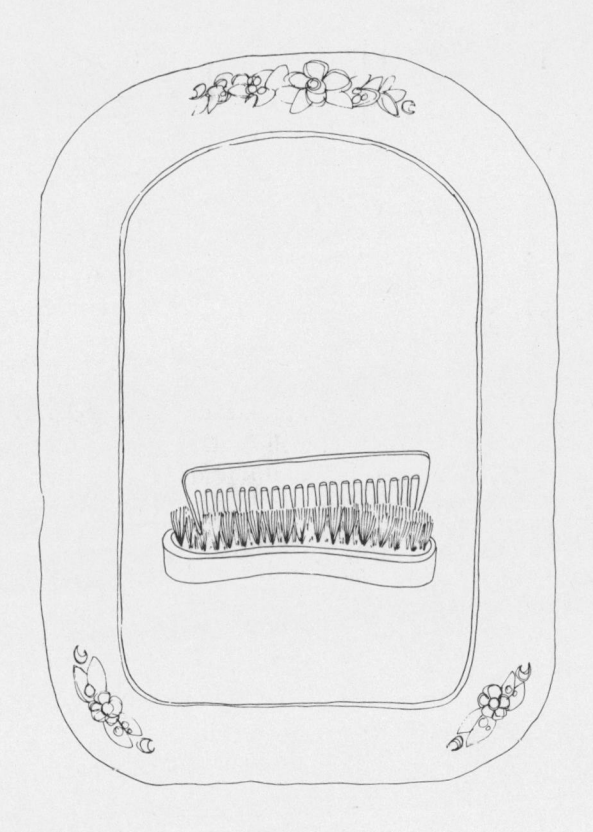

Old mirror frame of yesteryear

Comb and brush holder

HOW TO

This piece was made to be dainty and quite feminine. The mirror frame has scroll work and also flower designs which lends to the general theme. Small yellow rose buds are used for the arrangement in the comb case along with baby's breath and tiny velvet green forget-me-nots. Small greenery is also included to fill in the background. The cherub figure molded from lead was purchased at a flea market several years ago thinking it might have use some day and it fits in nicely for this piece. Other innovations can be used of course with the same effect.

First clean and repair the mirror frame as needed. Then we used antique satin spray paint and applied several coats. Next go over the surface lightly with a fine grade of steel wool to retain the "old" used look. To the backside top center of the frame nail a sawedge hanger. Then a piece of plywood (1/4" to 3/8") is cut to fit the insert on the backside of the frame. This board is covered with contact gold velvet paper and then secured to the frame with small nails.

The comb and brush holder was sprayed a soft green and allowed to dry well and then antiqued with burnt umber. Next center the comb case 1" from the bottom of the frame. Attach the case with small nails at a place that will be covered with the filling of greenery and flowers. At the top of the comb case there is usually a 1/4" hole for hanging to the wall. We covered this with an old cherub made from lead. A hole was drilled into the backside of the cherub to insert a dowel rod and it was secured to the piece with same. The cherub was painted gold and "antiqued" by rubbing lightly with steel wool. If you do not have something ornate to use for this purpose we suggest a small white porcelain knob be inserted in the comb case hole.

The glass from the vanity hand mirror was removed by taking out the reed ring around the edge. Then the front was sprayed with the white antique satin paint and after drying "antiqued" with steel wool. The mirror frame minus the glass was placed on the velvet and secured using small nails through the part that the mirror covers. Then the glass was glued in the frame and the "ring" to hold same. The piece is now finished except for filling the comb and brush case.

Tyrofoam was put in the bottom of the holder and covered with moss. Then we used 2 - 3" greenery along with baby's breath to carry out the daintiness theme. The small yellow roses (1/4" buds) were then added along with the velvet green forget-me-nots to complete the arrangement. A unique piece that will surely bring compliments from your friends.

Trivets

The iron trivet was originally designed to keep pans of food warm over the fireplace coals. These were made with three legs as the hearth base was seldom even and three legs would adjust better than four to prevent wobbling. Later the trivet was used to prevent hot pans of food from burning the table and as these became a sort of decorative piece many elegant designs were made. Some foundries that cast the trivets would use their name molded into the design for advertising purposes.

The trivet used for the plaque shown dates back to the early 1800's and has a most intricate design. At the top of the trivet, which would serve as a handle, there is a double heart and this is a symbol of Spring. In addition to symbol designs, trivets were also cast to depict animals, birds and the like. Sometimes you will find trivets made of brass and silver which were particularly for use when guests were present.

Mrs. Potts sadiron was advertised and widely used in the later part of the 19th century. Ironing in those days was quite a task for mother and meant heating the iron on the stove and then carrying this heavy item to the ironing table before even starting the work. Perhaps trivets were first used to place the hot iron on near the ironing board however regular iron stands were sold for this purpose. Many of the iron stands will have a slight "lip" near the pointed end of the stand which helped to keep the iron from slipping off. The Mrs. Potts iron was promoted as a set consisting of three sadirons, one removable wood handle and the iron stand.

Both trivets and irons make very interesting conversation pieces to remind us of the lack of conveniences in the good old days. The iron shown in our smaller companion piece plaque is only five inches in length. At first glance these appear to be a toy but actually this one is the Mrs. Potts sleeve iron and made small for this particular purpose.

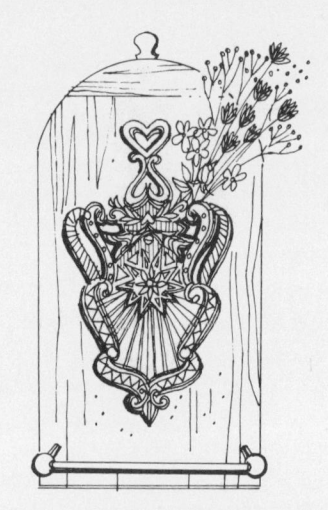

HOW TO—Trivet

The board used is 8" x 16" and rounded at the top as shown. Sawedge hanger is attached backside. Stain board as desired and then add the towel rack. See page 163 for detail.

As the legs for the trivet make it stand out about 1" from the board, we made a flower holder which is concealed when the trivet is permanently positioned. A length of pipe about 2" long and 1/2" in diameter works nicely and this probably can be found in father's junk box or buy a piece at the hardware store. As indicated in the drawing put a small dowel plug in the bottom end of the pipe and twist wire around the pipe at both ends. Then holes are drilled through the board and the wire stapled on the backside. This arrangement makes it quite easy to change the flowers to fit the particular season of the year.

The trivet is attached with black wire by drilling small holes through the board.

Flowers can be changed seasonally

Pipe length-threaded each end wire twisted and fastened through drilled holes to back of piece

Wooden dowel plug

HOW TO—Iron shelf

The companion piece is optional of course and any small lightweight iron can be used on the shelf. The board is 8" x 12". Use two hangers on the backside and a knob on the top edge and then stain as desired. Details for attaching shelf on page 162. The shelf board is 3" x 6" and the brackets 2" x 2".

Old 'Lava' Soap Box

Enamelware soap dish (1890)

Lava soap box board

Who would have ever thought fifty years ago that one board from an old soap box would be worth $5 to $6? That's right if the stenciling (usually black India Ink) is still in readable condition. Maybe the box used by those famous "soap box orators" would be worth even more. Scarcity and renewed interest in things of the past makes the difference.

The piece illustrated is a side board from an old box that contained bars of Lava soap. It is stenciled.

In the early 1900's the corner grocer simply displayed and sold many items from the shipping crate by removing the top, and placing the box next to the counter. When the box was empty, it was tossed into a store room at the rear of the store. Such empty boxes were sought after to use for storage of items in the home or farm and particularly desired by the young boys to use for making wood toys. The wood such as pine and poplar used to make these shipping crates was thin and light weight making it easy to saw and nail. Now and then Father would have access to some of these boxes to quickly split some kindling for a fire in the cook stove on a cold winter morn.

The enamelware soap holder is of the type that many times was nailed on the wall near the kitchen pump or wash basin stand. Soap holders were made in many shapes and sizes with some of fancy design with a loop affair to hang on the bath tub rim. Also others were of galvanized iron and in a large size to hold the one pound bars of soap for the laundry. These were made with a hole to hang on the wall and also so that the soap dish would stand up on a table or even on the rim of the wash tub.

HOW TO—Old Lava soap box

As the Lava "sign board" measures 6-1/2" x 18", we used a full size cutting board 16" x 22". It was stained with antique maple. Next attach two sawedge holders to the backside of the board for hanging purposes. Also a large white porcelain knob is placed in the vertical end of the bread board. The "Lava" soap board was stained with honey maple for contrast and to bring out the black stenciling on the board. The soap board was attached to the cutting board in each corner by using 1/8" dowel rods. Stain the top of the dowel before pounding in flush to the board top.

The enamelware soap dish is attached using two white knobs through the holes in the back of the dish. For the greenery holder, we had an old wood bowl of 10" diameter with a large crack in same. This was cut in half and secured to the board with dowel pieces. See page 162 for detail. The bowl is filled with greenery and baby's breath. A "modern" bar of lava soap is used in the container. A delightful piece for a country kitchen.

Kitchen Funnels

A vessel (usually an inverted cone) with a tube at the point through which liquids, powders, etc. may be run into another vessel. —Webster

Years ago the items carried by the village store were mostly in bulk form. At that time commodities such as canned goods and other staples in small packages had not reached the commercial stage. Bulk liquid products were sold by the gallon in kegs or by the barrel. The funnel then was an aid to pour from a large container into the smaller one for any immediate household need for the liquid item.

Funnels were made with copper, tin, aluminum and enamelware, with the latter being more familiar for kitchen use. Many of the funnels had handles like a coffee cup such as the handle on the tin canning funnel and the enamelware funnel shown in the drawings. Some of the "Sweden" funnels had only a small handle as shown and with a hole in same to hang on a nail. Many of the tin funnels were made without handles and usually have a tin "ring" about the size of a dime attached to the top rim for the purpose of hanging the funnel when not in use.

Some funnels were made special for canning purposes and were called "Fruit Jar Fillers."

The fruit jar funnel shown was patented in 1897 and has "threads" so that it would fit into most any screw top jar. This made it easy to fill the jar with the processed fruit or vegetable right from the kettle and also had the advantage of keeping the threads of the jar covered so the juice wouldn't spill on same. Otherwise one had to wipe the threads with a cloth before securing the regular lid. If the sugary juice was left on the threads and the jar lid tightened this would act as a "cement" making the jar hard to open or possibly cause it to break when the canned item was to be enjoyed at the dinner table. However, other canning funnels were designed and used without the threads.

A large enamelware or wooden spoon would have been used to transfer the "makings" from the kettle to the jar. Sometimes a ladle would also be used for this purpose and to transfer the fruit or vegetable from the kettle without the liquid, a pierced ladle would be preferred.

Fruit jar funnel — 1897

HOW TO—Canning jar funnel
(An old tin cup can be used in place of the funnel)

The bread board used measured 10" x 13" and was stained a light maple color. Attach sawedge hangers to backside and white knob on the end of board.

The funnel is placed about 1/2" from the top and left side of the board as shown. Then nail the funnel to the board through the tin part that touches against the board. Then 3/4" below the funnel bottom edge drill a small hole in the board to put the greenery end through and secure on backside. Then work this up around the funnel and through the handle. Also a smaller piece of greenery is placed inside the funnel back of the opening for the nest. Make a small nest of excelsior and position inside funnel and then add two small birds and position as if they are talking to each other.

The half bowl is glued to board (see page 162 for detail) and placed about 1/2" from bottom and side of board. Fill the bowl with plastic eggs and artificial strawberries to give a bright spring look.

HOW TO—Funnel with string

This makes a practical as well as attractive kitchen piece and you will always know where to find a piece of string.

The board should be about 10" x 13" in size. Finish as desired and then attach hangers to backside and the knob to board as indicated. This funnel with a rounded bottom is best to hold the string. Near the top edge of the funnel drill two 1/16" diameter holes and place funnel so the tube part will be free from the board and the top edge in a horizontal plane. Then nail the funnel to the board. The bowl is attached and filled as for the other plaque shown.

The string used should be the type that unwinds from the center of the ball.

HOW TO—Alternate canning jar funnel

Some may prefer to make a smaller plaque as shown. This makes a delightful piece to use, for keys, potholders or just to hang about anything small in size.

The board is 5" x 13" in size. Attach the funnel as for previous piece described except center on board. The metal screw hooks are painted black before attaching. Place these 1" up from the bottom of the board. The middle hook is positioned in the center and the other hooks 1" in from each edge.

Butter Paddles

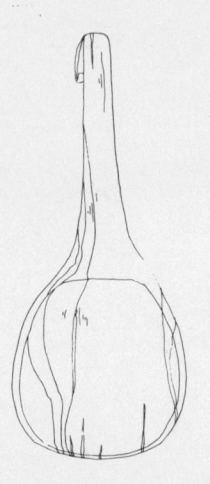

Butter ladle (hand made of buckeye wood and 75 years old.)

Butter paddle

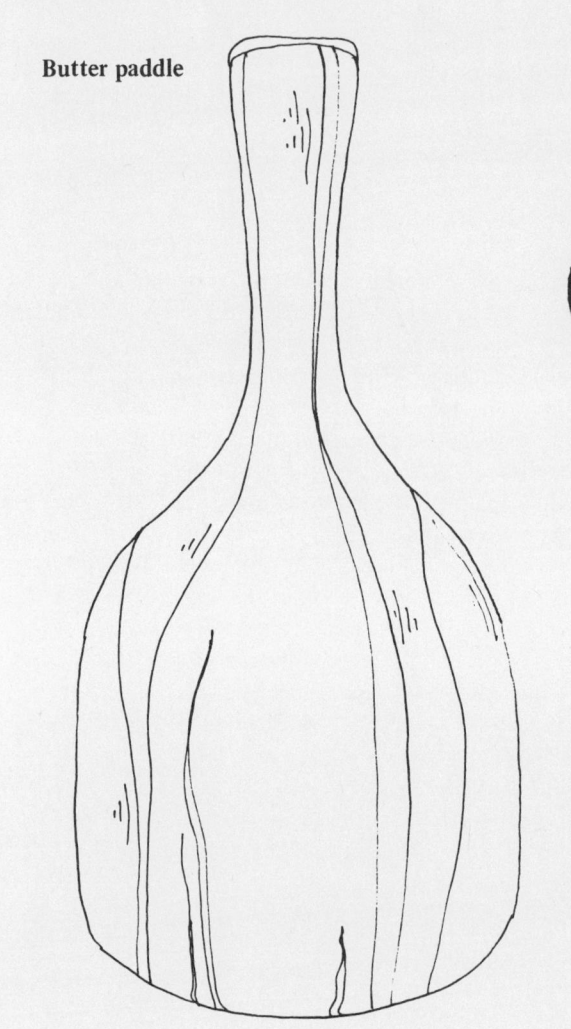

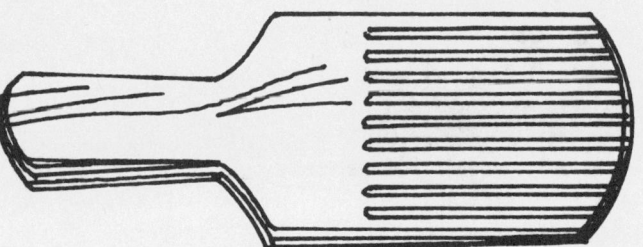

Butter spade

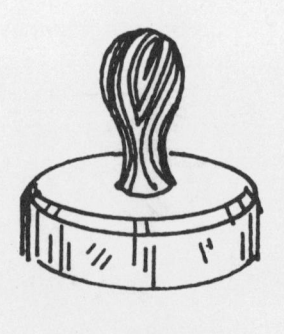

Biscuit Cutter

History

Butter "tools" were made in various shapes for working the butter and were called: Ladles, Paddles and Spades. Most of these are about the same size having a width of 5" and 9" in length.

Before the extensive growth of dairies, the whole milk taken from the cows was allowed to cool and then after the cream had risen to the top, it was "skimmed off" with one of many different style skimmers. The cream was a most precious commodity and used primarily to churn into butter with the resulting by-products of cottage cheese and buttermilk. During the churning process the butterfat in the cream was, so to speak, "kicked out" or separated resulting in globs of butter. To perfect the butter, the paddle was used to "work" the butter further after the churning chore was finished. Use of the paddle was for kneading or forming the butter and this also removed any excess milk in the butter.

HOW TO–Using butter spade

The board was cut to a size of 12" x 15". After sanding the board as desired, attach a sawedge holder to top backside and drill hole for the porcelain knob to fit on the top edge of the board. At this point stain the board as preferred. There are many different sizes and shapes of biscuit cutters, some of all tin or aluminum and others with wood handles. The one used had an attractive wood handle which was sanded and restained. If your "cutter" is all metal, drill a small hole in the edge and attach to board with a nail. If the "cutter" has a wood handle, attach same with a dowel rod. Details for securing the 1/2 wood bowl are covered on page 162. The bowl can be stained to contrast with the board or use acrylic paint such as burnt umber. Make a small nest from excelsior for the biscuit cutter and insert along with egg and bird.

The bowl is filled with excelsior and 5 to 6 plastic eggs. A sprig of baby's breath and bits of greenery add to the overall appearance and this finishes the wall piece.

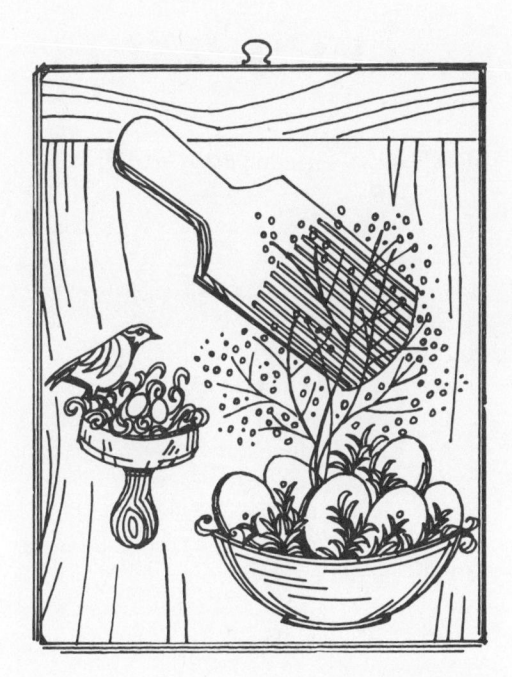

BUTTER PADDLE–With one side broken off

Sometimes we feel a greater enjoyment and accomplishment in creating with an item that is damaged or broken, than in using a primitive that is in good condition. Such was the case in working with this butter paddle. Due to extra hard use in preparing butter (or perhaps when used as a disciplinary tool) one side of the paddle part was missing. This didn't stop someone from offering it at a flea market and we were the willing customer for the grand price of $1. The handle was complete and the broken edge of the paddle part well rounded indicating it still functioned for a time even after broken. From a side angle these butter paddles have an elegant graceful look and that is how we used this broken item on a small simulated bread board.

HOW TO

The board used was cut to a size of 5" x 13". After the board is sanded well, stain a dark color to contrast with the "honey color" look of the paddle. Attach a sawedge hanger to the middle top of the backside of the board and drill hole in end of board for knobs. If wood pull is used instead of porcelain knob, paint it white.

In two places on the broken side of the paddle drill holes for 1/8" diameter dowel rod to extend out 1/2". Position on board and drill receptive holes for dowels and secure with glue. Just above the edge of the paddle drill a hole for the stem of a clump of artificial fern. Secure the stem to backside of board with staple. Nest is made of excelsior and placed in position with a small piece of stickum. Add a perky bird and this piece is ready to hang.

A most enjoyable hour long project resulting in an unusual and attractive piece for kitchen or dining area.

Old Eggbeaters

Make delightful conversation piece for display

Early rotary eggbeaters were made with handles, shank, and gears of cast iron. The trade name and patent date were in raised letters on outer edge and spokes of the crank wheel.

It was not until the 1870's that the first mechanical operated eggbeater was invented. One of the early models and still found today is the "Dover" trade name. See drawing No. 1. Before this time the housewife used long tines, wood spoons, and wire or tin whisks to beat the eggs. Webster defines the "whisk" as "a small culinary instrument for whisking or beating eggs, cream, etc. To beat or whip lightly; as to whisk eggs into froth." An interesting innovation is found in some of the wire whisk handle designs. The handle serves a dual purpose as it was made up of four heavy wires held together with a wire ring. See drawing No. 3. By sliding down the wire ring the four wires or prongs spead out. With the handle in this position a small cleaning rag was inserted and then the ring slid forward to hold the cloth tightly. This made it handy to insert the cloth into a glass chimney of a kerosene lamp, or other similar glass items, for cleaning purposes.

From the first rotary eggbeater with blades until the all tin ones of 1923 (A & J Brand) there have been many innovations of this piece of familiar kitchen equipment. Such names as Dover, Taplan, Holt and Cyclone are found on the "wheel" of the early crank type eggbeaters. Included with the name one will likely find patent dates of 1881, 85, 88 & 1903. A Taplan beater patented in 1903. A Taplan beater patented in 1908 had the trade name "Light Running" stamped into the wheel which turns the tin beating blades. The Dover company was apparently one of the first to experiment with the wood handle as their model with patent date of 1888 has a small wood handle and the iron crank wheel. In 1912 the different style "Turbine" eggbeater was patented. See drawing No. 2.

It seems that many of the early manufacturers of the rotary style eggbeaters changed or improved the design of the beaters frequently as well as the size in length or beating blades. This was probably brought about by competition of the different brands. For instance the Dover Co. beaters have four different patent dates from 1881 to 1903. One "improved" Dover model beater of 1903 had very small beating blades. There were usually different size beaters in length at that time with three being of the household type (9, 10 & 12") and one exceptionally large for hotel or bakery use.

Also desirable collectible beaters are the small "Baby Bingo No. 68" (Mfg. by A & J) and the "Betty Taplan" so identified on the tin wheel and advertised to use for mixing small quantities of ingredients in a cup or small bowl. See drawing No. 4. These small beaters are not toys and were so designed for regular kitchen use.

The more plentiful eggbeaters found today at antique shows, flea markets and the like are the "A & J" brand tin rotary beaters patented in 1923, and with wood or metal handles. The wood handles are usually painted with black or red enamel and a few with a combination of blue and white with an attractive antique look from usage.

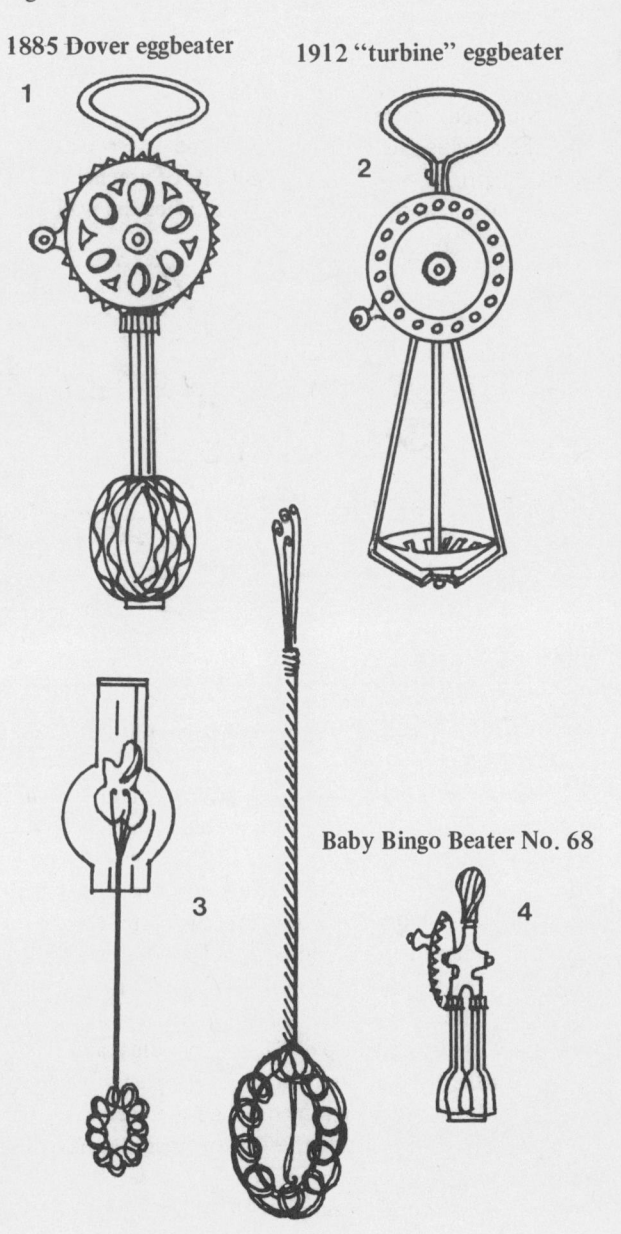

1885 Dover eggbeater   **1912 "turbine" eggbeater**

Baby Bingo Beater No. 68

Wire whisk—early wire spoon eggbeater with handle designed to hold cleaning cloth

HOW TO—Old eggbeaters

About any old eggbeater (or new one with sentimental value) can be used to make this wall plaque and most people have a favorite one to display. What could be a better way to keep and enjoy a treasured item such as this that has been in the family a generation or so.

It's preferred to use an old cutting board if available or facsimile and cut to a size of approximately 8" x 15". The board may have a used antique look and won't need stain. Otherwise use a light maple stain such as honey maple to obtain the desired results. Round the board as indicated at the top and then attach a saw tooth hanger to the top middle backside for hanging purposes.

Next drill a small hole in the top edge of the center of the board for the small porcelain knob.

For the wooden bowl, use an old salad bowl of 5 to 6" diameter and cut it in half. In the bottom rim of the cut edge of the bowl drill two 1/8" deep holes. Then cut two 1/8" dowel rods into 3/4" lengths, glue and insert into bowl. Paint or stain the bowl to contrast with cutting board. Then place bowl on board and mark to drill receptive holes and attach using glue. See page 162.

Place eggbeater in bowl and near the top of the handle drill two small holes through board to attach beater securely with a piece of small wire. Place 5 to 6 plastic eggs in bowl and garnish with bit of greenery and/or star flowers. The piece is now ready to hang for all to see and enjoy.

Other Ideas for Using Plastic Eggs

No eggbeater needed

If an old eggbeater is not available or you prefer a plaque without one, here are some other ideas for using eggs to make a cute kitchen or dining room piece.

This first plaque provides a shelf to show off other culinary items old or new and would make a handy place to store your recipe box. The board used is 8" x 16" and rounded at the top as shown. By starting the cut 2-1/4" from the top of the board, this will provide the correct shape for your board and at the same time give you the 2 brackets to support the shelf. After cutting the board, attach the sawedge hanger to the top backside and the 1/4" strip. Next cut the bowl in half.

The shelf is 3" wide and 7-1/2" long and slightly rounded on the outside edges. Glue the shelf to the board with the top edge of the shelf 3" up from the bottom of the board. The brackets are glued into position at this time and 1" in from each side of the shelf.

After the glue has dried, place a piece of styrofoam in bowl with "stickum" and position eggs as desired. Garnish the arrangement with bits of greenery and or star flowers. Place your favorite kitchen "keepsake" on the shelf and the plaque is ready to hang. For our shelf an old Thompson's malted milk miniature "coffee pot" was displayed.

The second plaque shown is made in a similar manner as above except the half bowl is placed lower and a towel bar replaces the shelf. See page 163 for making towel bar. An old wooden spoon is then placed on the board at an angle as shown. This is done by drilling 2-1/8" holes in the backside and just deep enough to hold the dowel rod. Cut 2-1/2" dowel pieces and glue into the spoon, position on board and drill receptive holes and glue in place. If it is preferred to use and old "whisk" attach by drilling holes in board an attach with wire. Old wood spoons that are discolored from use help to give this wall plaque an old country look. Sometimes you will find the old spoon with scorched places on the handle.

The basic plaque for the third idea is made the same as for the above piece with the wood spoon. For the decorative old collectible, a twin match safe is used instead of the spoon. Nail the shelf to the board from the backside to give it sufficient strength. Next attach the bowl with glue.

Old Moonshine Still

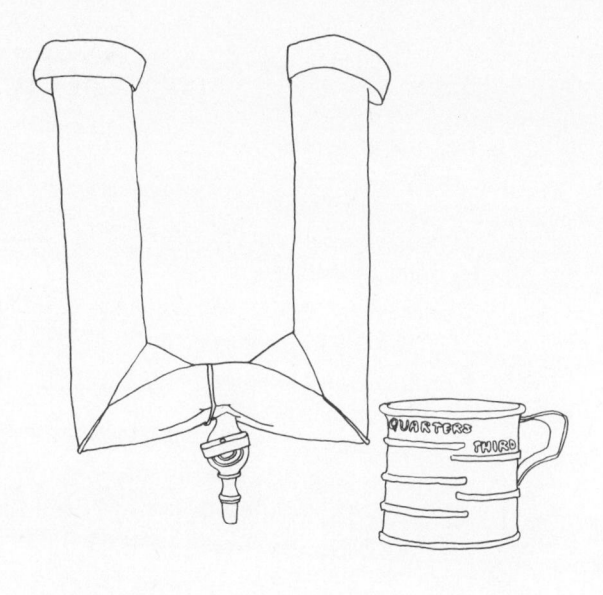

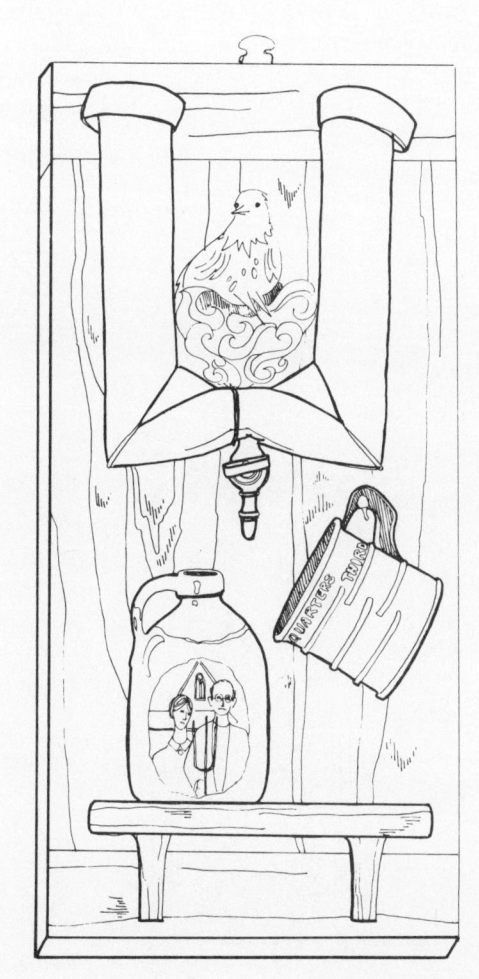

Baking powder tin lids were used as vapor deflectors

We understand that Baking Powder was not one of the ingredients used to make "moonshine" but at least two lids from old baking powder cans got into the act. The lids were used for an innovation piece to make the whiskey still function properly. This Still part illustrated was picked up at an old general store. The proprietor recognized this piece to be of interest and had it on the counter for sale.

It is made from tin "pipes" soldered together to form a "U" and with a brass petcock valve at the bottom. The baking powder lids served as a top to the outlet pipes and soldered so that the lids covered the two openings but not airtight so the vapors could escape. No one of course will admit (if they knew) just how a Moonshine Still worked but we have heard some theories that seemed quite logical for the function of this particular piece. The boiler used for the Still would likely have a pressure gauge but not an automatic safety valve. The piece shown then would have been a homemade mechanical safety valve. A tube from the boiler would have attached to this valve and when the gauge registered in the danger zone, the petcock would have been turned to the open position to release the pressure. The baking powder lids were attached to the top of the pipes so that the vapors would be deflected downward and not rise so rapidly in the air to avoid detection by the revenue agent. Although crude materials were used for this makeshift valve, the workmanship looked very professional. Probably the person involved had made several of these in his day.

This old piece of Moonshine equipment has perked its last batch and is now a very cozy place for mother bird to nest. The old tin measuring cup shown was a familiar item for Great-Grandmother and dates back to the late 1800's. It was marked in raised lettering "Quarters and Thirds" to note the heading for the measuring marks. When browing one day through some old recipe books it was interesting to read that when reference was made to a cup of liquid (8 oz.) it also expressed this as "2 gills." A gill being a wine measurement of 4 ounces. The tin cup in this instance may have been used by the "moonshiner" to add just that right amount of secret ingredient to the batch or for testing the liquid. The cup is hung on an old square headed nail in a characteristic position.

The pottery jug which is not necessarily old adds atmosphere to the general theme of this piece.

This Moonshine Still piece we know will not be easy to find like other primitive items, but you can have fun asking for such a piece as you travel around.

Household Graters

THE NUTMEG GRATER

Nutmeg is familiar to every housewife as a favorite spice, particularly for that Thanksgiving treat pumpkin pie. This spice comes from a very aromatic nut that is actually the seed from a tree. This nut being about an inch long and with a one-half inch diameter.

The grater shown in our drawing was called a "box grater" as it had a little box affair at the top with a hinged lid. This compartment will hold one or two small nuts and the purpose of same was to allow one to conveniently carry with them the grater and nuts (the graters are 2" wide and 5" long) wherever they ate. It was not uncommon in years gone by for a dinner guest to pull from his pocket the tin grater and add a little nutmeg "grindings" if one felt this would add to the tastiness of the food. Apparently the hostess expected this and was not insulted. (Would you dare try this today?)

RADISH GRATER

The "radish" grater was actually used for about any kind of fruit or vegetable that needed to be finely ground before using. These were available in different sizes from 3" x 6" up to 12" in length. The one in our illustration is 3" x 8" and with a wood handle. They were used to grate horse radish, pumpkin, coconut, squash, lemons, crackers, etc.

REVOLVING GRATERS

The revolving grater shown in the third plaque illustrated had a cutting edge on the cylinder similar to the radish grater. Again, it was used for a variety of fruits and vegetables. The inside cylinder was connected to the handle with a small threaded shaft. In this way it can be removed for cleaning by unscrewing from the handle. One of these we have has the word "Baby" in raised letters on the frame and no doubt was used to grind the food for tiny tots. These graters vary in size but most have an overall length of 9" and the cutting cylinder is 2" in diameter. There were also "revolving slicers" made in a similar size to slice cucumbers, potatoes, pickles and the like.

The "feeding" chambers on the top are round or square and with a lid to push down the fruit, against the cutting edge. Quite often the lids have been lost but one can be easily made from a scrap piece of wood and small knob.

Most people recognize the small nutmeg graters and these are still rather plentiful and readily found at antique sources. The grater is used by holding the nut in the fingers and rubbing same against the cutting edge to make the finely ground spice for food. One drawback to the little box grater was that you could not grind down all of the nut for fear of cutting the fingers on the sharp edges of the grating surface. For this reason there were improved graters made with a mechanism to hold and also turn the nut against the graters cutting edge. One such grater is shown and these are rather rare and dear in price. This type of grater of course was more expensive than the box type and was promoted with the claim that "it won't scratch your fingers and better yet no finger nail pieces will get in your pies, pudding etc." The mechanical grater was truly an improvement over the box type.

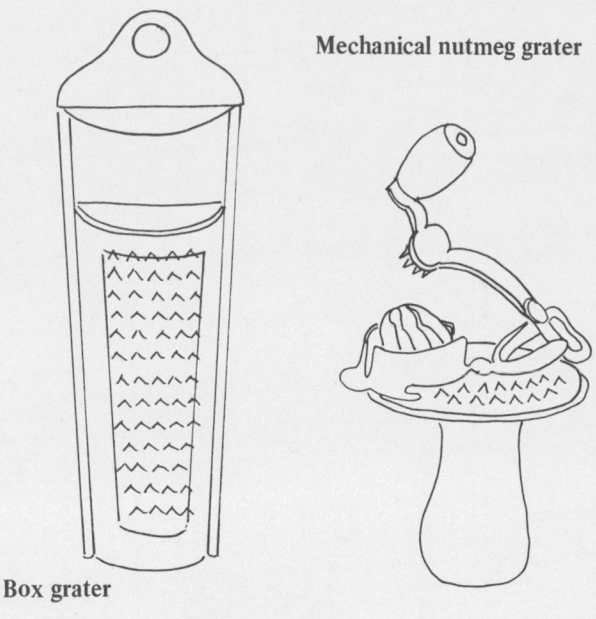

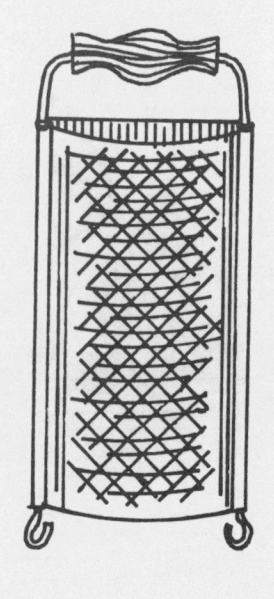

Mechanical nutmeg grater

Box grater

Radish grater

HOW TO—Nutmeg Grater

The nutmeg grater can be used to compliment any other old kitchen collectible. For this particular plaque we were fortunate to find a cylinder cardboard container that was used long ago for packaging the ground nutmeg spice.

The board used is 9" x 11" in size. Hangers were attached to the backside and white knob to the end of board as shown. Stain as desired. The shelf is 3" x 5" and the single bracket 1-1/4" x 1-1/2". See detail on page 162. The grater is simply attached by using small brads through the tin edge. With the lid open fill with flowers as desired and then place your favorite kitchen item on the shelf.

HOW TO—Radish grater

This piece takes a full size bread board 11" x 16". The board was used with its natural finish. Two hangers are nailed to backside and attach the knob on length end of board. The 1/2 wood bowl is stained to contrast with the board. Detail for attaching on page 162. The old wood spoon was secured by drilling small holes on backside and inserting pieces of dowels. Then place on bread board and mark to drill receptive holes.

The radish grater has a very ornate handle and this was sanded and stained walnut. Spray the tin grating part with flat black. Attach to board with small black wire. Birds nest is made of excelsior and stuffed in top of grater. Fill the bowl with excelsior, eggs, greenery and baby's breath.

HOW TO—Revolving grater

First you will need a board about 9" x 10" in size. Round the two top corners slightly and attach hangers to backside. Knob goes on top of board. The shelf is 3" x 7" and the bracket 2" x 2". Detail on page 162. The shelf is attached 1" in from the left side to give proper balance to the piece when grater is added. Above the shelf drill hole for greenery stem and attach to backside. Then clamp grater on shelf. Also include any other item of your choosing to go on shelf. We used a toy potato masher and put nest in same. Bird is peeking out from inside the grater. The lid for the food chamber was made from a scrap of board and with small porcelain knob attached.

Revolving grater

Firetorch (1800–1850)

Fire mark

Fire engine torch

Brass fire hose nozzles, fireman's hats, brass fire torches (from horse drawn fire equipment) are some of the main items sought after by collectors of Early Americana.

In the early 1800's only those home owners that had fire insurance were protected in case of fire. Fire brigades were organized to work for the insurance companies and they were paid only for fighting fires. So that the fire fighters could quickly determine if a house had proper coverage, the insurance companies issued iron plaques to each policy holder and these were called "Fire Marks." These were prominently displayed on the front of the house. These varied in size and shape and a typical one would be 6" x 10". These iron castings had identifying figures, names or symbols originated by the insurance carrier. See illustration. In those days the alarm was sounded by a trumpet instead of the screeching sirens we hear today.

Fire marks are available as reproductions and can be used in addition to a real collectible to give added interest to a display of early fire equipment. This was done in our plaque with the old brass fire torch.

The brass fire torch shown was from a horse drawn "pumper" and made by the Pioneer Brass Co. of Indianapolis. It was made to fit in a "ring" on the horse drawn equipment and could be removed to carry at the scene of the fire. The top part unscrews to replenish the fuel and the wick when necessary.

In the "Engine House" the harness for the horses hung over the stalls suspended like a web, so that when the alarm was sounded it could be dropped and snapped in place. Also when the alarm was heard one fireman had the duty of quickly starting the fire in the steam pumper so that it would be ready to function when reaching the fire.

HOW TO

A board 10" x 13" was used for this plaque. Attach sawedge hangers to backside and wood knob on top edge and then stain as desired. The fire torch is 2" in diameter and with a 1/8" ring 4" up from the bottom of the torch. A block of 1" thick wood measuring 2-3/4" x 3" was used to support the torch. In the center of this piece of wood cut a 2" diameter circle and the torch will slip into this opening to rest against the "ring" part of the torch. This was slightly rounded on the two front corners. Then on the back edge drill 2 holes 1/4" in diameter and 3/8" deep. Cut 2 pieces of dowel 3/4" long and glue in holes. Next position on board and drill receptive holes for dowel. Glue in place and let dry well.

The fire mark has holes for mounting at the top and bottom. Use 3/4" long black screws to secure.

For the companion pieces shown we mounted two small fire marks on wood plaques (painted red) and the third piece is a brief history of fire marks decoupaged on wood.

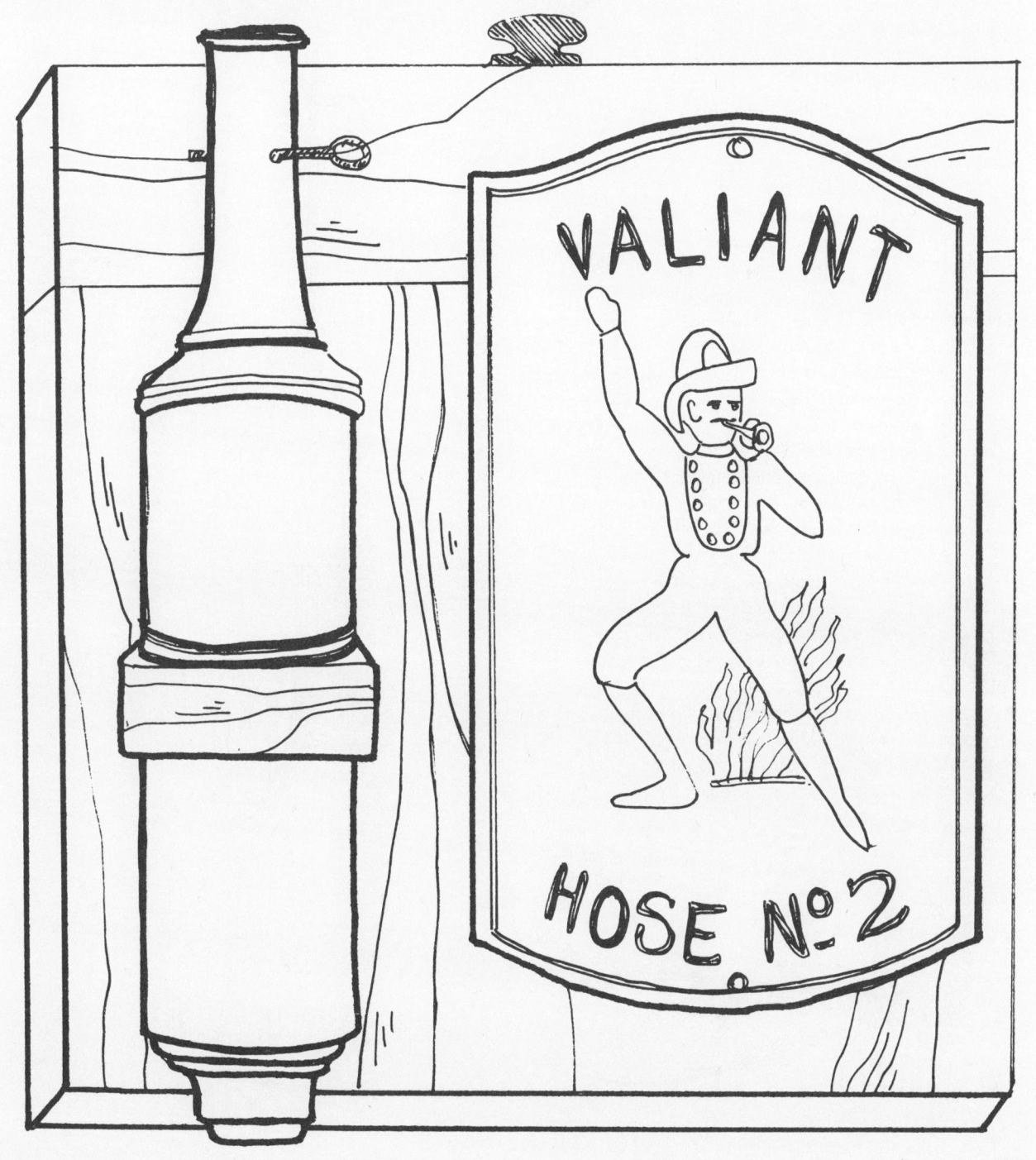

Old Railroad Keepsakes

Trainman's oil can, baggage man's cap and old time train schedule make unusual wall decor

The old cap illustrated was used by a New York Central baggage man. Railroad conductors and engineers also wore special caps and these were available in the late 1800's from mail order supply houses. The fancy nickel plated cap badge with the appropriate wording could be purchased separate and attached to the cap easily. The cap visor was often made of black patent leather to give stiffness and added wear.

In those antique shops that specialize in railroad items in addition to the old long spouted railroad oil can, one is likely to find old kerosene lanterns, torches that predate the lanterns, and oil or kerosene cans. These items are usually identified on the handle or bottom of the can with the railroad company's initials and have most interesting shapes. Any of these articles make nice display pieces.

The oil can shown is identified on the handle as "B. & O.R.R." The torch shown has a wick running down the long spout and into the can which held the liquid fuel. It was used to inspect the underside of the rolling stock and also at night at the switchman's station to identify the railroad that the car belonged to. Sometimes the light had to be extended four to six feet under the car and for this purpose a wood handle about three feet long fit in the hollow end of the opening.

Many safety rules were to be followed by railroad employees and these were published in small booklet form. Rule No. 4025 in a booklet for the Pennsylvania Railroad is of interest stating "Scuffling, horse play or playing jokes on fellow employee by air pressure, by electric shock, or by other means, either on or off duty, while on company property is prohibited." The rules of course were for safety reasons and to protect the welfare of the employee. Old railroad time tables dating back to 1910 were also used in the display box.

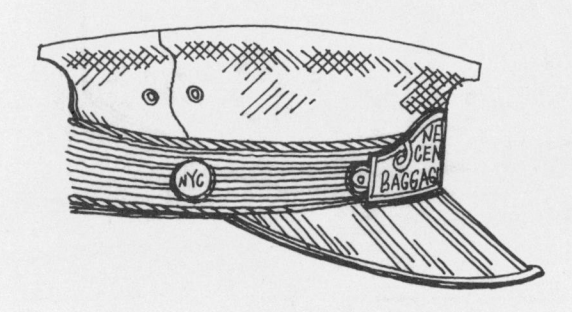

HOW TO

To start the project, attach two sawedge hangers to the backside of a full size bread board. The one we used was 16" x 24". To reduce the amount of exposed wood on the plaque we used a piece of gold colored contact burlap 14-1/2" x 22-1/2" on the bread board. For the box to hold the train schedule we used an old dovetailed cornered box 5" x 12" and 1" deep. Across the bottom attach a thin board 2" x 5" in size to hold in the pamphlets. Position the box on the board and attach with small brads. If desired, cover the inside of the box with burlap. A metal hook hanger is then attached to the board to hold the baggage cap.

Due to the size and shape of the engineers oil can, we made a shelf for same to hang just below and to the right of the other plaque illustrated.

The shelf is large measuring 6" x 14" and the wood brackets 4" x 5" in size. See page 162 for construction detail.

For an added touch you may be able to find a length of toy railroad track to use under the caboose. The caboose is a reproduction.

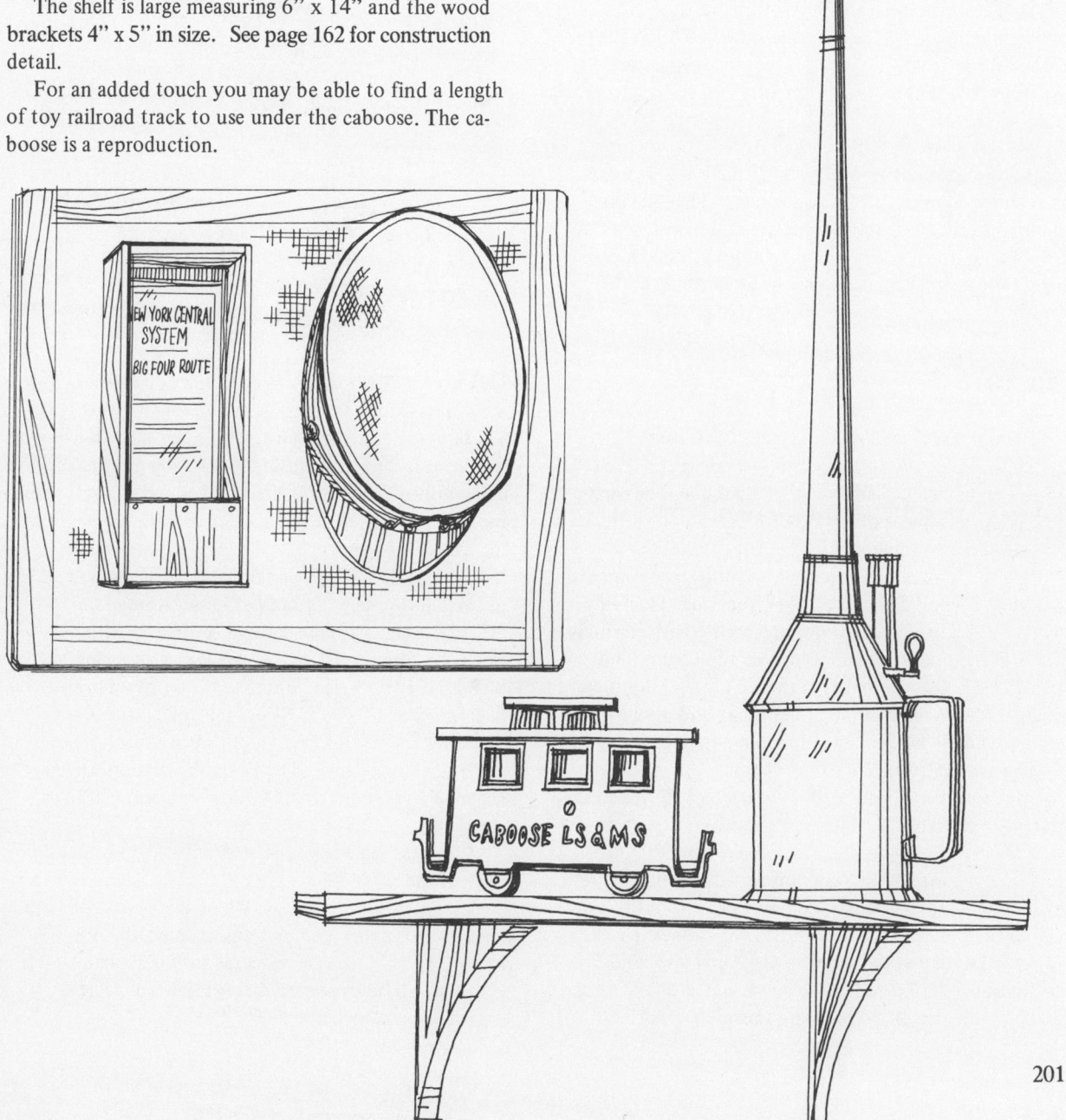

Abraham Lincoln Book

Improvised ink stand

This patriotic and handsome piece is centered around an old book entitled A. L. Lincoln, An Essary by Carl Schurz. The first copyright for the book was in 1871 and the last by Carl Shurz in 1919. Fortunately a very striking picture of Abraham Lincoln is included in the book about two-thirds of the way through, and the book was opened at this place to use in the plaque. Books on Lincoln are now somewhat hard to find and at a dear price. Any book of one's favorite great American would be appropriate to make a most unusual wall piece similar to this for den or library. The only thing contemporary about this wall piece is the brass plated eagle with its claws resting on the top page of the book.

The ink bottle is "Carters" and dated 1897. It sits on a stand made from an old round wood chair leg rest which in turn is mounted on top of a curved leg piece from an old candle stand table.

The eye glasses are left in the original case and are bifocal. Benjamin Franklin invented the bifocal glasses as a matter of necessity for his own use. The "backing" material in the piece is brown velvet and of course either red, blue or green velvet would be appropriate depending on the general color scheme of other items in the room.

HOW TO

The old frame used was painted a flat brown. It measures 21" x 27" in size. After preparing the frame, attach two sawedge hangers to the backside. The next step is to cut a piece of 1/4" or 3/8" plywood to fit the frame. The velvet material is then cut 2" wider and longer than the plywood. Stretch the velvet over the smooth side of the wood and staple to the backside. Then insert the velvet piece into the frame and secure with finishing nails. The round leg rest is placed on top of the candle stand "leg" piece and secured through the top with a dowel rod. You may want to improvise and design your own ink bottle holder depending on materials available.

The assembled holder for the ink bottle is now ready to attach to the velvet board. First drill a 1/8" hole into the bottom part of the "leg" and insert a piece of dowel rod letting it extend out about 1-1/2". Hold the bottle rest on the board so that the top part that holds the ink bottle will be in a level horizontal plane. From this you can determine the length of the dowel rod needed. We inserted the dowel rod into the "leg" and also used a small drawer pull through the dowel rod as a decorative piece to take the plainness from this rod support. Drill a 1/8" hole in the board to receive the dowel rod end. A word of caution: To prevent the velvet from twisting and pulling before drilling any hole, use a small nail as a starter. Also hold the cloth down tightly around the hole being drilled. The top of the wood round will rest against the velvet and need only be attached with a small finishing nail at this point.

The eye glass case is added next. This case was made of tin and the velvet lining was loose. A small hole was drilled through the case to hold the glasses with black fine wire. The top lid of the case was then nailed to the board under the velvet and then the cloth was glued back in place to hide the finishing nail heads.

Position the book and nail through the hard back cover in several places. Then glue the edges of the pages together and to the cover, to hold in open position at the picture.

The brass eagle is placed with the claws on the top edge of the book. The eagle will usually have a hole in each wing tip for mounting. We used a dowel rod forced into the holes provided and pushed in flush with the wing. Cover the ends of the rods with brass paint and one has to look closely to discern how the eagle is attached.

202

Notes

Notes

Notes

Notes